Governing global networks argues that ̶ ̶ ̶ ̶ ̶ ̶ ̶ ̶ ̶ ̶ ̶ ̶ ̶ ̶ ̶ ̶regimes are grounded in states' mutual interests, and not in the dictates of the most powerful states. It focuses on the regimes for four important international industries – shipping, air transport, telecommunications, and postal services. Of particular importance to these regimes have been states' interests in both the free flow of commerce and their policy autonomy. The authors examine the relationship between these potentially conflicting goals. In particular they trace the impact of "deregulation," which has led some states increasingly to place gains ̶ain a high ̶line of the ̶ysis is an ̶eorealists" ̶tions and

CAMBRIDGE STUDIES IN INTERNATIONAL RELATIONS: 44

Governing global networks

Editorial Board

Steve Smith (*Managing editor*)
Ken Booth   Christopher Brown   Robert Cox
Anne Deighton   Jean Elshtain   Fred Halliday
Christopher Hill   Andrew Linklater   Richard Little
R. B. J. Walker

International Political Economy
Roger Tooze   Craig N. Murphy

Cambridge Studies in International Relations is a joint initiative of Cambridge University Press and the British International Studies Association (BISA). The series will include a wide range of material, from undergraduate textbooks and surveys to research-based monographs and collaborative volumes. The aim of the series is to publish the best new scholarship in International Studies from Europe, North America and the rest of the world.

CAMBRIDGE STUDIES IN INTERNATIONAL RELATIONS

Series list continues after index

Governing global networks

International regimes for transportation and communications

Mark W. Zacher
with Brent A. Sutton

Institute of International Relations
University of British Columbia

CAMBRIDGE
UNIVERSITY PRESS

Published by the Press Syndicate of the University of Cambridge
The Pitt Building, Trumpington Street, Cambridge CB2 1RP
40 West 20th Street, New York, NY 10011–4211, USA
10 Stamford Road, Oakleigh, Melbourne 3166, Australia

First published 1996

Printed in Great Britain at the University Press, Cambridge

A catalogue record for this book is available from the British Library

Library of Congress cataloguing in publication data

Zacher, Mark W.
Governing global networks: international regimes for
transportation and communications / Mark W. Zacher with
Brent A. Sutton
    p.   cm. – (Cambridge studies in international relations; 44)
ISBN 0 521 55045 9 (hard.) – ISBN 0 521 55973 1 (pbk.)
1. Maritime law. 2. Aeronautics, Commercial – Law and legislation.
3. Telecommunication – Law and legislation. 4. Postal service – Law
and legislation. 5. International economic cooperation.
6. International cooperation. I. Sutton, Brent A. II. Title.
III. Series.
K4015.4.Z33 1996
341.7'5 – dc20 95–7671   CIP

ISBN 0 521 55045 9 hardback
ISBN 0 521 55973 1 paperback

Contents

Preface

The research for this book began with a recognition that in certain international issue areas cooperation is continuous and durable, and in others it is infrequent and fragile. We recognized, in particular, that there are many aspects of international economic relations where there are relatively stable international regimes. We decided to analyze the development of several international economic regimes and the reasons why the regulatory arrangements have been strong or weak for different aspects of an issue area. We chose the regimes for international shipping, air transport, telecommunications, and postal services because, as infrastructure industries, they are central to the operation of the international economy.

In seeking to understand why states have mutual interests in cooperation in certain areas and not others, we consulted literature in economics and political science. A great deal of the economics and political science literature on regulation assumes the existence of a government and is therefore of limited utility. However, writings from neoclassical economics theory concerning the benefits that flow from the regulation of "market failures" proved to offer considerable insights into why international regimes are created. The theoretical literature from international relations concerning mutual interests in cooperation tends to be very general and does not offer the insights into the likelihood of *particular types of international cooperation* that we hoped to find. Still, there are useful commentaries throughout international relations writings.

We set our theoretical perspective against the backdrop of the current debate between advocates of neorealism and neoliberalism, and we develop a theory of international regimes that falls largely into the neoliberal school. As noted above, our theory draws significantly on the economics literature on market failures. A brief overview of our theoretical orientation is presented in chapter 1, and a much more developed version of it is in chapter 2.

Chapters 3–6 are devoted to the international regimes for shipping, air transport, telecommunications, and postal services. Each chapter begins with an overview of the international industry and the relevant international organizations. There are then separate sections on the norms and some of the general rules for four policy sectors: jurisdictional rights, damage control problems, technical and procedural barriers, and prices and market shares. Chapter 7 focuses on the normative continuities among the four international regimes, the mutual interests underlying the norms, and some of the implications of the findings for international relations theory.

One of the biggest problems that we faced in writing this book was providing a proper balance between the general characteristics of regimes and the mutual interests underlying them and a comprehensive description of the four international issue areas and the norms of their regimes. In order to provide understandings of four quite complex international industries and the regulatory arrangements that have evolved over approximately a century, it is necessary to provide some fairly "thick description." Some international relations scholars may find some of the analysis too detailed about international economic issue areas about which they have only passing knowledge. On the other hand, some experts in particular industries or spheres of international law may think that we give inadequate attention to their area of expertise. It is always difficult to achieve the correct balance between the forest and the trees.

Within the four international service industries the two policy sectors that have evoked the greatest political interest are jurisdictional rights and prices and market shares, and the two sectors in which there is less "political" analysis are damage control problems and technical and procedural barriers. The public international law of jurisdictional rights concerns the fundamental legal/political structures of the interstate system, and the regulations concerning prices and market shares have attracted considerable political attention recently because of the trend toward deregulation or competitive markets. The telecommunications industry is the one industry where damage control problems and technical barriers have been highly politicized, because radio interference issues involve competition for radio frequencies and because technical barriers are tied to national manufacturers' competition for large international markets.

We hope that readers will take from this book an understanding of the important and long-standing regulatory regimes in the four international industries and their importance to the global economy. We also hope that readers will appreciate the salience of mutual economic and political interests to the strength and durability of the regimes and the implications of these underlying interests for international relations theory. While our approach and findings are generally supportive of the liberal theoretical tradition, we also draw some insights from realist writings.

Acknowledgments

There are a variety of individuals and organizations whom we would like to thank for the assistance that they provided during the course of our writing this book. We received generous financial assistance from the Donner Canadian Foundation, the Trustees of the Killam Endowment, and the Social Sciences and Humanities Research Council of Canada. The Centre of International Studies and Clare Hall at Cambridge University and the international relations faculty and St. Antony's College at Oxford University were hospitable in providing stimulating environments in which to work over two six-month periods. This research project started during the last year that the late John Vincent was at Oxford, and we will always remember his generous support and his friendship. During our research the Institute of International Relations at the University of British Columbia, and particularly the director Brian Job, provided support in many ways.

Trevor Heaver, Alan Cafruny, Ed Miles, and officials of the US Federal Maritime Commission and the International Maritime Organization provided information for and critiques of chapter 3. Martin Dresner, Vicki Golich, Michael Tretheway, and officials of the International Civil Aviation Organization provided information for and critiques of chapter 4. Jonathan Aronson, Peter Cowhey, Jonathan Galloway, Jeffrey Hart, Paula Murphy, M. J. Peterson, John Quigley, James Savage, and officials of the International Telecommunication Union provided information for and critiques of chapter 5. David Bullock and officials of Canada Post, the United States Postal Service, and the Universal Postal Union provided information for and critiques of chapter 6. Comments on drafts of one or more chapters were provided by David Armstrong, Claire Cutler, Ron Deibert, Mark Graham, John Haslam, Robert Jackson, Craig Murphy, Richard Price,

Michael Webb, and Robert Wolfe. We are also grateful to Eva Busza, Lesley MacGregor, Simon Read, and Ivana Stjepovic for research assistance. Comments from participants in panels and seminars at the American Political Science Association, the International Studies Association, the University of California (Berkeley), Oxford University, and the University of British Columbia were also helpful. We also benefited from the advice and assistance of John Haslam and Michael Holdsworth of the Cambridge University Press.

1 International regimes and global networks

It is clear to most observers of world politics that there is a great deal of order in international relations as well as conflict and disorder. A central issue for the scholar is to understand why there are orderly relations and regimes in some issue areas and not in others. One answer to the query is that regimes evolve quite simply when the most powerful state or states believe that particular regulatory arrangements would promote their interests. It is an answer that appeals to those who view the international politics of our century as having been shaped by the strength, and especially the military strength, of the great powers. They view it as naive and inherently harmful to think that the interests and power of the major states do not establish the fundamental parameters of international relations. Statesmanship in the eyes of individuals with such a perspective is about the great powers understanding what strategies and tactics will best promote their interests – particularly military security – and the large number of weaker states managing their relations with the stronger states in order to survive and prosper.

This is an inaccurate portrayal of the politics of international cooperation. There are too many international regimes that all or most states regard as in their interests to accept the above perspective. First, there has been a great deal of cooperation in sustaining a system of sovereign states that has lasted for three-and-a-half centuries. Not only has the death rate of states been quite low – except by voluntary political integration with other states – but the birth rate has been growing rapidly in the last half of the twentieth century. States show a great deal of respect for the sovereignty of other states, and they follow a host of conventions that protect each other's independence. States' support for "an international society" seems the only way to explain the fundamental continuity and stability of the legal and political order in the world. This book does not focus on this level of international order, but the general elements of order do provide the underlying structure for a great deal of the cooperation on which this book focuses. Without states' acceptance of each other's sovereign authority within defined territorial domains, their network of diplomatic conventions for communication and international law-making, and their obligations to comply with international agreements and to assure compliance by their citizens, it would be impossible to generate the kinds of specific regimes that are increasingly prevalent and important in many spheres of international relations.[1]

Second, as indicated above, there is a host of international regimes governing a myriad of issues – especially economic – that most states seem to support quite strongly. Such regimes vary in scope and strength, but they certainly contribute important elements of order to international relations. It would be foolish not to recognize that they are shaped in part by the interests and power of the larger states, but it seems equally foolish not to appreciate their promotion of the interests of the great majority of weaker states. One indication of the gains by smaller states is that they have tended to grow economically at rates roughly comparable to the rates at which the major powers grow. It is also, of course, wrong to think that states' mutual interests in all or even most issue areas are stronger than their conflicting interests and that therefore strong regimes are likely to be pervasive in international relations. The political world is a complex pattern of mutual and conflicting interests among states of varied power, and in certain issue areas there are quite simply not the common interests to sustain significant forms of cooperation. However, from the complex pattern of interests and power, mutual interests and international regimes in some issue areas do arise.

An important issue in the study of specific international regimes, as noted above, is whether many or most regimes are grounded in mutual interests among all participating states, or whether they rest on the interests and power of a dominant state or small group of states. Proponents of the former, neoliberal, position believe that in most circumstances states find a way of resolving distributional issues if they share important common interests in cooperation. They also think that the "anarchical" international system does not impose insuperable obstacles to cooperation since there are a variety of international institutions that provide opportunities for generating information, coordinating policies, monitoring compliance, and penalizing violators of rules. There is another point that is shared by most neoliberals, and that is that interdependencies and mutual interests in international cooperation are expanding. In particular, the possibility of gains from cooperation are growing sufficiently for states to be increasingly willing to trade off policy autonomy for economic welfare. Overall, neoliberals view the world as permeated with a growing network of international regimes.

Proponents of neorealism, on the other hand, argue that mutual interests are not the crucial foundation on which international regimes are built, but they do not claim that they are immaterial. In fact, they believe that while most states often benefit from cooperation when it occurs, mutual interests and gains are not the *sine qua non* of regime development. What is crucial is the existence of a dominant state or group of states, which generally gains more than the weaker states, and has the power to impose acceptance of the regime and compliance on other states. Neorealists also believe that international cooperation is infrequent because states find it difficult to agree on the distribution of relative gains, fear defection from agreements by other parties, and resist the development of high levels of interdependence. They posit that in an anarchical or self-help international system there is a natural tendency of states to avoid significant dependence on other states if it can possibly be avoided. In other words, in the world of interstate "anarchy" the prospects for mutual interests and regime formation are very limited, and mutual interests do not constitute the crucial political foundation of international regimes.[2]

The central thesis of this book is that many important international regimes are grounded in mutual interests among states and not on imposition by a hegemonic state or a grouping of the most powerful countries. Most of the mutual interests relate to the promotion of states' economic welfare, but some concern states' desire to protect their policy autonomy in certain issue areas. As will be elaborated in subsequent chapters, the regimes can be explained in terms of a theoretical approach that draws largely on neoliberalism, but integrates certain insights from neorealism.

The regimes that are covered in subsequent chapters concern the international industries for shipping, air transport, telecommunications, and postal services. They were chosen because, together with financial services, they constitute the major infrastructure or service industries that link national economies. The analysis of such regimes should reveal clearly a great deal about states' perspectives on the governance of the global economy and the nature and importance of the mutual interests that underpin international economic cooperation. The regimes for the four issue areas are, in fact, quite similar in that the nature and strength of their norms generally mirror each other. Norms are the most general obligations and rights that states accept in a regime, and they should be distinguished from moral standards. Also, a single set of norms that is common to a number of international regimes can be referred to as "a meta regime" and, as implied above, there is a meta regime of virtually identical norms in the case of the four transportation and communications regimes.

In examining the norms in the four international industries (and hence the meta regime linking them) it is desirable to break up each industry into four policy sectors: jurisdictional rights, damage control problems, technical and procedural barriers, and prices and market shares.[3] The character of the norms across the four industries can be described as follows:

Jurisdictional rights and obligations

- Open access to international spaces
- Innocent passage through territorial spaces
- Prerogative to exclude foreign firms as well as goods and services

Damage control problems

- Accident prevention
- Crime prevention
- Pollution prevention
- Reasonable compensation

Technical and procedural barriers

- Technical interconnection
- Facilitation

Prices and market shares

- Cartel (through mid-1970s)
- Limited competition (weak with uneven adherence since 1980s)

What these norms in all four international industries have done is to promote two highly prized values. The first is the removal of impediments to the international movement of transportation carriers and communications – and hence to the flow of international commerce; and the second is state control over important policy sectors. Among the norms in the meta regime the majority are related to facilitating the flow of commerce, but at least one of these norms (the cartel norm) was regarded for many years as simultaneously promoting the international flow of commerce and state policy autonomy. The key norms relating to the protection of state policy autonomy are the jurisdictional norm relating to the right to exclude foreign firms and services, and the cartel norm. As will be discussed at some length in subsequent chapters, the breakup of the long-standing cartels in the four industries, which started in the 1970s, poses the possibility of a new liberalized commercial arrangement throughout the world that will greatly enhance international openness. However, at the moment there are still significant differences among states concerning the regulation of prices and market shares, so that a strong norm favoring international competition is unlikely to emerge in the near future.

This book is organized along the following lines. At the end of this chapter there is a brief discussion of the four international industries and certain features of their regimes which provides an overview of subsequent chapters. Chapter 2 provides a discussion of the concept of international regimes as well as their components (principles, norms, rules, and decision-making procedures). There is then a discussion of theoretical approaches to international cooperation, hypotheses concerning conditions under which intergovernmental collaboration is likely to occur, and ways of determining the importance of mutual interests to the creation and longevity of international regimes. Chapters 3–6 analyze the regimes for the four international service industries. Each chapter is organized along similar lines. There is first an introductory section which includes the major features of the industry, the key international organizations involved in the development of the regime, and finally a chart of the norms of the regime. Each of these four chapters is then divided into sections on jurisdictional rights, damage control problems, technical and procedural barriers, and prices and market shares – with the analytical focus being on the relevant norms of the regime. The seventh and concluding chapter analyzes the similarities among the norms governing the four industrial issue areas, the importance of mutual interests in sustaining the regime norms and rules, and the implications of the findings for international relations theory.

Overview of the four industries and their regimes

Shipping

The most dramatic changes in the international shipping industry in recent centuries occurred in the nineteenth century with the advent of steel hull and engine-powered vessels.[4] In recent decades the industry has seen important technological changes such as dramatic increases in the size of vessels (especially supertankers) and the introduction of containerization on most liner vessels, but the technological changes have not been as dramatic as they have been in the other industries under study. Goods can be shipped more quickly and at lower rates than in the past, and this has influenced the growth of shipping; but the basic services of the industry have remained rather stable. Shipping tonnage is presently almost ten times what it was in the early 1920s, and it doubled over the 1970s and 1980s. Revenues from shipping services in the 1980s exceeded $100 billion annually, and more importantly ships carried over 95 percent of all exports by weight. The world of international commerce still depends very much on the shipping industry despite important developments in air transport, railroads, and trucking. It is, however, notable that many goods are carried by several transport industries between their points of origin and destination, and there has been a marked increase of multimodal transport firms since the 1960s.

Some of the most important early developments in international public law occurred with regard to international shipping. While the modern law of the sea had its roots in the seventeenth century, it was not until the nineteenth century that it was clearly recognized by the great majority of independent states. The legal norms of freedom of the high seas and innocent passage through territorial waters set a basic pattern of opening the arteries of world commerce that was followed in the subsequent development of international law in the other international service industries. The expansion of the global economy would certainly not have taken place as it did if the law of the sea had not assured the free flow of maritime transport. States have, of course, reserved the right to refuse entry to foreign vessels because they have complete jurisdiction over inland waters (e.g. ports). They seldom do refuse entry, but the right is there.

With regard to damage control problems and technical barriers in the shipping industry, international cooperation developed in the nineteenth century when many countries accepted British practices and laws. However, by the early twentieth century a multilateral law-making process in these areas had begun to develop – with the first crucial step being the formulation of the International Convention on Safety of Life at Sea in 1913. There are now a multitude of international conventions dealing with accidents, pollution, and barriers to the flow of maritime commerce. Most conventions are developed by the International Maritime Organization.

Unlike the other international industries analyzed in this book, the great majority of firms in the shipping industry have always been private. From the late nineteenth century until the 1970s most liner shipping firms (as opposed to bulk-goods shipping firms) were members of route-specific cartels called shipping conferences that established sailing schedules and fares. Governments were basically supportive of the shipping conferences because they assured regularity of service. Since the late 1970s there has been a marked decrease in shipping lines' participation in the conferences, and even in the case of those shipping lines that have remained members, they do not control fares in the way that they used to control them. Most shipping markets are now very competitive.

Air transport

The international air transport industry was limited to the carriage of small amounts of mail and a few passengers before World War I, but after the war it began to grow steadily.[5] Still, the small size and limited range of aircraft restricted its growth. Important changes in carrying capacity and range occurred in the late 1930s and early 1940s so that by 1946 the industry carried eighteen million passengers annually. Since the end of World War II the growth in the industry has been phenomenal, and in the mid-1990s the figure is over one billion passengers. Of tremendous importance to the expansion of international air transport was the introduction of jet aircraft starting in the late 1950s and of wide-bodied jets in the early 1970s. The air transport industry, of course, carries most international business travellers and international mail today, and in addition it carries an increasing volume of freight items that must be delivered quickly. The total annual value of international air transport services today is close to $250 billion.

Both immediately before and after World War I states established their sovereignty over adjacent or national airspace and freedom of access to airspace above the oceans. During the 1920s and 1930s there were some moves in the direction of a norm of innocent passage through national airspace, but it was not until the International Air Services Transit Agreement of 1944 that states began to move formally toward the right to overfly foreign states and to land for refueling and emergency reasons. Not all countries have accepted these rights, but the movement is in this direction. In the case of air transport the right to deprive foreign carriers of the right to land is much more important than it is in shipping because most states are so committed to the maintenance of national airlines. By insisting that they control a half of the traffic involving their country as a price for the right to land, states can assure the viability of their national airlines. Turning to safety and technical barrier issues, the International Commission on Air Navigation, which existed throughout the interwar years, was quite active in developing regulations, but in the postwar years the International Civil Aviation Organization greatly expanded the scope of international regulations concerned with preventing accidents and reducing barriers to the flow of airplane traffic. The number of safety regulations contained in the annexes to the International Convention on Civil Aviation is very large.

For over three decades after World War II the basic commercial parameters of the international air transport industry were quite stable, but since the late 1970s there have been some marked changes in regulatory arrangements relevant to prices and market shares. From 1946 until the late 1970s almost all international airlines (most of which were government-owned) operated within an international cartel that both set guidelines for the division of passengers and established passenger fares. The setting of fares occurred in regional and interregional conferences of the International Association of Transport Airlines. Key to the dominance of a cartel norm was the commitment of most countries to the existence of a national flag carrier. Over the last decade and a half there has been a decline of the cartel as countries have allowed more competition with regard to airplane fares and, to a lesser extent, market shares. The industry is very much in a state of transition at this time with increasing movement toward liberalization. There are, however, still too many important differences in the commercial arrangements among various groups of states to judge that a new norm has replaced the old cartel norm.

Telecommunications

Since the middle of the last century the expansion in the variety and volume of international telecommunication transmissions has been revolutionary.[6] The telegraph was introduced in the middle of the nineteenth century; the telephone in the latter part of the nineteenth century; and radio in the early twentieth century. While their use increased dramatically in the first half of this century, it was the integration of computers and telecommunications and the inventions of satellites and fibre optic cables in the 1950s and 1960s that caused a true explosion in telecommunications. This expansion has been accelerated by developments in digitalization and data compression in the late 1980s. The international telecommunications services industry now generates over $500 billion in annual revenues but, more importantly, it has revolutionized almost all other industries. Data transmission, e-mail, and facsimile have brought about fundamental changes in the operation of the global economy.

Except for outer space, there have not been treaties dealing with jurisdictional issues concerning the frequency spectrum, but informal understandings on jurisdictional rights and obligations have evolved during the course of states' promotion of the efficient use of the frequency spectrum and their prevention of interference among transmissions. These informal understandings basically prescribe open access to the spectrum in international airspace and an obligation not to interfere with international transmissions traveling through national airspace. Where international telecommunications differs from the other industries examined here is that there is some ambiguity with regard to the right of states to prevent (or jam) foreign transmissions to their populations. A good number of states give significant weight to the free flow of information, and in addition it is increasingly difficult for states to prevent foreign transmissions from reaching their populations.

One of the central regulatory issues in international telecommunications is damage control or the prevention of interference among transmissions. In telecommunications "accident prevention" largely refers to the reduction of radio interference through setting down guidelines for the use of certain radio bands for certain purposes (e.g. shortwave radio) and reserving particular frequencies for particular countries. A great deal of the work of the International Telecommunication Union (ITU) focuses on these matters. The ITU probably spends even more time on the regulation of technical barriers, since states are committed to an interconnection norm that involves ensuring that equipment standards are developed to assure the feasibility of international communications. Because the technical standards that are chosen sometimes have significant financial implications for national manufacturing industries, there are serious international conflicts on these occasions. Still, standards for the elimination of technical barriers are almost always accepted by the appropriate ITU body.

From the mid-nineteenth century until very recently the commercial world of international telecommunications services was dominated by a cartel of state-owned corporations (often referred to as post, telegraph, and telephone administrations or PTTs). The intergovernmental cartel divided the market and established guidelines for rates and the division of revenues. Since the 1980s, states, especially in the developed world, have become increasingly supportive of a competitive market for at least certain telecommunications services so that the commercial world of telecommunications is undergoing a significant transformation. The earliest movements toward liberalization occurred with regard to services that were of particular concern to international businesses such as data transmission, but now there is a growing movement to liberalize international telephone services. In no other international service industry has the impact of technological change been so profound.

Postal services

At the heart of the international postal services industry has been the exchange of letters and packages, but in recent years there has been some overlap with telecommunications.[7] In particular, the transmission of written messages by facsimile (fax) and electronic mail (e-mail) has challenged the traditional definition of postal services. Some government post offices or postal administrations have begun to offer electronic services, but to date they are not viewed as "postal services" by most people. Regardless of whether fax and e-mail are included in the definition of postal services, telecommunications firms are dominant in the provision of these electronic services, and they are taking an increasing percentage of total international messages from state postal administrations. The heart of postal services is still the transportation of letters and packages – the great majority of which are delivered by state postal administrations. Today approximately ten billion items are exchanged across state lines each year, although the volume sent within countries is around forty times that amount.

The key jurisdictional provision with regard to international postal services is that states must not impede the transit of mail across their territories (a kind of innocent passage norm). Of course, within states of origin and destination local government authorities have complete jurisdiction over the mail. With regard to the regulation of damage control problems and technical barriers, there are much more extensive regulatory arrangements than some observers might expect. The Universal Postal Union produces a great array of regulations to ensure that mail is not damaged and that states reduce technical and procedural obstacles to mail flows. Turning to the central commercial issues of prices, revenue, and market shares, since 1874 state postal administrations have basically operated a cartel within the context of the Universal Postal Union. The cartel has, however, been a lot stronger on setting fees for services required in the transport of mail and protecting the monopoly position of state administrations than in setting postal rates. Since the 1970s the postal cartel has also been in a state of decline as a result of competition from private delivery firms and electronic services and as a result of some attempts by postal administrations to take business and profits from each other. As with the other international service industries the recent popularity of "deregulation" has also had a significant impact on trends in the industry. The old world of postal services, which was dominated by state postal administrations, is definitely fading.

As is clear from this brief review of the four industries and their regimes, there have been significant similarities in the regulatory trends among them, and this includes a parallel decline in the cartels in the four industries over the past two decades. While the mutualities of interests that have sustained the central norms with regard to jurisdictional rights, damage control problems, and technical and procedural barriers have remained relatively robust or even grown in strength, the common interests that sustained the cartels in the four industries have obviously weakened. Technological change, the emergence of new competitors from the developing world, and the *zeitgeist* of neoclassical economics and deregulation have taken their toll on the cartels. It is also possible that we are witnessing a willingness on the part of states to accept more impingements on their policy autonomy for the sake of

11

economic gain than existed in the past. This may represent quite a notable change in the international political economy and the international political system. The analysis of the emergence and decline of the cartels offers a very interesting lens for understanding contemporary political change.

2 Mutual interests and international regime theory

This chapter is divided into four sections. The first addresses the concept of international regimes and the ways in which the regimes for the four international service industries are described in subsequent chapters. The second section discusses neorealist and neoliberal theories of international cooperation – focusing on their perspectives on the role of mutual interests. The third section analyzes those conditions under which regimes are likely to provide all or most states with gains in economic welfare or political autonomy. The fourth section presents some specific hypotheses concerning regime development in the four policy sectors of international service industries. The hypotheses are, of course, linked to the more general analysis in the previous sections. The concluding section summarizes the key features of the theoretical approach and also discusses some of the strengths and shortcomings of "functional" theories of international cooperation.

The character of international regimes

A central purpose of this study is to describe the regimes for the four international service industries in systematic terms – focusing on the norms.[1] Therefore it is important to address the concept of an international regime at this point. Since the late 1970s international relations scholars have devoted considerable energy to conceptualizing systems of international cooperation – what they have generally referred to as international regimes. While scholars have offered a number of definitions, the one formulated by the contributors to the volume *International Regimes*, edited by Stephen Krasner, remains a very good definition.

13

> Regimes can be defined as sets of implicit or explicit principles, norms, rules and decision-making procedures around which actors' expectations converge in a given area of international relations. Principles are beliefs of fact, causation, and rectitude. Norms are standards of behavior defined in terms of rights and obligations. Rules are specific prescriptions or proscriptions for action. Decision-making procedures are prevailing practices for making and implementing collective choice.[2]

The only slight modifications to the above definition that are employed in this study are amplifications to the descriptions of the key regime components which clarify their hierarchical character or their variations in levels of generality. *Principles* are general standards of behavior to which states attach varying degrees of importance and which often have conflicting policy implications. Because of these conflicting policy implications, tradeoffs among principles are required in formulating binding norms. *Norms* are the most general prescriptions and proscriptions relevant to an issue area that states feel an obligation to obey, and they should be distinguished from another use of the term "norm" – namely, moral values or standards. *Rules and decision-making procedures* implement norms and are hence at a lower level of generality. Norms are also often shared among specific regimes, and when the norms are the same or very similar among a number of regimes, it is possible to say that a "meta regime" exists.[3] For example, the four international regimes that are analyzed in this study have virtually identical norms such that it is possible to say that they are embedded in a meta regime for international service industries.

If the notion of integrating conflicting principles in a regime seems strange, it is important to realize that jurisprudential scholars have long recognized the existence of conflicts, if not a polarity, between principles in any legal system. Ronald Dworkin writes that "principles have a dimension that rules do not – the dimension of weight or importance"[4] and that "rules often represent a kind of compromise among competing principles."[5] He also notes:

> When principles intersect . . . the one who must resolve the conflict has to take into account the relative weight of each. This cannot be, of course, an exact measurement, and the judgment that a particular principle or policy is more important than another will often be a controversial one. Nevertheless, it is an integral part of the content of a principle that it has this dimension that it makes sense to ask how important or how weighty it is.[6]

14

In fact, legal scholars often regard rigid attachment to single principles as dangerous. The jurisprudential scholar Paul Freund has written that "single minded decisions suffer from a loss of insights that the cross-lights of competing principles would offer" and that it is important "to work out accommodations that will be tolerable because they recognize a core of validity in more than one position of the combatants."[7] Principles are thus not actually binding on states in their pristine form – norms being the most general prescriptions and proscriptions that are binding. Rules and decision-making procedures, of course, implement the substantive and procedural norms of a regime.[8]

In each of the four following chapters there is an outline of the regime that starts with a list of the salient principles (which are the same for all four regimes). There is then a list of the norms that have guided and constrained states' behavior in the four policy sectors: jurisdictional rights, damage control problems, technical barriers, and prices and market shares.[9] Below each norm there are subheadings for the nature and strength of that particular norm. *Nature* refers to those principles or values that the norm promotes, and the principles are listed in the approximate order of their importance or weighting. The orderings are products of judgments of the intentions of the states that formulated the norms. *Strength* refers, in general terms, to the extent to which the norm governs states' and firms' behavior with regard to a particular problem. Indicators of strength are the comprehensiveness of the rules designed to implement the norm and, more importantly, the extent to which states' and firms' behavior is guided by the purposes of the norm as well as the implementing rules. The key indicators of a norm's strength are the comprehensiveness of the injunction as it pertains to a particular issue and the extent of states' support for and compliance with the injunction. (It is possible to make a judgment of the overall strength of a regime which is a composite judgment of the strength of all of the norms. Such evaluations must, of course, be very general.)[10]

The following four chapters focus on the norms of the regimes rather than the rules because it is impossible to analyze the rules in great detail when covering the evolution of regimes over a century. Regime norms are often not stated explicitly or formally in legal texts. They therefore must be deduced from an overall analysis of the legal texts and states' policies and practices. To quote the definition of regimes presented above, regime injunctions can be both "explicit and implicit." On this issue Friedrich Kratochwil and John Ruggie note that "norms need not 'exist' in a formal sense in order to be valid" and that regimes exist when actors "exhibit principled and shared understanding of desirable and acceptable forms of social behaviour."[11]

One aspect of the regimes that is not covered in this book is the procedural or decision-making dimension. It is excluded in order to focus on the very extensive substantive dimensions of the regimes for the four international industries. Another study could profitably be devoted to the procedural dimension.

Mutual interests and international regime theory

This book makes a number of major points which are linked to its theoretical orientation toward international regimes, and therefore, before discussing regime theory, it is valuable to summarize these points.

(1) The existence of important mutual interests in cooperation in particular issue areas generally assures the creation and durability of international regimes. It is perfectly compatible with this stance to recognize that the nature of regimes, as opposed to the existence of regimes, is influenced by divergent state interests and power relationships. Also, it is compatible with this assertion that a few states may not share the mutual interests of the great majority.

(2) In some issue areas states have conflicting interests with regard to cooperation that override any common interests that they may share. That is to say, at least one important group of states will suffer losses in utility from any possible type of regime. States' interests do change, and these changes can alter states' opposition to or support for particular regimes.

(3) Because of states' concern to increase their populations' economic welfare, many important international regimes are based on facilitating the flow of international commerce (e.g. reducing impediments to the flow of international transportation and communications). However, as a result of states' concern to maintain their policy autonomy in certain politically important issue areas, some regimes or aspects thereof are designed to protect states' decision-making powers and to exclude foreign actors from intruding into these areas.

(4) Situations in which states are likely to share mutual interests in regimes can be identified. With regard to mutual economic

benefits these situations are often referred to in neoclassical economic theory as "market failures." States may also have mutual interests in protecting their political autonomy, but there is currently no body of theory that addresses conditions under which *particular types* of protective accords are likely to emerge. However, it is possible to posit a number of such conditions based on a reading of the international relations literature.

Reflections on international relations theory and cooperation

General theoretical approaches toward the study of international relations, and more particularly international cooperation, are often divided into realist, liberal, and Marxist traditions; but there are not presently a large number of scholars who identify themselves as Marxist international theorists. At the heart of realist theory is a conception of world politics as basically cyclical with recurrent periods of intense conflict and war, on the one hand, and periods of moderate conflict and peace, on the other. Central to liberal international theory is a view that there is progress in world politics – with progress defined in terms of greater freedom for individuals from violence, want, and oppression. Most writers associated with the liberal tradition do not see the emergence of an era of perfect harmony of interests, but over the long run they do see progress despite periods of serious conflict. One frequently noted difference between the two traditions is that realism is attached to the primacy of the state in international relations, whereas liberalism is associated with the view that nongovernmental actors are increasingly becoming more important on the world political scene. This view is open to dispute since it confines realism's relevance to eras in which states or at least politically autonomous units are the dominant actors and since it rules out the possibility that liberals' image of growing freedom for individuals might be best realized within a world of sovereign and relatively autonomous states.[12]

In recent years variants of these two major traditions have emerged – namely, neorealism and neoliberalism. The meaning of neorealism is relatively clear since it is associated with the theoretical position of Kenneth Waltz. There are, however, variations in neorealists' views, as Waltz has recognized.[13] Neorealism accepts states as the dominant actors and survival as states' overriding goal, and it posits the distribution of power as the major influence on the pattern of international relations. Neoliberalism is more difficult to define. It first emerged as a label that a neorealist, Joseph Grieco, applied to other scholars, and the one scholar who was centrally associated with the school is no longer using the title. (Robert Keohane now defines himself as an "institutionalist" rather than a "neoliberal institutionalist.") Still, the term has been used often enough to associate it with certain positions. Neoliberalism accepts states as the dominant actors that seek to maximize their own utility, but it does not privilege a goal of survival or security – at least defined in terms of a high degree of policy autonomy. In fact, it accepts that states are likely to have important mutual interests in cooperation, that international institutions within an anarchical world can facilitate cooperation, and that states are increasingly entering regimes that constrain their policy autonomy. One thing that is clear about both neorealism and neoliberalism is that they are basically time-bound to our present historical era. There is nothing wrong with this limitation since there should be theories that seek to understand international relations within particular historical contexts. Still, it is important to recognize that more appropriate titles might be "Westphalian realism" and "Westphalian liberalism."[14]

Before elaborating on neorealism's and neoliberalism's perspectives on international regimes, which form the theoretical backdrop of this study, it is valuable at least to note what they do not include. They do not encompass an understanding of those forms of cooperation that constitute the basic legal and political structures of the Westphalian system of sovereign states. Among contemporary international relations scholars this is something that writers in the *international society school* address more clearly and insightfully than any other group, although it is certainly touched on in the writings of some traditional realist and liberal writers.[15] It is precisely these general legal and political structures that make possible the kinds of cooperation or regimes that are analyzed in this book. Connected to the failure of neorealism and neoliberalism to address these general structures is an absence of any explicit treatment of transformation in the international system as well as the changing role of moral values. Traditional liberal theory, in both the Kantian and utilitarian moulds, certainly addresses the transformation of international political institutions; and a case can be made that it is an implicit part of neoliberalism which flows from the utilitarian tradition. While the subsequent analysis in this book does not focus on system transformation and moral values since it is assuming certain existing international political structures, it does consider them to a limited degree in the analysis of the movement toward "deregulation" and the willingness of states to sacrifice internal policy control in exchange for increasing economic welfare.

The neorealist perspective

The central theses of neorealism concerning international cooperation are that there are significant obstacles to the development of international regimes and that when regimes are created, they rest fundamentally on the interests and power of a hegemonic power or group of powerful states. While these perspectives reflect the views of the major neorealist writers, it is probably the case that at least some regimes based on mutual interests in the safeguarding of sovereignty and political autonomy are compatible with neorealist theory. Before dealing with the latter issue it is important to elaborate on existing neorealist perspectives on international cooperation since they form the backdrop to a great deal of the contemporary debate on regime theory.

Neorealists posit that there are three major interrelated obstacles to the development of international regimes. First, states are very reluctant to develop dependencies on other states (e.g. by accepting international regimes) since they want to preserve their freedom to defend their interests and particularly their survival. The drive to maintain a very high degree of autonomy is viewed as a natural condition of anarchic or self-help systems, and states therefore resist enmeshment in interdependencies and regimes – even if they provide the possibility of significant short-term gains.[16] In some realist writings maximization of decision-making autonomy is viewed implicitly as a state value in-and-of-itself – and not just as a means toward realizing the power of self-help. This statist orientation flows from neorealism's acceptance of the unitary character of states, the absence of other important actors in the international system, and the preeminence of security and survival in any lexicon of state interests.[17]

Second, and closely related to the previous point, neorealists believe that states are more concerned with relative gains than absolute gains because larger gains for other states increase their leverage in future bargaining confrontations – most importantly, when military security is at stake. Consequently, because any regime is likely to reward certain states more than others, it is very unlikely that the great majority of states would support a particular regime.[18] As indicated in recent work by Joseph Grieco, some neorealists accept that there are situations where relative gains are not likely to be very important, but on the whole they are tied to the view that in most areas of international relations states' concern for relative gains matters and thus impedes cooperation.[19]

Third, neorealists posit that the absence of strong international institutions for monitoring compliance with regimes and imposing sanctions on violators of regime injunctions creates fears of cheating and hence impedes acceptance of regimes – especially in important issue areas such as arms control or macroeconomic coordination.[20] While Waltz admits that world politics "is not entirely without institutions or orderly procedures" and is, in fact, "flecked with particles of government,"[21] these elements are not viewed as adequate to reduce fears of cheating.

Neorealists, of course, recognize that some regimes based on mutual interests exist; but they view them either as having little impact on the major trends of international politics or as flowing from the interests and power of the most powerful state or group of states. They assert that a hegemonic state or grouping may support a regime because it sees the regime as promoting greater relative gains for itself or at least protecting its existing power position. This argument is sometimes explained in terms of a Pareto optimality curve which is a set of points where the amount of a good available to two states is greater than at any other point on the inside of the curve, but where one party may enjoy more of the good than the other. At least an implicit view of some neorealists is that not only the nature of a regime (or the point of agreement on the Pareto curve) is affected by the most powerful state(s), but also the ability of states to accept a regime (or the movement out to the Pareto curve).[22]

Ironically, an important kind of regime based on mutual interests may be compatible with the theoretical postulates of neorealism: regimes based on the protection of states' political autonomy through recognition of their rights to control activities within their territories and within areas adjacent to their territories. Such regimes are certainly compatible with the neorealist perspective that states' preeminent goal is survival or security. Also, regimes that are based on protecting states' rights to thwart foreign activities on their territories or in adjacent spaces do not face the obstacles to cooperation identified by neorealists. First, they do not promote dependence on other states. Second, they do not have to rely on monitoring and enforcement by international

20

organizations because states generally have bureaucratic, police, and military capabilities to oversee activities in these areas. Finally, they do not affect states' relative power in a major way. If any states would gain from such legal proscriptions that protect their autonomy, it would be the less powerful. Such gains for weaker states vis-à-vis the more powerful states could be an obstacle in establishing such regimes, but at the same time great powers are likely to see important benefits from such regimes with regard to relations with each other. One thing, however, that would not be compatible with neorealism is if states' concerns for internal policy autonomy and for the capacity for self-help abated. These state goals are seen as natural conditions of an anarchical international system.

The neoliberal perspective

In presenting the neoliberal riposte to the neorealist stance, it is important to comment on both the issue of the extensiveness of mutual interests and the barriers to cooperation. With regard to the scope of mutual interests, neoliberals do not view states as being obsessed with limiting the development of interdependencies because of a fear that asymmetric interdependencies will lead to dangerous vulnerabilities. Neoliberals believe that the issue areas in which asymmetric inter-dependencies could lead to security threats are not as extensive as neorealists argue. Most international *economic* issue areas, in particular, do not engender serious concerns of relative gains. Also, neoliberals project that growing interdependencies in our contemporary era are likely to lead to expanding mutual interests in cooperation – especially in the economic realm. The dramatic surges in international trade, investment, and capital flows over the last half-century are notable in this regard.[23]

Unlike neorealism, neoliberalism tends to downplay the barriers to cooperation. First, neoliberals do not think that states have always been and always will be strongly concerned with maximizing their decision-making autonomy either as a core or instrumental value. They accept that states' core and instrumental values change in importance over time, and that they trade off autonomy or the power of self-help at times to realize other important interests. This position is implicit in many neoliberal writers' analyses of international cooperation.[24]

Second, an important outlook of neoliberalism is that there is not a large number of issue areas where states fear that gains by other states will pose serious threats to them. Hence a concern about relative gains is seldom a major obstacle to cooperation. The neoliberal position is clearly stated by Keohane when he writes that opposition to cooperation because of a fear of relative gains by other states is "theoretically implausible when applied to situations in which substantial mutual gains can be realized through cooperation and in which governments do not expect others to threaten them with force."[25]

Flowing from their belief in the primacy of absolute gains in most international bargaining contexts, liberals reject the notion that most regimes are products of imposition by the strongest states. Rather, they see most regimes as based first and foremost on mutual interests or the pattern of state preferences. Neoliberals accept that the nature of a regime and the distribution of benefits are affected by the distribution of power among states, but they believe that all states usually gain to some extent. Relevant to this point are the argument of Keohane that reciprocity is the central foundation of international cooperation among egoistic states and the assertion by John Ruggie that the ubiquitous multilateral regimes of the postwar era have been grounded inter alia on "diffuse reciprocity" where states gain over long periods of time even though they must forbear periodic losses.[26] For neoliberals it does not make sense to say that states first agree to move out to the Pareto optimal curve (where all states gain but where the gains vary) and then say that they become absorbed by the issue of relative gains. If they first agree explicitly or implicitly to move to the Pareto curve (i.e. accept that they will form a regime where all will gain), they are obviously not consumed by relative gains.[27]

Third, neoliberals believe that there is a network of formal and informal institutions in world politics that facilitate the negotiation of mutually beneficial accords, promote greater transparency in states' compliance with agreements, and help states coordinate sanctions in some cases. Most neoliberal writers would judge that the strength of international institutions varies by issue area and over time, but most are quite clear that organizations and normative frameworks assist states in reaching and preserving mutually beneficial accords that might not be created and sustained without their presence.[28]

The key point to derive from the above discussion of neoliberalism is that while there are significant obstacles to the creation and maintenance of international regimes, they are generally overcome when states share significant mutual interests in an issue area. Related to this, neoliberals do not think that regimes require the imposition of a hegemonic state or group of states. A good statement of this perspective is provided by Oran Young:

> There is nothing in theories of bargaining or negotiation as such to justify the conclusion that a hegemony is needed to produce agreement, so long as a contract zone or a zone of agreement exists. On the contrary, the usual assumption embedded in such theory is that rational actors will find a way to realize feasible joint gains.[29]

A comparable point is made by Andrew Moravcsik about international liberalism:

> Liberal theory analyzes international relations primarily in terms of the patterns of conflicting and convergent state preferences . . . convergent state preferences beget interstate cooperation; divergent state preferences generate interstate conflict. Metaphorically speaking it is the pattern of "demand" for certain international outcomes, not the specific institutional and geopolitical constraints imposed by the international political system on the "supply" of these outcomes, that imposes the fundamental constraint on state behavior. For Liberals, state purpose, not state power, is the most essential element of world politics.[30]

Hence, it is on the importance and character of mutual interests underlying international regimes that this book focuses.

In investigating neorealist and neoliberal positions on regime formation a crucial question is: what would constitute proof that mutual gains were or were not important in the creation and maintenance of a regime? The following are offered as indicators of the importance of mutual interests:

(1) durability of a regime and its norms over a long period of time during which there were significant changes in the international distribution of power and axes of conflict;

(2) adherence to the regime by states that are hostile to each other in many important international political issue areas;

(3) evidence that all or most states gained from the regime and no evidence that one group of states lost a great deal as a result of the regime;

(4) no indications that one group of states had to use sanctions to force another important group to join the regime or to comply with its injunctions;[31]

(5) existence of conditions where social science theory or international relations scholarship indicates that intergovernmental

23

intervention would increase total welfare (e.g. market failures) – and hence the probability that all would gain from a regime.

All of these conditions are important indicators, but the most central one is the first – the durability of regime norms over many years during which time there were significant changes in axes of conflict and the distribution of power among states. It would be difficult to argue that regimes were not grounded in mutual interests if these conditions held.

Conditions under which regimes can promote mutual interests

Any theoretical exploration of the role of mutual interests in regime formation must address the question: under what conditions do regimes promote particular mutual interests? Since economic welfare and state political autonomy are probably the two most important interests that states seek to realize, this section explores the conditions where intergovernmental regulation promotes mutual gains in these two values.

Mutual interests in promoting economic welfare

The hypotheses concerning the conditions under which regimes enhance all states' economic welfare are drawn from neoclassical economic theory. Economists have long been interested in the efficient allocation of scarce resources through market mechanisms and have identified several conditions that must be satisfied if socially optimal amounts of resources are to be produced. These conditions, which form the nucleus of the neoclassical model, are: (1) perfect information; (2) zero transaction costs; (3) atomistic markets (no single agent can influence market outcomes); (4) perfect factor mobility; and (5) actor rationality in the pursuit of utility maximization. Neoclassical theory then posits that when these conditions do not exist, governmental regulation will enhance total welfare gains, and hence the probability that most actors will benefit, by promoting these conditions.[32] A great deal of domestic regulation in states throughout the world has been justified and implemented on these grounds.

The circumstances or conditions in which the ideal neoclassical model does not hold or the market cannot operate efficiently are commonly referred to as "market failures."[33] In fact, four market failures concern the operation of markets, and another four concern characteristics of goods that prevent markets from operating efficiently. The first four, which are direct violations of the conditions laid out above, are: (a) uncertainty concerning costs and commercial opportunities (or imperfect information); (b) high transaction costs in negotiating private and intergovernmental agreements; (c) impediments to factor mobility, particularly barriers to the flow of goods, services, and capital; and (d) collusive arrangements among producers or consumers. In the case of *uncertainty* regimes can provide more information to market participants and governments so that they can better understand the costs and benefits of accords. When there are *high transaction costs* for commercial actors and states in concluding accords, regimes can reduce the time and resources expended on negotiating accords, and in so doing they facilitate agreements on regulatory arrangements that would otherwise fail to develop.[34] When there are *impediments to the movement of factors of production*, which include transportation and communications services, regulations can require the removal or reduction of the barriers. In the case of *collusive arrangements* where producers are extracting high fees or rents, regulation can restrict or regulate collusion among producers. In the presence of these four market failures, prices are generally higher and output is generally lower than would be the case of perfectly functioning markets. As a result of these outcomes, government intervention has been justified as a means to enhance economic welfare through the more efficient allocation of resources by market mechanisms.[35]

The final four types of market failures concern characteristics of goods that require governmental intervention in order to assure the efficient operation of the market. In the case of the last three, they can be viewed as the result of inadequate property rights. The four are: (a) economies of scale or a natural monopoly; (b) externalities; (c) scarce common property resources; and (d) public goods. The market failure of a *natural monopoly* exists when there are economies of scale such that production costs can be minimized by a single producer. Economies of scale are most likely to exist in sectors that have high fixed costs and undifferentiated products, such as utilities, communications, and transportation. Competition, left unchecked, results in either the emergence of a single monopolist that is able to charge higher prices than those that would prevail in a market with many producers, or a state of "ruinous" or "destructive" competition where supply is characterized by recurrent cycles of excessive and insufficient production and the attendant problem of unpredictable changes in prices and availability. Regimes in such circumstances can promote efficiency by creating and regulating a single producer, whether it be an individual firm or a cartel of firms.

Externalities exist when a good has unintended negative (or positive) side-effects on third parties, and these unintended costs (or rewards) are not taken into account in the production costs. The result of this divergence between private and social costs is that resources are misallocated, and the system does not maximize welfare.[36] The most common international externality that is analyzed in this book is transboundary pollution. In such a case regulation can require preventive action or compensation to injured parties. *Scarce common property resources* exist when there are no restrictive property rights for a scarce resource – and consequently there are overexploitation and resource misallocation. Regulation can in such circumstances assure that exploitation is controlled so as to produce maximum (and sustainable) output in the long term. Public goods exist when they can be consumed by everyone at no extra cost (jointness of supply) and no one can be excluded from consuming the good (nonexcludability). In such a situation there is a tendency to let others take responsibility for the production and financing of the good (that is to say, to be "free-riders"). As a result, there is a proclivity for underproduction of such goods in the absence of some kind of community regulation that assures contributions by everyone.[37]

A central assertion of this book is that where these eight market failures exist to a significant degree, regimes directed at their "correction" will probably increase total welfare gains and hence the likelihood that all or a large majority of states will realize benefits. Consequently regimes will be accepted. It is, however, important to note that it is quite possible that the mutual gains will not include all states and that a few states may lose. These latter states generally have to be threatened with sanctions or offered side-payments to secure their compliance.

While the general character of the eight market failures is relatively clear, it is important to explore some of their indicators. It is these indicators on which a study should focus in determining the existence of market failures and hence mutual interests in cooperation.

  (1) Uncertainty of costs and commercial opportunities
      (a) absence of clear accords concerning what rules govern particular transactions or activities;

(b) lack of procedures for determining and discovering costs of goods or services;

(c) possibility of damages to parties or goods involved in transactions;

(d) lack of legal liability and insurance;

(e) lack of clarity with respect to legal recourse in case of non-performance;

(f) lack of knowledge as to the interests and activities of commercial and state actors.

(2) High transaction costs (private and public)

Private:

(a) absence of clear procedures and institutions for negotiating accords;

(b) absence of specificity in the laws to which transactions are subject;

(c) multiplicity of laws governing transactions between different parties.

Public:

(a) absence of negotiating forums in which to negotiate accords with other states;

(b) high level of generality in the relevant laws;

(c) multiplicity of laws governing different international relationships.

(3) Impediments to the flow of factors of production

(a) government constraints on exports and imports (e.g. tariff and non-tariff barriers);

(b) technical inability of carriers and equipment to inter-connect;

(c) possible interference with transactions from third parties;

(d) multiple and unclear laws applicable to movement of goods and services and commercial transactions.

(4) Collusive arrangements to control supply and prices (except in a situation of a natural monopoly)

(a) formal or informal producer cartels;

(b) supply and price control arrangements between producers and consumers.

(5) Natural monopolies

(a) studies and statements by economists, firms, and governments indicating existence of economies of scale;

(b) acceptance of monopolies (including cartels) by commercial actors and governments .

(6) Negative externalities (harmful effects to third parties)
(a) unintended damages caused by one country's industries to the industries, people, or resources of another state (e.g. transborder pollution).

(7) Scarce common property resources
(a) depletion of resources in international space;
(b) evidence that there is more demand than supply for the resources in international space.

(8) Public goods
(a) no or minor additional cost for consumption by additional parties (jointness of supply);
(b) inability to exclude consumers from consumption of good (nonexcludability).

Among these market failures, one is more central to this study than any other – impediments to factor mobility and particularly the flow of services. In fact, uncertainty of costs and high transactions costs could be included as impediments to the flow of goods and services. The meta regime that encompasses all four international service regimes basically concerns keeping open the arteries of international commerce. Other market failures that loom as important in aspects of the four regimes are natural monopolies (economies of scale) and negative externalities.

Mutual interests in protecting political autonomy

This section, on conditions where international regimes can protect states' political autonomy, is not very long because strangely there are no works in international relations theory that focus on conditions under which states are likely to agree on specific regime norms to establish areas of state jurisdictional and operational control.[38] As noted above, the neorealist literature has overlooked the possibility of regimes that protect states' policy autonomy in certain areas despite the fact that they are quite consistent with general neorealist understandings of international politics.

This gap in the literature on international regimes is strange because, as Terry Nardin has written, "the purpose of international law must be to maintain the equivalent of agency at the international level, that is, the independence and sovereignty of states."[39] Likewise David

Armstrong in his study of the socializing effects of the international system on revolutionary states wrote: "It is crucial to remember that the modern international society was not just a society of sovereign states but a society for sovereign states, with its most basic role that of legitimizing and protecting their sovereign status."[40] At another point he comments that the society of states should be viewed "in origin as an association drawn together by a single common interest – sovereignty itself – and accepting, in the first instance, only such common rules and institutions as would protect and enhance sovereignty."[41] Perhaps the best summation of this argument that we should expect a great deal of international cooperation grounded in states' concern to protect their political autonomy is the comment by Inis Claude that international organizations (and regimes) are "designed to contribute to the capability of states to stay in business and to save the multistate system itself."[42]

Hypotheses relating to states' cooperation to protect their political autonomy must be deduced from a knowledge of the basic features of the international system and the general interests of states in a certain time period. In particular, it is important to start from the assumption that states are concerned about protecting their political autonomy from military incursions, from major economic and social intrusions by foreign organizations, and from excessive dependence on foreign states for their well-being. States have, of course, been willing in varying degrees to accept the intrusion of foreign firms and a degree of dependence on other states, but they would still prefer a high degree of policy autonomy in governing their own societies and conducting their foreign relations.

There are several conditions or circumstances where states are likely to have strong common interests in protecting their political autonomy and where there are unlikely to be significant problems with regard to either detection of violations or dramatic losses from defection. There may be more, but these provide good indications of the types of hypotheses that might be generated with regard to the development of regimes based on mutual interests in political autonomy. The two hypotheses below are particularly relevant to international service industries.

(1) When the military security and economic well-being of states can be threatened by foreigners' activities in *adjacent geo-graphical spaces*, states will adopt regime norms that recognize

29

national control over these spaces. Jurisdictional control gives states the right to exclude from the area foreign persons that might harm them, to circumscribe the activities of foreign persons, and to take action against foreign parties.

(2) *When an industry has widespread effects* on states' economic welfare, their independence from control by other states, and the political attitudes of their citizens, states want to assure control over that part of the industry that particularly impinges on their welfare and political autonomy. Therefore, they are likely to back an international regime that gives all states the legal power to exclude foreign industries from their territories and gives the collectivity of states the power to divide the international market so as to control international linkages.

Hypotheses concerning regime development in four policy sectors

Because the analyses of the four international regimes are divided along the lines of the four main policy sectors, it is appropriate to develop hypotheses concerning the probability of regime development for each of the four sectors. The hypotheses are based on the likely occurrence of the conditions that were discussed above. In the case of certain policy sectors there will be several hypotheses because of the need to take several economic and political conditions into account. Also, while most of the hypotheses relate to the likely occurrence of strong regimes, some concern the actual character of the regimes.

Jurisdictional rights

These refer to the rights of individual states or the international community of states to legislate for different activities in particular geographical areas and to enforce the laws. It is quite possible for different political authorities to have rights to legislate for different activities in a particular geographical area.

(a) Strong international regimes for jurisdictional rights are likely since states and private actors like to know whose rules they have to obey in different geographical areas. That is to say, a lack of clear jurisdictional rights creates high uncertainty of costs, high transaction costs, and impediments to the flow of goods and services.

(b) States will establish an open access norm for international spaces between them because it reduces impediments to the flow of goods and services. Also, by establishing a common property status for international oceans space and airspace, states are predisposed to create uniform laws for both international and national jurisdictional zones, and this reduces the costs of conducting commerce.

(c) States will establish state sovereignty over areas adjacent to their territories (air and sea) since other states could threaten their security and internal control if they had unrestricted access to these areas. However, they will accept a right of "innocent passage" for foreign states. That is to say, they will allow transit through their sovereign domains as long as foreign parties do not threaten their "peace, good order, and security."

(d) States will not compromise their legal prerogative to control the activities of commercial enterprises on their territories since it may be important to exclude foreign firms in order to further the welfare and independence of their citizens. This, however, does not mean that they will not accept constraints in international conventions from which they have the legal power to withdraw.

Damage control problems

Damage control issues can concern unintended damages or accidents, and they can also involve intentional damages or crimes. Most of the efforts of international organizations have concerned the prevention of unintentional damages (e.g. collisions, pollution, and interference between radio transmissions). Other damage control issues are liability for damages as well as requirements concerning prosecution of violators of international laws.

(a) The prevention of accidents and crimes pertaining to international commerce as well as compensation for losses will be strongly regulated because commercial parties do not want high uncertainty of costs which constitutes an impediment to the flow of commerce. Also, firms and states want to avoid having to deal with such problems on an ad hoc basis because this involves high transaction costs.

(b) States will accept some responsibilities for promoting the compliance with international laws concerning safety, crime, and pollution, but they are likely to eschew obligations to apply particular penalties. Unfettered control over criminal justice systems is central to their conception of independent statehood, and they resist incursions on their autonomy in this area.

Technical and procedural barriers

An important market access issue is the ability of equipment employed in international service industries to interconnect with equipment in foreign countries. Another market access issue concerns "facilitation" or the reduction of administrative and procedural obstacles involved with the entry/exit of goods and services into/out of countries. Particular facilitation issues are customs procedures, health inspection, and immigration procedures.

(a) Technical equipment standards are very likely to be regulated by international bodies if such standards are necessary for international interconnection between transportation carriers and (air)ports or between the senders and receivers of communications. Such regulations eliminate impediments to the flow of international commerce, and of course they also reduce uncertainty of costs and transaction costs.

(b) Procedures affecting the speed at which goods, services, and people pass through international gateways (ports, airports) are likely to be regulated since states generally want to facilitate the flow of commerce. Regulations can reduce uncertainty of costs, transaction costs, and impediments to the flow of goods and services.

Prices and market shares

Central issues in any area of commerce are the prices of the goods or services and the market shares of different producers. Prices define the central terms of the relationship between producers and consumers, and market shares define in significant ways the relative success of different producers. Intergovernmental regulation can take different forms under different circumstances.

(a) One circumstance where prices and market shares are likely to be regulated is where there is a natural monopoly or economies of scale. In such a situation it is, of course, beneficial for all states to create a single entity to produce the good (which, of course, could be a cartel of existing firms).

(b) Another circumstance where prices and market shares are likely to be regulated is where states are committed to maintaining complete control over an industry's operation within their territories because of its salience to their internal political and economic control. For example, an international cartel that divides the market and discourages competition facilitates states' control of the national industries in question.

(c) An international regime based on economic liberalization (no regulation of prices and market shares) is likely to develop if states are not committed to maintaining a particular industry and if there is a belief in the economic benefits of liberalization.

Conclusion

In concluding this chapter it is valuable to reiterate a number of the key points concerning the explanatory analysis and then to reflect on the general theoretical approach. First, in analyzing the strength and nature of the regimes the focus is on general trends and not particular decisions. This strategy is best both for describing the overall character of the regimes, and for evaluating the importance of mutual interests in sustaining the regimes.

Second, the book focuses on the general purposes or functions of regimes (e.g. reducing uncertainty of costs and barriers to trade) – and not on the distribution of benefits that flow from the regime injunctions (e.g. greater benefits for the industrialized countries than for developing states). There will be some mention of distributional conflicts, but largely to highlight that despite these differences in rewards states continued to maintain loyalty to the regimes because they performed functions that were valued by all. There are also discussions of certain circumstances where regime norms were not accepted because of conflicts of interests and distributional issues.

Third, the key indicators of our claims concerning mutual interests are: the existence of the conditions that have been identified as generating mutual interests in cooperation (e.g. market failures); regime norms or functions clearly directed at resolving these problems; and the durability and functional stability of the regimes over periods when there were major changes in political axes of conflict and power relations.

In closing this discussion of the theoretical framework it is valuable to consider a criticism of this approach other than the general neorealist challenge described above. It concerns the theory's limitations as a "functional" theory which posits that under certain circumstances states support regimes or institutions because they perform certain tasks or functions that benefit all states.[43] Stephan Haggard and Beth Simmons have identified the shortcomings of functional theories as follows. First, such theories identify the conditions under which regimes are demanded by many states, but do not specify the conditions under which they are likely to be supplied or when precisely they will be created. Second, they assume that because regimes perform certain functions, the regimes were established for those reasons. Lastly, they ignore the distributional consequences of regimes on their development and the fact that regimes "are certainly more likely to reflect the interests of the powerful than the interests of the weak."[44] Elaborating on this last point from a realist perspective Stephen Krasner has written that "Market failure [or functional] analyses, which have dominated the literature on international regimes, pay little attention to power." He goes on: "For a power-oriented research program, power is exercised not to facilitate cooperation [i.e. to realize joint gains] but to secure a more favorable distribution of benefits."[45]

The first assertion that functional approaches do not identify those circumstances when particular regimes will be created is certainly correct, and it is a shortcoming. On the other hand, the ability to identify those circumstances when states tend to favor regimes with certain purposes is an important contribution to regime theory. A comprehensive regime theory would have to encompass facilitative conditions. However, to reiterate the point made above, the ability to identify those conditions under which all or most states are likely to realize absolute gains is not a minor accomplishment. It is especially not minor if one finds that regimes are generally established under these conditions.

The second assertion that functional theories are wrong to assume that regimes were created to perform certain functions just because they performed them after their creation introduces an appropriate element of circumspection on this matter. However, if certain conditions identified as creating mutual interests in cooperation (e.g. market failures) exist prior to the formation of the regimes, if states indicate a concern for modifying these conditions, and if the regulatory arrangements are clearly designed to alter them, it is a reasonable conjecture that the regimes were formed to perform certain functions.

34

The third criticism that functional analysis ignores the impact of the distribution of power on regimes has to be broken down into two assertions: first, power relations affect the *nature* of regimes and, second, they affect the *existence* of regimes. On the first point, proponents of functional analyses accept that the particular shape or nature of regimes is bound to be affected by bargaining power. On the second point, the functionalist position is that while some regimes may be dependent on the most powerful states' realization of greater relative gains, this is not the case with regard to most regimes. If regimes endure over many decades during which time international power relations and axes of conflict change and if there is a great deal of continuity in their norms, it would be very difficult to judge that states did not consider the regimes to be in their mutual interests.

At this point it is important to restate the key assertion of a functional and neoliberal theoretical approach that when there are significant mutual interests in cooperation (i.e. all states realize absolute gains), distributional issues and power relations will usually not block the creation of regimes. It is on this argument that this study rests. The next four chapters focus on the importance of mutual interests underlying the norms of the international regimes for shipping, air transport, telecommunications, and postal services. The final chapter reviews the commonalities in the structures among the four regimes and the mutual interests that sustain them. It also comments on some implications of the findings for international relations theory.

3   The international shipping regime

International shipping services and the regulatory framework

Shipping has been crucial to the growth of the world economy for two related reasons. First, as world production expands, international transportation services are required to carry many raw and intermediate goods to manufacturing plants and finished goods to consumers. Second, shipping is a more cost-effective method than land and air transport for moving most bulk goods between states. Without inexpensive, efficient oceanic transportation, world trade would not have grown as fast as it has because higher transportation costs lessen opportunities for exploiting comparative and competitive advantage.

While the importance of international air transport has grown markedly in recent years, with passenger travel and priority mail now almost entirely handled by the aviation sector, shipping continues to dominate the movement of most goods internationally. In the late 1980s, about two-thirds of all international trade by value (and 95 percent by weight) was transported by ship. It is thus not difficult to appreciate how vital world shipping is to international trade and commerce. Shipping is also in itself an important industry – earning about $140 billion annually and employing one million individuals in the late 1980s. The shipbuilding industry earns another $20 billion annually.[1]

The growth of international shipping has been steady and dramatic over the past two centuries. At the end of the Napoleonic Wars in 1815 there were 2.3 million deadweight tons (dwt) of ships involved in foreign trade. By 1870 there were 23 million dwt; and 82 million dwt by 1922. During this period about two-thirds of shipping tonnage was registered in Britain.[2] By 1970 the tonnage of vessels involved in foreign trade had jumped to 326 million dwt, and by mid-1989 it was 638 million dwt.[3] In the years 1970–89 the annual average rate of increase in deadweight tonnage was 16.4 percent.[4]

An important aspect of recent developments in the industry has been changes in the distribution of tonnage registered in different groups of countries. Between 1970 and 1989 the share of the developed market economies dropped from 65 to 32 percent; that of open registries (or flag-of-convenience states) rose from 22 to 35 percent; that of the developing countries rose from 6 to 21 percent; and that of the then socialist states went from 7 to 10 percent. Vessels registered in flag-of-convenience states are largely owned by Western financial interests which register their vessels in these countries to reduce their taxes and operating costs. The two key open registry states are Liberia and Panama which account for close to 80 percent of the tonnage of this group. In the case of the increase of the tonnage of the developing countries this is largely accounted for by the growth in the fleets of small Asian states. In the developed world Japan, the UK, the USA, Norway, and Greece have the largest fleets. Another important characteristic of the present world fleet is the distribution between bulk and nonbulk (or liner) carriers. Around 75 percent of global tonnage is composed of bulk carriers with about half of that accounted for by oil tankers. Of the approximately 25 percent that are nonbulk cargo (or liner) vessels, a high percentage of the tonnage is now accounted for by container vessels.[5]

As indicated above, there are two basic types of vessels and hence of shipping services (liner and bulk). *Liner* shipping generally provides scheduled service at fixed rates between two or more ports and usually carries manufactured goods such as electronics. As a result, liner vessels account for close to 70 percent of global exports by value, but only 25 percent by weight.[6] *Bulk* shipping, on the other hand, operates mainly on a charter basis and specializes in the carriage of liquid and dry bulk commodities such as oil and grains. For most of the past century liner shipping markets have been dominated by cartels or "shipping conferences" of private shipping firms although they are definitely on the decline; and bulk markets have generally been quite competitive.

There are a number of environmental factors, both political and economic, that influence the international shipping regime. In the economic realm, the shipping industry is often plagued by surplus capacity – particularly in recessionary times such as the periods 1981–85 and 1991–92.[7] An important consequence of this surplus capacity is the increasing politicization of the industry as some states attempt to preserve their domestic maritime capabilities in the wake of shrinking and increasingly competitive world markets. Another economic factor shaping the liner shipping industry is the move towards containerized vessels and the establishment of enormous multimodal transport operators which offer point-to-point shipment through interlinked truck, rail, and shipping services. These operators have emerged most notably in the Pacific and North Atlantic trades.[8] In addition to the greater efficiency of intermodalism, it has also dramatically increased the capital requirements for entry and continued operation in the industry, as well as the need for greater managerial skills. These higher capital requirements have led to the establishment of a number of multimodal consortia and mergers among transportation firms.[9] (These developments are all discussed in greater depth in the subsequent section on prices and market shares.)

A significant aspect of international maritime transport, which is found in all international transportation and communications industries, is the legal characteristic of joint sovereignty.[10] By its very nature international shipping requires that two or more states allow exit and entry to a vessel before it can engage in shipping services. However, this "bilaterally shared sovereignty can give rise to policy conflict between different national regulatory regimes – the more so when some countries more aggressively develop or protect their maritime transport capabilities."[11] Therefore it is necessary for states to enter into agreements in order to regulate different aspects of the transactions.

International shipping is sometimes viewed as a bastion of laissez-faire principles and practices, free of international regulation. However, this image does not accord well with reality. The international shipping industry is governed by a plethora of regulations administered by many different national and international organizations and institutions. Many aspects of shipping operations such as jurisdictional issues, damage control problems, and technical barriers, are subject to extensive international regulations, and this was true in large part for prices and market shares in the past. It is on the vast array of these regulatory arrangements that this chapter focuses.

Important international bodies

There is no single intergovernmental organization that is charged with governing all aspects of international shipping. Rather, there are a number of both public and private international organizations that regulate or coordinate governments' and firms' behavior in different parts of the issue area. The structure, function, and orientation of the three most influential will be discussed here although passing reference will be made to others.

The *International Maritime Organization (IMO)*[12] is a United Nations specialized agency, the aim of which is to facilitate cooperation among governments on technical matters of shipping. The governing bodies of the IMO are the Assembly and the Council (consisting of thirty-two members). Most of the diplomatic activity relating to the development of international regulations in the IMO occurs in a number of committees, the most important of which is the Maritime Safety Committee. Other important IMO committees include the Marine Environment Protection Committee, the Legal Committee, the Technical Cooperation Committee, and the Facilitation Committee. The committees are charged with examining practices and technical standards and making regulatory proposals.

Numerous conventions and resolutions have been adopted by the IMO. Since 1959, twenty-three international conventions (as well as many amendments and resolutions) have been adopted, twenty of which are currently in force.[13] The most important IMO conventions are those concerned with safety, and the provisions contained in these conventions are in force in almost all maritime states. The IMO has also adopted a number of conventions designed to prevent marine pollution and to ensure that victims of marine accidents and pollution receive adequate compensation.

The *Comité Maritime International (CMI)* is a private organization of international maritime lawyers which was founded in 1897. Its purpose is to promote the unification of private maritime law and practice. Located in Belgium, the CMI has traditionally formulated draft conventions on primarily private aspects of maritime law and then submitted them to the Belgium government which, in turn, convened an international conference to consider the matters. The preparation of draft conventions within the CMI is a lengthy process. It involves soliciting the views of its members (national maritime law associations) on harmonizing national maritime laws or developing laws on new problems and then convening international meetings to reconcile national differences. Today the CMI works closely with the IMO, the United Nations Commission on International Trade Law (UNCITRAL), and the International Institute for the Unification of Private Law (UNIDROIT).[14]

Since the beginning of this century, twenty CMI conventions have been adopted, and the vast majority of them are in force or have been replaced by other conventions. These conventions have been largely formulated in the private law field and have concerned issues of liability and compensation, ship financing (maritime liens and mortgages), salvage, and certain criminal jurisdictional issues. The generally strong support for these conventions reflects the desire of most states to create a legal environment that is conducive to the facilitation of international shipping and trade. Uniformity is an essential precondition for a growing maritime industry because it promotes both certainty of costs and factor mobility.

The *United Nations Conference on Trade and Development (UNCTAD)* is the newest and most controversial international organization concerned with the shipping industry. Established in 1965 to address commercial issues of concern to developing countries,[15] one of its goals is to examine all aspects of commercial shipping with a view to promoting the development of Third World fleets and ensuring that existing shipping practices do not exploit developing countries. The work of UNCTAD in the shipping field was supervised largely by the Committee on Shipping until 1992. Since then deliberations on shipping have taken place within the Standing Committee on Developing Service Sectors. Although the developing countries – especially some aspiring maritime states – have sought the approval of new regulatory arrangements for a number of dimensions of the international shipping industry, they have not had a major impact on shipping markets.

In addition to the above international bodies, there are a number of industry associations that have influenced the regulatory structure of international shipping, most of which have offices in London. Of particular note is the work of the International Chamber of Shipping (ICS). The ICS is composed of about forty national shipowners' associations, and it participates in the development of technical shipping standards with other nongovernmental bodies and the IMO. Also, the Council of European and Japanese National Shipowners' Associations (CENSA) has been an influential body in the shipping field. It focuses

largely on commercial issues such as government policies toward shipping conferences. Both of these organizations as well as a considerable
number of other nongovernmental organizations actively participate in
the formulation of maritime conventions.[16]

Overview of the international shipping regime

Most aspects of the international shipping regime (outlined in
Table 3.1) have been quite stable over time, and this can be attributed
significantly to states' dedication to the principle of the free movement
of commerce. The norms relating to jurisdictional rights provide
considerable protection for vessels in plying the world's oceans
although coastal states are given limited political control over adjacent
waters. The damage control norms are, as one might project, founded
on both the principles of preventing transnational damage and the free
movement of commerce. The long-standing norms relating to technical
and procedural barriers are based on states' desire to promote the
principles of the free flow of commerce and economic efficiency.

The one area of the shipping regime where there have been some
significant changes is in the area of prices and market shares. Here a
cartel norm was central to the operation of liner shipping for many
years since it was seen as furthering efficiency and the free movement
of international trade. While the cartel norm continues to guide the
behavior of shipping lines on certain routes, there is presently a high
level of open competition on most routes. In the case of bulk shipping
the competition norm has always been accepted by states and shipping
lines since it has been seen as maximizing efficiency and not under-
cutting the free flow of trade.

Jurisdictional rights

Some of the earliest developments of international public law in the
modern state system concerned international shipping, and in fact there
were legal or quasi-legal understandings with regard to navigation on
the oceans going back millennia. The central jurisdictional issues in the
modern era have always been whether ships have rights of access to
different areas of the oceans and whether states have certain rights with
regard to vessels in their coastal zones. One implication of a right of
open access for ships to the high seas is that the regulation of ships'
activities falls to international conferences and organizations.

Table 3.1 *Outline of the international shipping regime*

Principles

Free movement of commerce: obligation of states to reduce impediments to the free movement of goods and services.

Free flow of information: obligation of states to allow the flow of information among peoples of different states.

Efficiency: obligation of states to provide goods and services to their populations at lowest possible cost.

Transnational damage control: obligation of states to prevent activities of their nationals from imposing damages on the nationals and property of other states and to provide compensation for any damages.

Internal political control: right of states to assert jurisdiction and control over activities within their territories and over "legal persons" outside their territories.

Equity: obligation of states to provide all states with a reasonable share of resources and financial returns from international commerce.

Norms

Jurisdictional rights

Freedom of the high seas: right of vessels to have open access to the high seas.
- Relevant principles: free movement of commerce
- Strength: very strong

Innocent passage: right of vessels to transit through the territorial waters of foreign states as long as they do not threaten the peace, good order, and security of those states.
- Relevant principles: free movement of commerce, state political control
- Strength: strong

State control over entry of foreign firms and ships: right to control ships' entry into internal waters (bays and harbors) and the local establishment of foreign shipping firms.

Table 3.1 (*cont.*)

- Relevant principles: state political control
- Strength: strong

Flag state jurisdiction: right of flag states to exercise jurisdiction over the actions of and activities on their flag vessels while on the high seas.
- Relevant principles: state political control, free movement of commerce
- Strength: strong

Damage control

Accident prevention: obligation to prevent vessel accidents that damage the vessels and the goods on board.
- Relevant principles: free movement of commerce, efficiency
- Strength: strong

Crime prevention: obligation to prevent intentional damage to or theft of goods carried by vessels.
- Relevant principles: free movement of commerce, efficiency
- Strength: medium

Spread of disease control: obligation to prevent the transmission of serious diseases among states as a result of movement of vessels and their passengers.
- Relevant principles: free movement of commerce, transnational damage control
- Strength: strong

Pollution prevention: obligation to prevent their own and foreign flag vessels from polluting the marine environment.
- Relevant principles: transnational damage control, free movement of commerce
- Strength: moderately strong

Reasonable compensation: obligation of flag states to assure that reasonable compensation is paid to nationals of other states for damages that have been caused by their flag vessels.
- Relevant principles: transnational damage control, free movement of commerce
- Strength: moderately strong

43

Table 3.1 (*cont.*)

Technical and procedural barriers

Technical interconnection: obligation to agree on common technical and procedural standards relating to vessels' loading and unloading goods in ports.
• Relevant principles: free movement of commerce, efficiency
• Strength: strong

Facilitation: obligation to reduce the financial costs and the time spent by foreign vessels in their ports.
• Relevant principles: free movement of commerce, efficiency
• Strength: moderately strong

National non-discrimination: obligation to allow vessels into ports regardless of their state registry (applies particularly to flag-of-convenience vessels).
• Relevant principles: free movement of commerce, efficiency
• Strength: strong

Prices and market shares

Cartel: obligation of firms to cooperate in controlling rates, division of revenues, and market shares in the international shipping industry.
• Relevant principles: free movement of commerce, efficiency
• Strength: in liner shipping, strong until mid-1970s – weak now except on a modest number of routes; in bulk shipping – very weak

Competition: obligation of firms and states to promote open competition among shipping lines
• Relevant principles: efficiency, free movement of commerce
• Strength: in liner shipping, very weak until the late 1970s – now moderately strong for most routes; in bulk shipping – always strong

===

There have been four central norms of the law of the sea as it relates to international shipping. They are: the *norms of the freedom of the high seas; innocent passage through territorial seas; state control over entry of foreign ships and firms;* and *flag state jurisdiction over vessels on the high seas.* They will be discussed in the context of a historical analysis of the evolution of the law of the sea. The norms reflect a balance between states' commitment to the free movement of international commerce and states' concern to assure political control over their territory and economic entities. Overall, however, priority has been given to the desirability of facilitating the international exchange of goods and services.

The legal notion of the seas as *res communis,* or an area open to all but not appropriable by any, had its historical origins in the era of the Roman empire. However, for more than a millennium after the fall of the Roman empire there was no clear legal order on the world's oceans and, in fact, prior to the seventeenth century states asserted a variety of claims over ocean space. There were times as well when piracy was quite prevalent.[17] This was, however, an era when international maritime commerce was quite modest and when vessels tended to stay close to their home countries.

With the expansion of international exploration and commerce in the sixteenth and seventeenth centuries as a result of progress in international ship-building it was logical that there would be an international debate on the law of the sea. This debate in the seventeenth century centered on the treatises of two Dutch and British legal scholars – Hugo Grotius and John Selden. Each defended his country's maritime interests of the time. Grotius' support for freedom of the seas or *mare liberum* reflected Dutch interests as the major trading state of the day, and Selden's position in favor of the right of coastal states to extend their control over shipping or *mare clausum* supported the British interest in restricting the shipping of the Netherlands and other countries in neighboring seas.[18] Britain, however, soon began to move away from its backing for national extensions of jurisdiction, and along with most other countries it soon embraced the right of "unmolested navigation."[19] Over the course of the seventeenth and eighteenth centuries there were a variety of modest claims to jurisdiction over shipping by coastal states as a result of periodic wars, but on the whole most states' interest in the freedom of international commerce as well as great powers' concern for naval mobility supported broad adherence to freedom of the seas.[20]

It was in the nineteenth century that the *norms of freedom of the high seas* and *innocent passage through territorial seas* were formally recognized by most members of the European state system, and they have endured to the present. Of great importance to the acceptance of freedom of the seas was the influence of Britain. As one author noted: "If the world's greatest commercial empire were the end, then shipping was the means, and freedom the great causal umbrella that heaped benefit on all who stood beneath it. There was now little need for coastal extension of state sovereignty – commerce and trade, of mutual benefit to all who could and would invest in it, took precedence."[21] While Britain was the most important supporter of the regime, virtually all independent countries supported it. Action against minor challenges to freedom of the seas was undertaken not only by Britain but by the other great powers as well for "it came to be universally accepted amongst the maritime states of Europe and America that the sea, constituting the great highway for commerce and communications between 'civilized' nations and the remotest regions of the earth, should remain unrestricted during the continuance of peace for the complete enjoyment of every nation."[22] Of course, peoples that were subject to European colonialism at this time might have taken a different view.

The norm of innocent passage through states' territorial seas (generally recognized as three miles at that time) was also of great importance to the freedom of navigation because it obligated coastal states to allow transit passage by vessels unless they threatened their "peace, good order, and security." This provision was particularly important for the free flow of commerce through international straits where the width was less than six miles. As one author noted, "The concept of innocent passage . . . is at once a restriction on the right of freedom of the seas for navigational purposes and *its guarantee*."[23] In other words, states had a right to act against vessels in their territorial seas only if there were clear evidence that they were posing a security threat.

A component of the public law regime that has existed for centuries is the *norm concerning the right to control the entry of foreign firms and ships*. The aspect of that norm that is key for our purposes is states' complete sovereignty over internal waters or waters within indentations along coastlines such as ports, harbors, and bays. These are areas that are not important for the flow of international commerce, and maritime interests have therefore been willing to accept that coastal states should have complete jurisdictional control.[24] Jurisdiction over these areas, however, gives coastal states the power to exclude foreign vessels from doing business in their countries. They do not often exert this right, but they do exert it on occasion. A non-commercial motive for this norm is that states recognize that it is from these areas that their security can be threatened most seriously by naval vessels; and they therefore want undiluted legal control of these waters.

A final norm that has been recognized for about the last two centuries is flag state jurisdiction or legal control by states of registry (flag states) over their vessels while they are on the high seas. It embodies a balance between the principles of free movement of commerce and state political control over national economic entities.[25] Also, it creates a sense of legal and hence financial certainty for shipowners in that they are clear as to whose legislation they have to obey when on the high seas. Relevant to this point one study has noted that freedom of the seas "would result in chaos, without the corollary principle pursuant to which every vessel sailing on the high seas must have a nationality and remains subject to the supreme and exclusive authority of the state whose flag she is entitled to fly."[26] A comparable point was made by another author to the effect that the principle assures that when ships are on the high seas, they neither find themselves in a "legal vacuum" nor subject to arbitrary coastal state actions.[27] What flag state jurisdiction also means is that international laws applicable to vessels on the high seas must be legislated by the community of states and enforced on vessels by their flag states. This implication of the norm provides the basis for the development and enforcement of international laws for the world's oceans, and while the community of states may not develop conventions for certain maritime problems and individual states may refuse to ratify particular conventions, the historical record indicates that states have developed quite effective international rules for many international maritime issues.

Since the development of a customary law of the seas pertaining to shipping and exploitation of marine resources in the nineteenth century there have been a number of attempts to revise different dimensions of it in the twentieth century. These attempts, however, have not posed serious challenges to the basic law pertaining to commercial navigation. Virtually all of the major challenges concerned control over the economic resources of the oceans. At the first major international conference on the law of the sea in 1930 states were not able to formulate a treaty because of differences as to whether the territorial sea should be kept at three miles or extended several miles. This impasse,

47

however, had little to do with states' views on navigation rights; it basically concerned rights over coastal fisheries.[28] The same scenario basically reoccurred at the First and Second United Nations Conferences on the Law of the Sea in 1958 and 1960. At these meetings states could not agree on the breadth of the territorial sea, but in the 1958 Convention on the High Seas they did affirm customary international law on innocent passage.[29] It should be stressed that the key reason that the maritime powers resisted the increase in the breadth of the territorial sea at prewar and postwar conferences was that they feared how the doctrine of innocent passage through territorial seas might be reinterpreted and used to restrict navigational freedoms – especially in international straits. They were not completely confident that coastal states would not try to expand the notion of threats to their peace, good order, and security in the future.

During the Third United Nations Conference on the Law of the Sea between 1973 and 1982 the international community finally accepted a treaty that covered virtually all issues concerning the law of the sea – namely, the United Nations Convention on the Law of the Sea.[30] They accepted an extension of the territorial sea to twelve miles, but they strengthened the freedom of navigation through the territorial sea by several means. First, a new right of passage through international straits called "transit passage" was accepted, and it gives littoral states almost no grounds for interfering with transiting vessels (Arts. 34–45). Second, coastal states are deprived of their previous right to legislate ship construction and equipment standards in their territorial seas, and this reduced possible grounds for intervening against vessels engaged in "innocent passage" (Art. 21). The only area of the world's oceans where coastal states are given any right to legislate unilateral standards is in ice-covered areas where they are allowed to impose environmental standards (Art. 234). It is sometimes portrayed that the developing countries conceded these navigational rights in exchange for jurisdiction over resources in the 200-mile Exclusive Economic Zone (EEZ), but this is somewhat misleading. The developing countries sometimes portrayed their acceptance of the navigation provisions as part of such a tradeoff because the maritime powers made their acceptance of the EEZ contingent on strong provisions on navigational freedoms. However, most Third World states (those bordering major international straits being the exception) were, in fact, in favor of navigational freedoms. Some had reservations concerning the movement of naval vessels – but not commercial vessels. They realized that they had strong interests in the free flow of maritime commerce – especially if they had any neighbors in a position to impede ships sailing to and from their ports.[31]

In developing a jurisdictional regime for the oceans states have built in certain components that serve their common interests in state control over commercial activities in their territories and over any possible attacks from adjacent waters. These components include complete jurisdiction over vessels in inland waters, the right to intervene against ships in territorial waters if they threaten state security, and jurisdiction over flag vessels on the high seas. However, the dominant principle underlying the law of the sea is the freedom of vessels to ply the world's oceans to engage in international trade. As one author has noted, "the freedom of the high seas is not a self-contained legal principle, but is ancillary to and dependent upon another norm – the right to commerce and communication."[32] A different phrasing of the same point is that "the open (or high) seas provide a necessary means of communication between nations and . . . free use of it is indispensable for international trade and commerce."[33] Over recent centuries states have realized this connection, and this was particularly clear at the Third United Nations Conference on the Law of the Sea. As a study of the politics of national enclosure in the world's oceans noted: "Any nation that benefits from international trade has an incentive to recognize that jingoistic restrictions on navigation amount to an effective tariff against its own imports and exports as well as those of other countries."[34] The ability to engage in maritime transportation without concern for intervention against transoceanic carriers and the ability to gauge costs of transportation are central to the operation of international commerce, and they are the foundations of the prevailing jurisdictional regime. To resort to the terminology of economic theory, the jurisdictional norms are grounded in a concern to reduce impediments to the flow of goods and services, uncertainty of costs, and also transaction costs for both commercial parties and states. On this latter point, global accords on jurisdictions reduce the number of agreements that firms and governments have to make in facilitating the movement of goods.

Damage control problems

The one dimension of the shipping regime in which the largest number of accords have been generated is that concerning damage control. The key damage control problems are the prevention of accidents that damage or destroy cargo and vessels, the prevention of theft of cargo, the control of pollution to marine and shore resources, the prevention of the spread of diseases by ships, and finally compensation for damages or losses. Damage control is the one general shipping issue where it is easiest to make the case that the regulatory regime is regarded as serving the interests of virtually all states. While some states are always interested in avoiding the costs of regulations or in affording their shipping industries a competitive advantage by not adhering to regulations, such states are generally not numerous; and even they recognize certain benefits from adhering to international rules.

There are five main norms relating to damage control: accident prevention, crime prevention, prevention of the spread of diseases, pollution control, and reasonable compensation. That concerning accident control is the strongest, and that pertaining to crime control is the weakest. As will be noted below, crime control impinges closely on states' domestic legal systems, and states are reluctant to accept incursions into such an important political domain. In discussing each of the norms it is only possible to touch briefly on the complex regulatory systems that have evolved over the past century (see Table 3.2 for outline of conventions).

The *accident prevention norm* was not particularly important in the international shipping regime in the nineteenth century – even the latter decades of the century when ocean-going steamships were beginning to take over from wooden sailing vessels. Shipping firms were reluctant to accept standards that would cut into their profits, and governments did not judge that it was their role to regulate such an international industry.[35] However, with the growth in the size, and hence value, of vessels and their cargoes and the rising number of maritime casualties which arose from the increase in international trade, Britain and then other countries began to legislate rules concerning collision prevention and ship standards. In fact, Britain's legislation tended to be accepted as "*de facto* international rules."[36] The first truly international convention in this area was the 1889 Washington Convention on Maritime Safety, and it largely concerned navigational practices.[37]

An important early step toward the acceptance of ship construction and equipment standards was the British Merchant Act of 1906 whose standards were applied to all vessels visiting ports in Britain and British colonies. But as is so often the case, it took a disaster to create the pressure for major change. This disaster was the sinking of *Titanic* in 1912 with a loss of 1,513 lives. It led to the formulation of the Safety of Life at Sea Convention in 1913 – a legal instrument that has been regularly revised since then.[38] In fact, today it is the backbone of the IMO conventions concerned with vessel safety and is accepted by states that account for 95 percent of the world's merchant fleet.[39]

The accident-control regulations, which have grown steadily since the early twentieth century, concern: (1) navigational aids;[40] (2) collision prevention rules;[41] (3) marine traffic control systems;[42] (4) load lines;[43] (5) radio regulations;[44] (6) vessel construction, equipment, and operating standards;[45] and (7) training and certification of seafarers.[46] In the case of the first five sets of regulations there have certainly been differences among states at international conferences, but on the whole the conflicts have not been very acute because they did not seriously affect the profits and competitive positions of shipping firms. This has not been the case with some vessel construction and equipment standards because shipowners are concerned about their ability to pass on the costs and because some states view their national fleets' adherence to international rules as undermining their competitive advantage. These are important reasons why international conferences sometimes end up in stalemate and why certain states seek to avoid acceptance of accords after they have been formulated. In the case of the issue of qualifications of ship officers and crew there has always been a great deal of difficulty in getting international agreements because crew costs are an important component of overall operating costs (and hence affect the profits and competitive positions of the shipowners), and because national training and testing programs vary a great deal. Consequently the 1978 convention dealing with the issue establishes goals more than it imposes requirements. Strong accords would be very difficult to reach in this area.

Most states as well as shipowners and shippers unquestionably have seen accident-control regulations as serving their mutual interests although they have wanted to minimize the costs of the regulations. Global regimes have reduced uncertainty of costs by establishing global rules and reducing the number of accidents and have lowered transaction costs for shipping firms and states by establishing a single international negotiating forum for most issues. There is also another tremendously important reason that global regimes are seen as both reducing cost uncertainty and promoting the flow of commerce, and this is the fear that if there are not broadly accepted international

Table 3.2 *International agreements concerning damage control, pollution damage, and compensation*

I. Damage control

A. Unintentional damage (vessel construction, equipment, and operating standards)

Collision Prevention Rules	1889
International Radiotelegraph	1906
(provisions re. use of maritime radio communications) (amended frequently by International Radiotelegraph Union and after 1933 by International Telecommunications Union)	
Collision Prevention Rules	1910
Safety of Life at Sea (SOLAS) (first)	1913
Safety of Life at Sea (second)	1929
Maritime Signals	1930
Manned Lightships Not on their Stations	1930
Load Lines	1930
Uniform System of Maritime Buoyage and Rules Annexed Thereto	1936
Safety of Life at Sea (third)	1948
Collision Prevention Rules (amended 1965)	1948
International Association of Lighthouse Authorities	1955
Safety of Life at Sea (fourth)	1960
Facilitation of International Maritime Traffic (amended 1990)	1965
Load Lines (amended 1971, 1975, 1979, 1988)	1966
Tonnage Measurement of Ships	1969
Special Trade Passenger Ships (amended 1973)	1971
Regulations for Preventing Collisions at Sea (COLREGS) (amended 1989)	1972
Safe Containers	1972
Carriage of Passengers and Their Luggage by Sea (amended 1976, 1990)	1974
Safety of Life at Sea (fifth) (amended 1978, 1983, 1988, 1991)	1974
International Maritime Satellite Organization (INMARSAT) and its Operating Agreement	1975
Carriage of Passengers and Their Luggage by Sea Protocol (amended 1990)	1976

Table 3.2 (*cont.*)

International Maritime Satellite Organization (INMARSAT)
   and its Operating Agreement   1976
Standard Marine Navigation Vocabulary   1977
Standards of Training, Certification and Watchkeeping
   for Seafarers   1978
Maritime Search and Rescue   1979
Safety of Fishing Vessels   1987
Salvage   1989

B. Intentional damage (crimes against vessels and goods)

International Maritime Bureau (gathers/disseminates info
   related to maritime crime; established by ICC;
   *not a convention)   1981
Maritime Fraud Prevention Exchange
   (established by UNCTAD)   1988
Suppression of Unlawful Acts Against the Safety of
   Maritime Navigation   1988

II. Pollution and disease control

Prevention of Pollution of the Sea by Oil
   (amended 1962, 1969, 1971)   1954
Civil Liability for Oil Pollution Damage (Brussels
   Liability Convention; amended 1984)   1969
Intervention on the High Seas in Cases of Oil Pollution
   Casualties   1969
Establishment of an International Fund for Compensation
   for Oil Pollution Damage (amended 1976, 1984)   1971
Prevention of Pollution from Ships (MARPOL)
   (amended 1978, 1989, 1990, 1992)   1973
Protocol Relating to Intervention on the High Seas
   in Cases of Marine Pollution by Substances other than Oil   1973
Oil Pollution Preparedness, Response, and Cooperation   1990
International Sanitary Convention (amended frequently)   1903
International Health Regulations (amended frequently)   1951

Table 3.2 (*cont.*)

III. Compensation

Unification of Certain Rules of Law With Respect to Collision Between Vessels	1910
Unification of Certain Rules Relating to the Limitation of Liability of Owners of Sea-Going Vessels	1924
Unification of Certain Rules Relating to the Bill of Lading (the Hague Rules) (amended 1967, Hague-Visby Rules)	1924
Limitation of Liability of Owners of Sea-Going Ships	1957
Tanker Owners' Voluntary Agreement on Liability for Oil Pollution (TOVALOP)	1969
Civil Liability for Oil Pollution Damage	1969
Contract Regarding the Interim Settlement of Tanker Liability for Oil Pollution (CRISTAL)	1971
Establishment of an International Fund for Compensation for Oil Pollution Damage	1971
Civil Liability in the Field of Maritime Carriage of Nuclear Material	1971
Carriage of Passengers and Their Luggage by Sea	1974
Limitation of Liability for Maritime Claims	1976
Carriage of Goods By Sea (the Hamburg Rules)	1978
International Multimodal Transport of Goods	1980

Sources: IMO News (various issues) and different books on maritime safety, marine pollution, and international health. See especially Nagendra Singh, *International Maritime Law Conventions*, 4 vols., 3rd edn (London: Stevens, 1983). Dates of amendments include both "amendments" and "protocols." The IMO also approves many recommendations and codes, and these are often subsequently integrated into conventions.

regimes, states will legislate their own unique schemes. And this will lead in consequence to problems in judging shipping costs, to higher freight rates, and hence to some reluctance to use shipping services. States, shippers, and shipowners generally have comparable perspectives on this matter.

There is, however, almost always a problem in gaining adherence of all states to conventions that impose significant costs on shipowners –

and the larger the costs of the regulations, the bigger the problem. Some states judge that if they do not accept a convention, their flag vessels will have a competitive advantage over those of other states that do accept it. Often the states opposed to adherence are less wealthy than the major maritime powers and see remaining outside shipping agreements as a way of promoting their shipping industries. The flag-of-convenience countries have pursued such policies of evading global standards at times. The resistance of such states, however, seldom succeeds in a major way because the maritime powers want to assure broad adherence so as not to place their industries at a competitive disadvantage and because they want to discourage unilateral legislative approaches to ship standards. The basic strategy that they use to prevent non-acceptance of international conventions is to require that all vessels using their ports meet convention requirements. If the major trading states enforce such a rule, virtually the entire world fleet has to comply.

Most international shipping conventions stipulate that in order for a convention to enter into force states accounting for between one-half and two-thirds of the world deadweight tonnage have to accept it. In fact, the support of the major trading countries is probably more important since they are in a position to enforce most ship standards in their ports. On the whole there is a basic agreement among the major maritime and trading states in most areas of ship standards that global rules are of the utmost importance because of the detrimental effects of a patchwork pattern of regulations among coastal states.

The *norm of maritime crime prevention* is definitely not as strong as that concerning accident prevention because it touches so directly on states' legal systems. This is in some ways surprising because maritime crime (e.g. theft and fraudulent payments) has grown rapidly – one estimate placing it at $13 billion annually.[47] There is no doubt that it has increased insurance premiums. The key problem in developing a strong international legal system, as alluded to above, is that the punishment of maritime crimes often requires the gathering of information in foreign states, and states often have quite different legal procedures and substantive views concerning the punishment of crimes. One legal scholar has concluded that "where evidence is overseas, the practical difficulties in securing it and the cost involved generally render it unattractive to pursue the matter" and that "the international fraudster who orders his business with a degree of care has virtual immunity."[48] Also, states find it very difficult to standardize legal procedures and criminal laws on matters such as extradition. These areas remain rather sacrosanct spheres of national jurisdiction. As one national official remarked, international criminal enforcement involves "many complicated issues that often step on state jurisdictions and governments do not want to accept restrictions on these matters."[49]

The one area of maritime crime that has been addressed in an international convention is terrorism, and that occurred in the wake of the *Achille Lauro* incident when Palestinians took control of the vessel and killed an American passenger.[50] One of its explicit purposes is that terrorism should not "seriously affect the operation of maritime services" (Preamble). Like other conventions dealing with terrorism the obligations to prosecute violators allow a choice as to where the violators should be prosecuted and a reasonable degree of latitude in the penalties imposed, but it does represent progress in building that aspect of the shipping regime dealing with maritime crime. The greatest amount of collaboration in dealing with maritime crime has come largely in the sphere of information sharing. In 1981 the International Chamber of Commerce established the International Maritime Bureau to gather and disseminate information relating to maritime crime, but it is composed of solely private businesses.[51] Also, in 1988 UNCTAD created the Maritime Fraud Prevention Exchange in London to serve as a clearing house for information in this area.[52] Presently UNCTAD is working on a draft of minimum standards for shipping agents whose practices are central to the control of maritime crime.

One important point concerning maritime crime is that many cases are prosecuted successfully in the states where they occur. Often adequate information to convict criminals is located there. However, cases where the victims are in one jurisdiction and the criminals are in another are common as well. Despite the common interest of shippers, shipowners, and governments in curtailing maritime crime, the regime regulations remain weak because of the reluctance of states to adjust their legal procedures and prescriptions.

There are two types of third parties that can be injured by international shipping. They are individual users of coastal facilities that are damaged by pollution and individuals who are victims of diseases carried by vessels. The plight of the latter is addressed by the *norm against the spread of diseases* whose origins date back to international conferences in the mid-nineteenth century. The international health problem at that time was that diseases such as cholera and yellow fever were transmitted by ships and their passengers – especially those traveling between Asia and Europe. In response to these developments European states, especially those most severely affected on the Mediterranean, enacted a variety of restrictions – the most important being the imposition of quarantines on vessels in their ports. These restrictions were strongly resisted by many shipowners who viewed the restrictions as imposing extra and often unanticipated costs. In some cases vessels were treated in a discriminatory fashion. For this reason, it was shipping interests that were the major advocates of uniform international regulations. However, at the first conference in 1851, and at another six in the next four decades, there was no agreement because of differences in interests between various shipping and trading states and because of scientific disagreements on the ways in which the diseases were transmitted. Finally, by the 1890s the problems for shipping interests were becoming sufficiently severe and medical knowledge had advanced enough that four international accords were concluded. These were superseded by the International Sanitary Convention of 1903. This convention was further developed in the following decades, and in 1951 the newly created World Health Organization (WHO) revised its terms and relabeled them the International Health Regulations. International health regulations that apply to shipping encourage information sharing, require that states have certain health facilities in their ports, and regulate the use of quarantines in the case of ships suspected of carrying diseases.[53]

In the case of control of the transmission of diseases by ships there are two sets of interests – those of the states where the ships dock and those of the shipowners. It is significant that the first thrust for international regulation came from the shipowners who were distressed by the varied and sometimes arbitrary regulations of the Mediterranean states. Shipowners were willing to accept uniform rules, but not to accept unexpected and non-uniform rules that affected their competitive advantage and that discouraged the use of shipping services.

The third-party damage problem in the international shipping industry that has achieved a higher profile than disease transmission in recent decades is *pollution control*. In large part the problem is one of fouling and poisoning of coastal areas from ship discharges and accidental spills – for the most part, from oil. There were some international meetings to consider the issue of intentional or operational discharges before World War II, but they were not successful in developing international controls. The first major convention was concerned solely with oil pollution control, and it was signed in 1954. It was revised several times by the IMO before being superseded by a convention that addressed all forms of pollution from ships in 1973 – the International Convention for the Prevention of Pollution from Ships. Before the 1973 convention and its amendments came into force in the 1980s, compliance rested basically on detection of discharges at sea or inspection at loading ports, and hence the levels of compliance were not particularly good. The 1973 convention and its amendments reduce the possibility of pollution because certain construction and equipment standards make discharges impossible and others make illegal discharges detectable at discharge terminals – largely in the industrialized nations. Compliance with discharge standards is now much higher than it was in the past. It is, however, important to point out that two compliance problems that have existed since the 1954 convention came into force still exist – albeit to a lesser degree. They are the unwillingness of some states to inspect foreign vessels in their ports and the reluctance of some flag states to prosecute their own vessels as diligently as they might. The inspection problem is not as serious a problem now because even a small number of conscientious inspectors in the industrialized world can have quite an impact. In the case of the willingness of flag states to prosecute their vessels for violations, a real problem remains, but it has definitely improved over recent decades.[54]

The pollution-control norm is relatively strong in the regime both because a good number of the most important maritime and trading states are recipients of pollution, and because virtually all maritime and trading states are concerned about the possible imposition of varied national controls on ships transiting coastal waters. These national controls could, in fact, include the assertion of jurisdiction over vessel activities in territorial seas beyond what states now have, and this is anathema to shipping interests. In fact, in the 1982 Convention on the Law of the Sea coastal states lost their previous right to legislate ship construction and equipment standards in their territorial seas because of a concern to assure freedom of navigation. The central concern of trading and shipping interests is that all countries accept international accords so that coastal states do not impose unilateral controls and assert new forms of jurisdiction. As Michael M'Gonigle and Mark Zacher note in their study of the politics of marine pollution control: "Considering the complexity and diversity of the industry's operations across numerous boundaries, unilateral action that would create a variety of national standards is anathema . . . For maritime interests, uniformity has been the battle cry in a struggle to retain free access to all of the world's oceans and to prevent the imposition of uneven costs."[55] One could say that coastal state interests have determined that there would be pollution controls on shipping, but maritime and trading interests have determined that these controls are global as opposed to national or regional.

A final issue related to the pollution control regulations is: to what extent are the regulations simply the product of the interests and power of the developed countries and particularly the United States? It is certainly the case that the regulations would not have developed as soon or been as strong if it had not been for the industrialized powers. However, it is important to realize that the developing countries are sensitive to impediments to commercial navigation just as the developed countries are – even if they may not attach the same weight to marine pollution control. Both the Third World and European states were swayed by the threat of unilateral US legislation in 1973, 1978, and 1990 when conferences of the IMO approved new equipment and construction standards for ships. The USA unquestionably obtained more stringent and expensive standards than the other states wanted, but they were all committed to one set of global standards. The most powerful state in the international oil transportation industry obtained largely what it wanted, but it too compromised to assure international uniformity in shipping standards.[56]

An important issue that cuts across all of the damage control issues previously discussed is that of financial liability. There has always been a struggle between shippers and shipowners as to the responsibility of shipowners for losses under certain conditions and the limit of the liability. More recently there has been a comparable struggle involving cargo-owners (e.g. oil companies), coastal states, and shipowners as to the liability for damages caused by accidental or intentional discharges. On the whole, there have been legal agreements that have determined responsibility for losses, and hence insurance requirements, because the various parties (and especially the shipowners) have wanted a high degree of certainty as to their costs.[57]

With the expansion of international shipping in the seventeenth century it was established that there should be a limit to the liability of shipowners. This was "probably one of the first instances of state support for its shipping industry,"[58] and it was viewed as "necessary to protect embryonic merchant industries from ruinous losses."[59] At first

59

the shipowner was liable in cases where he was responsible for an accident, but by the nineteenth century the shipping industry was successful in removing almost any liability from the shipowner's shoulders. Some governments, such as those in the USA and the British Dominions, responded by legislating a division of responsibility between the shipowner and shipper. Consequently the problems caused by a diversity in national standards as well as lobbying by shipper interests led to sufficient political pressure for a change.[60] The resultant agreement is known as the Hague Rules of 1924. While shipper interests thought that shipowners were given too many loopholes and that the limit of liability was too low, almost all states accepted the compromise division of responsibility between the two interests. This promoted a greater degree of financial certainty among parties in the industry and removed liability standards as a competitive issue. No longer could shipowners lobby their governments against the imposition of liability on the grounds that it would undermine their international competitive position.[61]

The Hague Rules were revised in 1968 and became the Hague-Visby Rules. They placed greater responsibility on the shipowner, but the responsibility was not heavy enough from the perspective of the developing countries. The latter pressed for their revision, and they achieved this with the formulation of the Hamburg Rules in 1978.[62] Because of developed country reservations concerning the burden placed on shipowners in the Hamburg Rules, they have not been ratified by enough countries to enter into force, and the Hague-Visby Rules are still the accepted guidelines for the industry. However, regardless of different states' and commercial interests' views on the shortcomings of these rules and a number of other conventions dealing with liability, there is a great deal of predictability in the industry as to actual and possible financial burdens.

Since the 1960s, and particularly since the sinking of the *Torrey Canyon* in 1967, the issue of liability for pollution damage has been an important issue. Every time that another oil tanker such as the *Argo Merchant* or the *Amoco Cadiz* discharges large amounts of oil after an accident, the liability and compensation question is examined anew. In fact, the basic framework of the present regime was put in place in conferences among governments and private industrial interests in the four years after the *Torrey Canyon* disaster. There was a tremendous amount of conflict over the distribution and extent of liability among shipping and cargo (i.e. oil company) interests, but there was virtually no question as to whether an international regime would emerge. Almost all participants were determined that there should not be a patchwork pattern of national regulations and that coastal interests should be provided with reasonable compensation for the damage and costs that they sustained.[63]

In reviewing what has evolved in those aspects of the shipping regime dealing with damage control, it is, first, crucial to recognize that except for the area of international maritime crime there are reasonably strong regulatory arrangements. In the case of crime, the fact that criminal acts can often be prosecuted in single national jurisdictions and that international regulations would impinge seriously on national systems of criminal law have impeded progress. However, cooperation in preventing and investigating maritime crime is growing.

With regard to accident prevention, pollution prevention, and compensation for damages, the key underlying principles are, of course, the free movement of commerce and transnational damage control. In order to promote these principles states have developed international regulations to reduce uncertainty of costs, transaction costs, and impediments to the flow of goods and services, and they have acted to curtail a negative externality (i.e. pollution). Some states have also favored an international regime because they have feared that the shipping fleets of some other states might be able to gain a competitive advantage if international rules were not developed. Overall the central goal of most states has been a uniform set of rules, and consequently they have discouraged diverse international laws. International uniformity certainly reduces uncertainty and transaction costs, and it also lessens the possibility that national laws and actions will impede the movement of international commerce.

Technical and procedural barriers

The key barriers to the flow of shipping services and their cargoes are the administrative procedures required for ships and goods in ports, equipment interconnection standards for ships and port facilities, and an unwillingness to allow flag-of-convenience vessels into ports. A particular norm addresses each of these problems.

The *facilitation norm* concerns the issue of administrative procedures that apply to vessels and their goods when they arrive in port. It prescribes simply that states should seek to reduce the work and time required for vessels in their ports. Shipping companies have always complained about delays in ports caused by regulations concerning the entry of ships, cargo, and passengers or by a lack of knowledge of these administrative requirements. A 1959 study noted that the shipping industry was drowning in "a sea of red tape" and that the documents required for planes in foreign airports were considerably less than what was required of vessels.[64] For the most part states have been receptive to the acceptance of regulations that reduce loading and unloading problems because of pressure from shippers. However, problems have been endemic because there are long-standing differences in national laws and a variety of government departments are usually involved.

The major international attempt at bringing some uniformity to the documentary requirements for ships was the 1963 American Convention of Mar del Plata which established simplified procedures for meeting customs, immigration, and health requirements.[65] At the time these problems were also being considered in the International Maritime Organization, and these deliberations eventuated in the 1965 Convention on Facilitation of International Maritime Traffic.[66] Its purpose is to "facilitate and expedite international maritime traffic and to prevent unnecessary delays to ships and to person and property on board" by "promoting uniformity in formalities, documentary requirements and procedures" (Arts. 1 and 2). It is, however, important to point out that the convention does not require that states adhere to certain practices. They are merely obligated to simplify and unify their customs and immigration standards along lines suggested in the treaty, and if they do legislate different or supplementary standards, they are obligated to inform the IMO so that the information can be distributed within the industry. This more flexible approach to international standardization is less "psychologically offensive to national sovereignty" in important policy areas such as customs and immigration controls and hence facilitates international accord.[67] The 1965 convention, in fact, entered into force in 1967 and is now accepted by close to sixty states. In addition, many non-ratifying states follow its prescriptions and proscriptions very closely. Overall, states still hold to the view which they shared at the time of the 1965 conference that it is very detrimental to the growth of international trade to allow delays of vessels and frequent rejection of goods in ports because of documentary requirements or inadequate dissemination of the national requirements.[68]

In international shipping the need to standardize technologies has been much less important than it has been in telecommunications and even air transport. Traditionally there was almost no need to standardize equipment between ships and port facilities because there was so little interdependency between the two. Ships tied up at docks, and cranes lifted the cargo boxes from the vessels. A few technical standards were developed (largely through the International Standards Organization), but they were relatively minor in importance. The *technical interconnection norm* only really came into play in a major way with the widespread adoption of containerization in the 1970s. Containers had to fit storage areas in ships, trucks, and trains, and in addition the cranes that loaded and unloaded the containers had to be built to handle containers of a set size. Standard parameters for containers were formulated by the International Standards Organization (ISO) since common dimensions are necessary for "interchangeability, compatibility and intermodality of containers and also for promoting effective use of container-handling facilities, ships and inland transport vehicles."[69] Now almost all containers are built according to these specifications, and there is no doubt that standardization has promoted the exponential growth of container vessels and multimodal transportation firms (e.g. US Lines, Evergreen, and K Line) in the last several decades.

Quite a unique issue of market access in the postwar era has concerned whether states should admit all flag vessels into their ports – and in particular those registered in "open registry" or "flag-of-convenience" states. The practice of shipping firms in developed countries registering their vessels in developing countries whose tax, crew, and other requirements are not as stringent as those in their home countries originated before World War II – but on a very minor scale. It was not until after the war that Western (especially US) shipping firms began to register significant tonnage under Liberian and Panamanian registries. The USA naturally became the leading proponent of the *national non-discrimination norm* according to which states are obligated to admit all flag vessels into their ports. During the 1950s the traditional European shipping powers were the first states to challenge flags of convenience, since the Liberian and Panamanian registered vessels, of course, undermined the competitive positions of their flag lines. In the 1958 Convention on the High Seas the European states were able to secure a provision that there must be a "genuine link" between the shipping firm that owned a vessel and the state of registry, but the meaning of the phrase was left unclear. Then, by the 1970s, Western resistance to flags of convenience almost disappeared as most Western shipowners realized that they could not compete with shipping firms registered in the Third World while adhering to their home states' legislation on issues such as crewing and taxes. Most of them, therefore, transferred their registrations to Third World states.[70]

Since 1970 the main challenge to flags of convenience has come from some Third World shipping states such as Brazil and India that see the flag-of-convenience states as an obstacle to their securing larger shares of shipping markets.[71] As a result of their pressure a rather general provision for a "genuine link" was retained in the 1982 Convention on the Law of the Sea, but it has not served to undermine flags of convenience because of most states' concern for cheaper shipping services.[72] Also, in the early 1980s some maritime developing countries pressed for the conclusion of a treaty that would elaborate on the meaning of "genuine link," and in 1986 a United Nations Convention on Conditions for Registration of Ships was concluded. However, the requirements for the registration of vessels are very general, and in addition states cannot enforce the convention against foreign vessels in their ports. Apart from the fact that the developed countries were not willing to retreat in their backing for open registry, the developing world was by no means united on the issue. Some aspiring shipping states were dedicated opponents of flags of convenience, but many benefited by the lower shipping costs afforded by flag-of-convenience vessels and opposed their elimination. This was especially true of countries that exported bulk commodities.[73]

Overall the open registry norm has been viewed by the majority of states as serving their interests. There has always been a small group of states that sought to protect their national fleets from competition from flag-of-convenience vessels. At first the challenge came largely from the European maritime states – and later a number of Third World countries. In the end the interests of shippers, consumers and a significant group of Western shipowners prevailed.

With regard to the three norms concerning procedural and technical barriers, it is clear that they are all relatively strong. They all reduce impediments to the flow of international goods and services and promote economic efficiency. States resist certain standardized procedures on issues such as customs and immigration, and a few maritime countries oppose open registries. The overall picture, however, is one of states' willingness to support the efficient movement of goods and people in their ports.

Prices and market shares

The issues of prices and market shares in the international shipping industry have been dealt with quite differently in the bulk and liner trades since the latter part of the nineteenth century. In the case of bulk trades there has generally been an acceptance of an open competitive market – hence the dominance of the *competition norm*. On the other hand, in liner trades there has been an acceptance of a *cartel norm* or cartels of shipping firms known as "shipping conferences" over most of the past century. Conditions supportive of shipping conferences began to erode dramatically in the late 1970s, and since then their share of liner trades has slipped from around 90 to 50 percent.[74] However, except on the small number of routes where only conference vessels operate, the conference lines do not have a strong influence over prices and market shares. It is important to note that while shipping conferences have been formed by shipowners, they have had the implicit, and often explicit, approval of governments (e.g. the US and Canadian governments have passed legislation exempting conferences from anti-trust legislation). In recent decades the support of governments as well as shippers for shipping conferences has weakened, but shipping conferences are still seen as very important in certain geographical trades.

A key issue in the regulatory arrangements governing international shipping is why states supported cartels for liner trades for approximately a century. One of the two *potential* bases of mutual interest in supporting liner cartels could be states' interest in protecting their shipping industries. More specifically, a cartel could be seen as assuring many countries' shipping industries sufficiently high prices and market shares that they could remain in business. In fact, this consideration has not been very important for most countries, although it has had some influence on a modest number of maritime states. The other potential basis of mutual interest is a perception that a cartel furthers efficiency and a free movement of commerce because of the existence of economies of scale in liner shipping. More specifically, there is the related fear that open competition would lead to widely fluctuating prices, periodic disruptions in service, and destructive competition that might lead to monopolies on some routes. This reasoning, in fact, had a major impact on most states' support for liner cartels until very recently, and even now it underlies states' support for shipping conferences in some trades. The fear of disruption in services has been particularly crucial to states' support for cartels for much of the past century because of the salience of shipping to the flow of international commerce. This traditional rationale is captured by the comment that "liner shipping operates in structurally unstable markets. This instability fundamentally conflicts with the economic function of liner shipping to support international trade."[75] Of course, as shipping conferences have seen their importance to the regularity of shipping decline, so have they seen a gradual fall in support for conferences from shippers and governments.

Bulk shipping

Bulk shipping, which mainly involves the shipment of commodities, accounts for around 75 percent of international shipping by weight but only about 30 percent by value. With regard to liquid bulk shipments petroleum has always dominated, and with respect to dry bulk shipments the dominant commodities have been iron ore, coal, grain, phosphates, and bauxite/alumina. Approximately 90 percent of all vessels involved in bulk trades are on long-term charter, and of those about a third are owned by the multinational firms that are involved in the export and import of the bulk goods. The length of charter arrangements between shippers and independent shipping firms varies considerably. The basic formats of the contracts are, however, spelled out in model contracts that have been developed by organizations such as the Baltic and International Maritime Council (BIMCO).[76]

Bulk shipping has always been quite competitive, and the great majority of states are committed to the competition norm. In both the long-term charter market as well as the single-voyage charter market, which accounts for about 10 percent of all sailings, there is strong competition. One study has noted that "Tramp shipping [chartering of vessels for single voyages] is an industry that has a market which functions under conditions that are not dissimilar to the theoretical model of perfect competition."[77] The increasingly specialized character of a good number of bulk carriers has undercut the competitive character of the market to an extent, but not to a serious degree.[78]

The reasons for the high level of competitiveness in the bulk sector are reasonably simple. Voyages by bulk carriers are generally between two ports, and vessels are usually chartered far in advance of a voyage. There are a large number of shipowners from many countries offering the services of their vessels, and a potential charterer usually has a range of firms from which to choose. If by chance a shipping firm goes out of business between the time a shipper charters a vessel and the time of the voyage, another vessel can be chartered on the short-term charter market. Therefore, competition does not threaten disruptions in the market in the sense that shippers do not suddenly discover that vessels are not available at certain times.

Beginning in 1979 some developing maritime states sought to obtain commitments by the developed countries to guarantee their shipping lines a share of the bulk market, but the developed nations would not be moved. Unlike the case with the liner market the developed countries argued that there are no institutional impediments such as shipping conferences to entry into the bulk market, and in addition there are no economic arguments that cartels would enhance global welfare. It was stated bluntly that if the developing countries could offer bulk carriers at competitive rates, they would be chartered. The developing countries argued about the obstacles created by the long-term charter arrangements between multinational firms and shipping companies, but their arguments were not viewed as convincing.[79] Some developing states have also tried to increase their market share by promoting the abolition of flag-of-convenience registries (in other Third World states!), but they have been rebuffed in this strategy.[80] One study has pointed out that, in fact, the great majority of Third World commodity exporters benefit from low shipping costs and have little interest in the proposals which would raise shipping rates.[81] There is basically a strong consensus among most states in favor of a competitive market for bulk trades.

Liner shipping

The modern age of international shipping began around the 1870s with the development of the steamship. This technological innovation coincided with the opening of the Suez Canal, and the two developments produced surplus capacity and, concomitantly, intense competition and rate wars among shipping companies.[82] In response to this situation a prominent British shipowner launched negotiations in 1875 to establish rates and divide the market among competing liner companies serving the Britain–India trade. This first "shipping conference," known as the Calcutta Conference, was soon followed by the steady growth of other shipping conferences that established rates and divided business on various routes. By 1900 there were 100

shipping conferences for different routes and trades, and in the 1970s
there were around 360. The number of lines in a particular conference
has ranged from two to forty. From the early twentieth century to
around the mid-1970s the network of shipping conferences controlled
about 90 percent of international liner shipping.[83]

Shipping conferences are composed of independent shipping lines
that enter into collusive agreements to establish rates and usually
market shares for particular routes, and they often engage in revenue
pooling. The membership of conferences often overlaps since particular
shipping lines frequently serve a variety of international routes. The
primary rationale for a cooperative agreement among liner firms
serving a particular trade route is to increase efficiency in production
and marketing or, in other words, to service a set of ports at regular
intervals at rates that are close to cost.[84] One common strategy utilized
by conferences to maintain the loyalty of shippers to conference vessels
is the use of tying arrangements or loyalty contracts. Loyalty contracts
generally include promises by shippers to supply cargo to conference
lines and promises by conference lines to give rebates and cheaper rates
to shippers, all of which are justified on the basis that they reduce risk,
promote regular service, and reduce costs.[85]

"Closed conferences," which predominated in the world liner
industry over the past century, control the entry of new members – and
generally require unanimity of existing members for the admission of
new firms. Apart from setting rates and sailing schedules, closed
conferences often pool revenues and use the same port facilities. "Open
conferences," which have operated in US trades since the US adoption
of anti-trust legislation for the shipping industry in 1916, are limited
basically to rate setting and must admit any vessel operators that want
to join as long as they meet certain conditions. The USA, in fact, has not
always rigorously imposed its anti-trust legislation on liner shipping
since it has sometimes wanted to support its own national shipping
lines and to assist the national lines of foreign allies. However, until
very recently it adopted a more pro-competition policy than did the
European states and Japan. On the other hand, it is important to recognize that the European countries, while permitting closed conferences,
generally did not adopt hostile stances toward independent or non-
conference lines and, in fact, exerted some pressure on conference lines
to meet the complaints of shippers. Hence, the traditional gap between
the USA and other industrialized countries has not been as great as is
portrayed by some observers. Very recently there has been an about-

face in the relationship between the European Union and the USA with the former adopting a more pro-competition stance than the latter.[86]

There have been criticisms of shipping conferences from the very beginning of their existence, and there have been a variety of government and academic studies that examined the criticisms. Just prior to World War I major British and US government studies were published. Both were basically supportive of the benefits of liner conferences although the American report was quite critical of certain conference policies.[87] A recent OECD publication noted that of the many government studies of conferences over the years, "Nearly all investigations concluded that, despite a number of drawbacks, the conference system was indispensable as a means of enabling shipowners to provide shippers with regular and efficient services at relatively stable freight rates." However, the OECD report observed that these studies did not agree on the desirability of particular government regulations concerning shipping conferences.[88] It is also important to note that most governments have supported counterweights to conferences in the form of both supporting regular negotiations between conferences and shippers' councils and providing access for independent lines to port facilities. These measures have helped to ensure that conference lines do not impose excessively high rates.[89]

The basic rationale for the conferences, which has been reiterated by many sources, is that in the case of liner trades an absence of regulation will lead to "destructive competition" (rate wars and interruptions in service after the collapse of firms) and that a cartel can best provide reliable service and stable rates. The economic characteristics of an industry that lead to destructive competition are economies of scale with high fixed or sunk costs, inelasticity of demand, and frequent excess supply.[90] The historical position of shippers, which has weakened in recent years, is that they supported conferences and paid premium rates in order to assure reliable and high quality service.[91] One thing that should be stressed about past and present analyses in favor of liner conferences is that they generally assume that the shipping industry should provide regular service to a large number of ports. They recognize that shipping companies might be able to increase their profits by concentrating on "thick" routes (often referred to as "cream skimming") but that this would come at the cost of less regular service and higher rates for the "thin" routes. Given the fact that shipping is an important infrastructure industry on which many other industries depend, both government and business officials put considerable weight on the reliability and comprehensiveness of the system.[92] A good summary of the above thinking appeared in a 1989 study by the US government: "Conference agreements have been justified on the basis that they provide stable and nondiscriminatory service and rates. While conference rates may be higher than they would be in purely competitive markets, conferences do offer a degree of certainty for shippers in terms of rate stability and regular sailings."[93]

Since the l960s shipping conferences have been criticized by many sources, but for the most part they have not constituted blanket indictments. A few critics have noted that the conferences' primary accomplishment has been to maximize profits for member shipping lines,[94] but such basic challenges have been infrequent. Shippers have always criticized conference practices on such things as rate-setting and scheduling, but for the most part they have sought to alter conference policies rather than to eliminate the conferences altogether.[95] There were extensive negotiations in the 1960s and early 1970s between Western shippers and the conferences, and they produced various recommendations as well as a set of guidelines called the CENSA Code. For different reasons the USA and the developing countries opposed the CENSA Code and prevailing conference practices. The former favored more competitive practices, and the Third World states wanted larger shares of conference business for their fleets.[96]

One of the major thrusts behind the attempts by Western shipowners and shippers to work out some understandings on conference practices starting in the late 1960s was the demand of developing countries that their national shipping firms be admitted to conferences serving their ports and be given equitable shares of the cargo. In the end they succeeded in securing approval of the 1974 UNCTAD Code on Liner Shipping, which provides their national lines with automatic membership in conferences serving their ports and assures them of a significant portion (40 percent) of their exports and imports. For a number of reasons the Liner Code has not had a major impact, but for the purpose of this analysis the key message to take from the UNCTAD deliberations is that the developing maritime states, while opposing certain conference practices, were strong backers of the shipping conferences. The government-blessed international cartels are excellent devices for sheltering developing-state firms by providing "equitable" market shares and high rates.[97]

While there was some movement in the 1960s and 1970s toward the settlement of conflicts between conferences, on the one hand, and both shippers and developing states, on the other, it was during this time that the share of liner shipping markets controlled by the conferences began to drop steadily. From over 90 percent before 1970 it dropped to around the 50 percent range of today. The most dramatic decrease actually occurred in the 1980s, and according to the OECD shipping conferences' share of the market on a number of major routes declined from 82 to 60 percent between 1985 and 1989.[98] The implications of this decline in the roles of conference vessels in many trades was expressed well in a 1994 study:

> conferences have difficulties to remain effective. Often, their market shares have declined so much that their capacity regulating function is no longer existing at all. In respect of prices, their role is sometimes hardly more than setting a reference level, giving full way to the tendency of marginal pricing by individual carriers.[99]

The routes where the conferences have particularly lost large shares to independent or non-conference lines and have had to follow the tariff policies of the independent lines are the "thick" or highly traveled ones such as the transatlantic and transpacific routes. About the only routes where the conferences appear to have rather stable positions are in those north–south routes where the volume of traffic is light and/or there are cargo-reservation agreements between exporting and importing states (for example, between Brazil and Argentina and their trading partners).[100] Apart from losing a significant share of the market the shipping conferences are finding that they have to establish rates very close to those of the independent lines, and according to the OECD this trend will accelerate in the future. Also, the conferences are facing serious problems of violations of rate agreements by member shipping lines. In fact, shipping lines are increasingly accepting the open market price because of "the staggering number of independent rate actions" by their own members.[101]

Some important examples of the recent decline of shipping conferences are the developments on the North Atlantic and the North Pacific. Turning first to the North Atlantic, the two major conferences, faced with declining profits or rising deficits in the mid-1980s, decided that they had to try to influence the rates of the non-conference lines. They persuaded most non-conference lines to form an organization called Eurocorde that would establish rate guidelines. This "discussion agreement" had some very modest effects on rates on the North Atlantic, but after dramatic losses in the early 1990s the conference lines formed a new organization in April 1992 with most of the non-conference lines (but not the largest, Evergreen) which is called the Trans-Atlantic Agreement (TAA). In 1993 there were nine conference and six non-conference lines in the TAA, and they accounted for around 75 percent of the transatlantic market. The TAA recommends rates and regulates capacity, and it has generally called on members to cut capacity by around 10 percent. In addition, it is involved in space sharing and the sharing of certain port facilities. The TAA has managed to reduce the shipping lines' losses, but there are significant variations in rates among TAA lines. One government official described the TAA as "a last gasp of an old era," and he could well be correct. Both the European Union and the USA have adopted more critical views of the TAA and market management more generally in recent years.[102]

In the North Pacific trades there are about ten lines belonging to two shipping conferences as well as a number of non-conference lines. Since the late 1980s there has also been a "discussion agreement" called the Transpacific Stabilization Agreement (TSA) which is composed of nine conference and four non-conference lines. The central function of the TSA is to buoy rates by regulating capacity, and in the early 1990s it generally withdrew about 10 percent of capacity. While the conferences and the TSA have had modest effects on rates and market shares, there has been "continued cut-throat competition between conference and non-conference carriers."[103] There has also been a lot of independent action by conference lines – that is to say, violations of their rate agreements. The market is presently even more wide open than it is in the North Atlantic.[104]

Why have the conferences lost such a large percentage of the market and their ability to control tariffs on many of the trades where they operate, and what are the factors that have affected the changes? The two key factors are the advent of containerization in liner shipping and the expansion of Asian shipping firms. Containerization, whose effects are multifaceted, started in the USA in the 1960s, and by the 1980s almost all large liner vessels in the world were containerized. In container vessels goods are packed in large steel containers at the point of origin, and the containers are usually not opened until they arrive at the final point of destination. In the case of containers with small shipments from many shippers they are opened at the port of destination, and the goods are dispersed by truck or rail.

The first way in which containerization weakened cartels is that it introduced competition among different modes of maritime transport.

In the 1960s and 1970s the introduction of container vessels, which now have about four times the carrying capacity of the older break-bulk vessels, caused differences in the cost structures of vessels with and without containers. This was due not only to the ability of the former to carry freight by ship at a lower cost but also their frequent use of more efficient multimodal ports.[105] According to one report written in the late 1970s, there was "substantial service competition between cellular container operators and break-bulk or semi-conventional operators" since the former "can offer security from damage and pillage, fast transit times, and reliable timetables."[106] It is of some importance that several new types of vessels (RO-ROs, LASH, and neo-bulk) have recently introduced an element of competition with containerized vessels in certain trades.[107]

Second, one of the most important impacts of the containerization revolution is that it opened the door to multimodal transport operators (ship, rail, and truck) whereby companies offer rates for point-to-point service. Thus, the cost of the shipping "leg" of a trip is not set separately, and the rates of shipping and multimodal transportation firms cannot be easily compared and regulated. Multimodalism has led to the creation of new larger conferences that often include both multimodal and purely shipping, rail, and trucking firms, but they do not eliminate the conflicts between the different types of firms.[108] Multimodalism has also led the major shipping lines to create global networks that encompass routes originally regulated by several conferences. This leads to conflicts between these global carriers and other carriers that specialize in regional routes.[109] In the words of one shipping official "Intermodal-services and -pricing mechanisms undermine tariff structures."[110] Another related effect of containerization and multimodalism is that it has facilitated the use of "land bridges" such as the trans-Siberian railway that has introduced yet another element of competition into international transportation networks.[111]

Third, related to the development of containerization and multimodalism is the emergence of fewer and larger shipping and multimodal firms and transportation consortia. An example of this trend is developments on the North Pacific where the trade went from forty-two liner companies in 1985 to ten joint ventures or consortia in 1993.[112] The capital required for large expensive container vessels and multimodal systems means that firms must have a much larger capital base than they had in the past. An indication of the extent to which multimodal firms are pushing out many purely shipping companies from the

73

industry is that between 1977 and 1989 the number of multimodal firms increased from 71 to 246. These new firms are so large that they are not threatened as easily by economic collapse as was the case in the past with the smaller and more numerous shipping companies. Therefore, there is not as serious a problem of disruption in service by allowing open competition.[113]

Fourth, a very important impact of containerization is that it has basically eliminated the difference in the quality of service offered by independent and conference lines. In the words of one shipping official, "outsiders offer[ed] inferior services" in the past and now "the quality of service of conference members and outsiders is largely equal."[114] In the past era of break-bulk vessels the quality of loading and other services of the independent lines was generally inferior, but containerization has been a great equalizer. Even though independent lines tend to be smaller than those belonging to conferences, their services are basically of a comparable quality.[115]

Along with the above effects of containerization another very important influence on the decline of conferences is the growth of non-Western shipping firms, which is related in part to the containerization revolution. Since the birth of the conferences in the nineteenth century there have been shipping companies that periodically sought to challenge the conferences on certain routes, and sometimes they succeeded sufficiently to be offered membership and market shares in the conferences. However, after World War II the Eastern bloc fleets and shipping companies from the developing world (especially East Asian countries) began to penetrate certain trades and pose larger challenges to the shipping conferences than they had ever experienced in the past. The Soviet bloc fleets often had to stay outside conferences to secure business since the quality of their service was on the whole not as good as that of the conference lines. The truly dramatic increase in non-conference lines started in the mid-1970s, and it can be accounted for largely by the growth of firms from Taiwan, South Korea, Hong Kong, and the People's Republic of China. They did not share any sense of identity with the conferences dominated by Western firms, and the new shipping technologies generally gave them the opportunity to provide equivalent or better service. They also had lower employee costs and were very innovative in developing services such as round-the-world service. In fact, according to one shipping journal, "The arrival on the scene of independent operators offering surprisingly attractive service products made the long-entrenched consortia look clumsy and out of touch."[116] The Taiwanese firm Evergreen is now the largest carrier in the world. Sometimes new shipping firms such as Evergreen seek admittance to particular shipping conferences, but on the whole they find it advantageous to stay out.[117]

Another factor that has contributed to the weakening of the cartels in international shipping is the growing acceptance of deregulation or economic liberalization since the 1970s. The impact of this trend is covered in greater detail in the analyses of the other international service industries in subsequent chapters. Apropos this judgment for the international shipping industry, an article in an industry paper recently commented about the European Union's increasing opposition to shipping conferences: "the Commission considers that the TAA, by harming the growth and competitiveness of the European economy and by threatening increased unemployment, creates an intolerable situation for the public interest."[118] What this article was stressing was that the European Commission judged that everything possible had to be done to reduce the costs of European exports in global markets and hence enhance the prosperity of the European economy. The traditional European deference to shipping conferences has almost completely disappeared.

In analyzing the decline of the conferences it is important to mention certain policies of both developing and developed states – if only to dismiss them as important factors in the decline of the conferences. As noted above, the 1974 UNCTAD Liner Code, which emerged as a result of pressure from Third World maritime states, has not constituted a challenge to the conferences. In fact, the Code is supportive of conferences. Also, the bilateral cargo-reservation accords that have been negotiated by some developing states with developed countries (for example, by Argentina and Brazil) have not had a serious negative influence on shipping conferences since such accords have played a modest and declining role in international shipping. They have particularly declined in the 1990s.[119]

Turning to the impact of the developed countries it is important to focus on the USA since it is sometimes portrayed as an enemy of conferences. The present policy of the USA can be traced back to the Shipping Act of 1916 which stated that only open conferences (those that set rates but cannot determine membership or market shares) could service American ports. The Act also set down some restrictions on conference practices. Since then the extent to which the USA has adopted restrictive policies toward conferences has varied, but it has always protected conferences to one extent or another. With regard to US policy after World War II, Alan Cafruny has argued that its support for conferences through the mid-1960s was due to its political sensitivity to the economic welfare of its Western allies with shipping industries and that the weakening of US support for conferences in the 1960s was due to an increasing recognition that it no longer had to provide economic assistance to its allies. With this reorientation in general policy, it is argued that the USA focused solely on the economic well-being of its national fleet and shippers, and consequently it moved to weaken shipping conferences. This stance captures certain elements of US policy at this time, but it overstates the change of US policy since the 1960s and its impact on the weakening of shipping conferences. The 1984 US Shipping Act has been interpreted by most observers as being more favorable to conferences than previous US legislation. For example, while the 1984 Act allows "independent action" or violations of rate agreements by conference lines, it favors conferences by placing the burden of proof of violations of the antitrust provisions on the government (a reversal of past policy) and legitimizes the setting of multimodal rates by shipping conferences. US shipping firms that belong to conferences are very supportive of the Act, and that indicates a great deal about US government policy.[120] Since the mid-1980s conference lines have been much more worried about possible antitrust actions by the European Union than by the US government. However, the Federal Maritime Commission's review of the TAA in 1994 may indicate a move in the direction of the recent policy of the European Union.[121]

The central rationale for the shipping cartel over most of the past century was a perception that only cartel arrangements or shipping conferences could provide reliable service over a vast network of ports. This is tantamount to saying that there is "a natural monopoly" in international shipping services. Few shippers and governments wanted to risk the possibility of interruptions of service and inferior service that would result from open and "destructive competition." One can presently challenge this economic analysis, but there is no doubt that past government and academic studies reflected this judgment. What has happened in the past several decades is that the multiple effects of containerization and the entry of well-financed and innovative firms largely from East Asia have turned around the traditional perception of the importance of conferences. This point of view is contained in an observation in a recent article on the North Atlantic route: "many shippers can see no need for or real benefit from the existence of the conference structure in the trade, owing to the abundance of regular reliable services in this trade, including those of independents."[122] There is presently, in fact, pressure from some national shippers' groups to eliminate the antitrust immunity that shipping conferences enjoy.[123]

One factor that it is important to dismiss as a crucial support for shipping conferences is states' commitment to maintain national fleets. Most states do not think that it is important to have significant fleets for their welfare or political power, and those that do want at least a modest fleet do not look to liner conferences as the best method of realizing their goal. A recent article on international shipping that is very sympathetic to developing countries' interests noted that the possession of at least modest national fleets is "the most appropriate way of avoiding . . . disruptions [in imports] and of ensuring the availability of adequate shipping services." It then went on to note that such fleets are "an important element of attaining and maintaining national independence" – implying in part their importance in promoting a sense of political independence.[124] There is, however, little indication that most governments see large shipping fleets as central to their sense of independence or national power, although some judge that they should maintain small fleets under their flag. Few countries regard it as a matter of national pride to have ships flying their flags in their ports – unlike the situation with aircraft at their airports. For major powers and some Third World states the possession of small fleets has had some importance for balance-of-payments, security, and symbolic political reasons, but they tend to use cargo-reservation schemes, control of cabotage, special registry regulations (e.g. Britain's support for an Isle of Man registry), and the subsidization of national shipping firms as more effective protectionist strategies than support for shipping conferences. After all, within shipping conferences their national shipping lines may not have adequate power to assure certain market shares.[125]

There is not presently a strong regime for liner shipping, but a regime based on a limited competition norm is definitely emerging. It upholds open competition supplemented by interfirm dialogues on excess capacity problems on thick routes[126] and cartel arrangements on thin routes. However, some states have instituted various measures to protect their national lines (particularly, cargo-reservation guidelines and subsidies) that do constitute exceptions to such an evaluation.

While some observers see an increase in maritime protectionism in the future, there has been a decline in protectionist trends such as cargo-reservation schemes and subsidies for national shipping lines in the 1990s. Governments are becoming increasingly reluctant to subsidize national industries.[127]

The somewhat "messy" situation that prevails is, however, not viewed with any significant alarm by shippers and states – basically because there are no serious possibilities of the disruption of shipping services. Also, shipping rates are generally at fairly competitive levels on most routes, and when they are not at such levels, it is often because of the protectionist practices of particular shipping states – not the shipping conferences. The patchwork pattern of commercial arrangements that exists today in liner shipping is likely to be acceptable to the great majority of countries because oceanic trade continues to flow – and at lower rates than was the case in the recent past. An international system of cartels no longer seems necessary to realize states' central goal of the free flow of commerce. There is a chance that a new regime based on a limited competition norm will grow stronger, and if this does occur, it is likely to have a number of exceptions to open competition embedded in it to take account of route-specific economies of scale and national protectionist policies.

The competitive market that has always operated in bulk trades and the cartel system that prevailed for a century in liner trades were not grounded on a mutual interest in state autonomy. The central common interest of states has been the free flow of commerce, and they have supported the arrangement that they perceived as most effective in removing impediments to the flow of goods and services. A secondary, but still high priority, goal has been economic efficiency or low shipping rates. In the last few decades shippers and states have perceived that it is possible to have both regularity and comprehensiveness of service and low competitive prices on most liner routes. Therefore, the liner shipping world is beginning to coalesce around what might be called a limited competition norm.

Conclusion

The international shipping regime has been dominated first and foremost by states' dedication to the principle of the free movement of commerce. In the case of jurisdictional rights, the principle of the free movement of commerce was modified to give states certain powers in coastal waters and over their flag vessels, but these powers do not threaten ships' freedom to move throughout the world's oceans. Also, the norm of flag state sovereignty can be seen in part as a means of achieving greater certainty concerning the creation and enforcement of international law which itself promotes the free flow of commerce. In establishing the importance of mutual interests underlying the juris- dictional norms, it is important to recognize that while the law of the sea is associated with the interests of the major maritime powers, it was traditionally non-great powers that were the strongest backers of open access.[128] At the three UN Conferences on the Law of the Sea in recent decades the majority of medium- and small-sized countries continued to manifest strong support for the freedom of commercial navigation.

In the case of damage control issues the principle of preventing transnational damages was, of course, central to the evolution of norms and rules. However, this principle was backed in part because it promoted the free movement of commerce, since *international* maritime safety and pollution control laws discourage states from passing *national* legislation that could hinder the free movement of vessels. To reiterate a point made by M'Gonigle and Zacher in their study of the international politics of oil pollution control, "For maritime interests, uniformity has been the battle cry in a struggle to retain free access to all of the world's oceans and to prevent the imposition of uneven costs."[129] It is also the case with regard to the highly developed regulations governing technical and procedural barriers that the domi- nant motivations are the reduction of cost uncertainty and of barriers to the flow of goods and services. While in negotiations over damage control and technical barrier questions there are always significant disputes over what particular rules should be adopted, the participants are almost always committed to the acceptance of some rules. With few exceptions states do not leave conferences without agreements on new requirements.

While those aspects of the shipping regime relating to jurisdictional rights, damage control, and technical barriers have increased in strength during this century with the growth in world trade, dimen- sions of the regime relating to prices and market shares have gone in the opposite direction in recent decades. The long-standing acceptance of the cartel norm and shipping conferences has seriously weakened, although there are indications that a new regime based on open competition in most shipping trades is emerging. The key reason for the decline of the cartel system is that as a result of containerization and the growth of Asian shipping lines the network of shipping conferences is no longer seen as important to regular reliable service or the free movement of commerce on most routes. In different terminology, shippers and states no longer think that there are economies of scale on most shipping routes and consequently that cartels are means to reliability and efficiency.

Looking at the international shipping regime from the perspective of reducing market failures, the key concern of states and commercial actors has been in reducing impediments to the free flow of goods and services. Linked to this concern has been the desire of states to reduce uncertainty of costs which result from an absence of clear rules and possible financial losses and to reduce transaction costs that are attendant on the lack of international laws. The issue of controlling negative externalities also arose in the context of dealing with the growing problem of ship-generated marine pollution. Finally, for approximately a century states and commercial actors judged that economies of scale existed on individual routes and that open competition would lead to "destructive competition" that would produce periodic disruptions in service. This perception, as noted above, has gradually disappeared in recent decades.

4   The international air transport regime

International air transport services and the regulatory framework

The age of aviation can be dated to 1903 when the Wright brothers in the USA and then Captain Ferber in France first flew engine-powered planes. In 1909 the first international flight between non-contiguous countries occurred between France and Britain. While there were important changes in plane technology in the years leading up to World War I, there was little commercial utilization of aircraft in these years. Over the course of World War I dramatic technological changes occurred, and it was these developments that opened the door to the birth of commercial air transport after the war.[1]

In 1919 a number of important legal and political steps were taken that laid the bases for the development of international civil aviation. An international conference granted states sovereignty over air space above their territories, and this meant that intergovernmental negotiations would shape the development of the international air transport industry. Also in 1919, states created the International Commission for Air Navigation, and airlines formed the International Air Traffic Association for the purpose of developing technical and safety standards. The distinctiveness of the two organizations tended to disappear during the 1920s and 1930s because most airlines outside of the USA were founded and owned by states. In fact, most states subsidized their airlines during the interwar years because of their importance to military power and the development of commercial networks. In looking back at the early expansion of international air transport it is important to note that in the 1920s international flights were confined largely to Europe. It was not until the late 1920s that flights between the USA and Latin America developed. With regard to transatlantic flights Lindbergh's crossing of the Atlantic in 1927 raised hopes that commercial transoceanic travel was around the corner. However, it was not until 1939 that the first commercial transatlantic flight took place. One important reason for the very modest growth in the airline industry in the interwar years is that before the introduction of the DC-3 and Boeing's Yankee Clipper in the late 1930s planes had a carrying capacity of only ten or less, and even the DC-3 had a carrying capacity of only twenty-one.[2]

During World War II the size and range of planes increased significantly, and starting in the early 1950s turbo-prop aircraft gradually replaced piston-engine planes. The former allowed the carriage of heavier payloads at faster speeds. However, both piston-engine and turbo-prop planes had carrying capacities of between fifty and 100 passengers. A dramatic change in speed and carrying capacity occurred with the emergence of commercial jet aircraft in the late 1950s. The Boeing 707 and McDonnell Douglas DC-8 with 150-passenger capacity soon became the most popular planes in the industry. By 1970 wide-bodied jets with capacities of 250–400 passengers became available. Over the next two decades piston-engine aircraft were phased out, and even turbo-prop planes dropped to a small percentage of the fleets of international airlines.[3]

These technological changes led to some striking decreases in flying times and increases in both the total number of passengers and, more specifically, international travelers. In the case of flying times, the president of Pan American Airlines Juan Trippe was able to go around the world in 1936 in a combination of flying boats and a Zeppelin in thirty-eight days. In 1947 Trippe again went around the world – this time in thirteen days and just 103 hours of flying time. Then in 1980 a British businessman circled the globe on scheduled flights in 44 hours.[4] The total number of passengers on scheduled airline flights increased from eighteen million individuals in 1946, to 106 million in 1960, 311 million in 1970, 748 million in 1980, and 1.1 billion in 1991. The growth rate was around 15 percent in the 1950s and 1960s, 11 percent in the 1970s, and 5 percent in the 1980s. This increase was due significantly to the fall in real costs per tonne kilometer which in 1990 were a third of what they were in 1960. International travelers as a percentage of all passengers has been quite stable in the 20–25 percent range in recent decades. Likewise international passenger-kilometers as a percentage of total passenger-kilometers has remained relatively stable at around

40–50 percent – rising to 51 percent in 1991. Actually, the airlines of only four countries in the world fly more miles domestically than internationally, but those four are the USA, the Soviet Union/Russia, China, and Brazil.[5]

There have been some marked changes in countries' shares of the world air transport market since the 1940s. The share of US scheduled airlines of total passenger-kilometers has dropped from around 60 to below 40 percent, and that of Europe has risen from just below 20 percent to above 30 percent since 1950. However, turning to solely *international* passenger-kilometers, the North American share for the period 1973–88 dropped from 28 to 22 percent; the Europeans' share went from 44 to 36 percent; and the share of the Asian and Pacific countries shot up from 14 to 29 percent. The dramatic growth of international air transport within the Asia–Pacific region is one of the most notable developments in the last two decades.[6]

In surveying the world air transport industry an important distinction in airline services is between scheduled and non-scheduled (or charter) services. Charter services accounted for a small percentage of international passenger-kilometers in the 1950s, but during the 1960s they grew rapidly so that by the early 1970s they controlled 40 percent. However, in the mid-1970s the scheduled airlines began to offer competitive fares so that by the 1980s and early 1990s the share of international passenger-kilometers accounted for by charter services had dropped to the 14–20 percent range. Of total kilometers flown by charter services, about one-half are flown by major airlines such as Air Canada and British Airways as opposed to independent charter firms. Today the differences in fares between scheduled and charter services are not dramatic on many routes.[7]

Turning to revenues earned by the world air transport industry, the global figure for 1985 was $112 billion and $218 billion for 1991; and between 80 and 85 percent of it came from passengers as opposed to cargo and mail. Most airlines carry some freight and mail, but there are some like United Postal Services, Federal Express, and DHL that specialize in the carriage of these goods. The profits of most passenger airlines tend to be quite modest, and one reason is that many of them are completely or largely government-owned. Even with the high airfares set by IATA Traffic Conferences some of them require government subsidies in order to survive. The great majority of airlines outside of North America were government-owned until the 1980s, but beginning in that decade quite a few airlines in the developed world and some in the developing world have moved toward privatization.[8]

Important international bodies

The two major international organizations in the field of civil aviation before World War II were the International Air Traffic Association and the International Commission for Air Navigation. The former was composed solely of airlines and the latter was composed solely of states. Both were created in 1919, and both were charged with promoting technical and commercial coordination and safety. In the postwar period they were succeeded by the *International Association of Transport Airlines* (IATA), which was created by the airlines in 1945, and the *International Civil Aviation Organization* (ICAO), which was formed by governments in 1944. The headquarters of both are in Montreal. The major difference between these bodies and their interwar predecessors is that IATA was given powers in setting passenger fares that the International Air Traffic Association never had.[9]

The ICAO is the UN specialized agency concerned with international air transport, and almost all states in the world belong to it. For several decades the socialist states refused to join; but in 1970 the Soviet Union joined, and in 1974 the People's Republic of China took the seat of China. The ICAO is responsible for passing most international regulations concerning interconnection, standardization, safety, and crime control. The regulations are attached as annexes to the ICAO convention and are regularly revised.

The plenary body of the ICAO is the Assembly which meets once a year. It elects the Secretary-General (who focuses basically on administration), the Council (composed of thirty-three states), and various committees. The technical recommendations that are approved by the Council and Assembly are not binding, but states are conscientious in seeking to implement them.[10] The Council President is the most important official in the ICAO, and there have only been three since World War II. A particularly important part of the ICAO Secretariat is the Technical Assistance Bureau which provides extensive assistance to Third World countries in developing safe and efficient air transport services.

The key commissions and committees are the Air Navigation Commission, the Committee on Joint Support of Navigation Services, the Air Transport Committee, the Legal Committee, the Finance

Committee, and the Committee on Unlawful Interference of Aircraft. The Air Navigation Commission, with its concern for air safety, and the Air Transport Committee, with its concern for facilitating the movement of passengers and cargo, are particularly central to ICAO's work. A large number of nongovernmental bodies are important participants in the deliberations of its committees, and none is more significant than IATA. While diverse interests come into play in the various ICAO bodies, on the whole the participants judge issues on their technical merits. In fact, members of the crucial Air Navigation Commission sit in their individual, and not their national, capacities. That is to say, they are not supposed to receive directions from their governments. The members, however, inevitably give some weight to national interests at times. The most important regulations developed by ICAO are included in the International Standards and Recommended Practices that make up the eighteen annexes attached to the International Convention on Civil Aviation. A "Standard" is regarded as necessary to the safety or regularity of civil aviation whereas a "Recommended Practice" is judged to be desirable, but not necessary. The Standards and Recommended Practices require approval of two-thirds of the members of the Council, and they are then included in the annexes as long as one-half of ICAO member states do not disapprove of them.[11]

When IATA was formed in 1945 by forty-two airlines, the conferees intended that the new organization would both provide information and policy suggestions to the ICAO on technical issues and focus on commercial issues such as the establishment of passenger fares. To fulfill these responsibilities the member airlines created a number of deliberative bodies. The top decision-making body in IATA (now with over 200 members) is the Annual General Meeting. It passes general policy resolutions and is responsible for electing a Director-General and members of the Executive Committee (composed of twenty-one airline officials). The Executive Committee provides direction and coordination to the many committees of IATA – notably, the Technical Committee, the Traffic Advisory Committee, the Legal Committee, and the Financial Committee. The Financial Committee is responsible for the standardization of accounting procedures and the settlement of accounts among airlines. It operates a Clearing House that balances credits and debits among airlines. The main concerns of the Legal Committee are liability for damages and crime control, and the main concerns of the Technical Committee are technical standardization, safety, and health.

The Traffic Conferences that set passenger fares for different regions operate under the Traffic Advisory Committee. Until 1979 there were three regional Traffic Conferences that set fares; since then there have been eleven. Until the 1970s the decisions of the Traffic Conferences were viewed as legally binding, and there was an IATA Compliance Office that monitored airlines' compliance and applied sanctions (fines) for non-compliance. However, the tariff-setting system began to weaken in the early 1970s because of overcapacity, the growth of new airlines, and the growing demands for lower fares, and it collapsed in a number of regions in the late 1970s. Now there is considerable variation in the extent of tariff-setting, decision-making arrangements, and compliance with conference decisions within the eleven regional Traffic Conferences. Even within those regional conferences where there is still a commitment to multilateral tariff-setting, negotiations tend to drag on throughout the year rather than being confined to a short period annually.[12]

The criteria for and categories of membership in IATA have changed over time. One requirement has always been that the state in which an airline is registered must be a member of ICAO. This has promoted the involvement of airlines and IATA in the international regulation of safety and other technical issues. In the immediate postwar decades members had to be scheduled (not charter) airlines and had to participate in the IATA Traffic Conferences. In 1974 the growth of charter airlines led to the admission of some types of charter airlines, and then at the beginning of the era of deregulation in 1978 it was decided that there would be two classes of members – those that participated in both facilitation and tariff-coordination activities and those that just participated in the former. These changes in the late 1970s were due significantly to pressure by the USA. By 1990 only eighty-three of IATA's 157 members were full participants in IATA's tariff-coordination activities. It was also in that year that some of the most important Asian holdouts finally joined IATA (Singapore International Airlines, Malaysia Airlines, Cathay Pacific, and Royal Brunei) since they were confident that membership would not entail any commercial restrictions.[13]

Overview of the international air transport regime

The principles that are embedded most deeply in the normative structure of the international air transport regime are those concerning the free movement of commerce and states' internal political control, although the principles of transnational damage control and economic efficiency are also reflected in a number of the norms (see Table 4.1).

The jurisdictional norms of the international air transport regime reflect first and foremost states' desire to control foreign airlines' access to their markets and hence their ability to protect their national airlines. States' right to control the landing of foreign aircraft at their airports, in fact, structures many other aspects of the regime. However, the jurisdictional norms do also promote the free movement of commerce by allowing flight over the high seas and national territories (although some countries do not accede to the latter provision). As might be expected, the norms relating to damage control and the reduction of technical barriers are directed primarily at promoting the free movement of commerce and the prevention of transnational damage.

With regard to prices and market shares there has been a dramatic weakening in the central cartel norm since the late 1970s, and this change reflects a change in states' relative allegiance to the principles of internal political control and economic efficiency. The old cartel norm was based first and foremost on states' determination to maintain the economic viability of their national airlines. Now the growing adherence by most of the industrialized world to a limited competition norm is based on the principle of economic efficiency – or a greater concern for lower fares and the elimination of government subsidies.[14]

Jurisdictional rights

The norms concerning air transport closely parallel those with regard to shipping, and there has not been a great deal of international conflict over them. First, there is the *norm of open access to air space above the high seas*. Second, there is the *norm of state control over adjacent air space and landings* which stipulates that states have jurisdiction to grant or deny permission to foreign airlines to overfly their territory and to pick up and deliver passengers at their national airports. Third, most states have accepted an *innocent passage norm* that foreign commercial aircraft should have the right to pass through their sovereign air space in order to shorten the distance of a flight and to stop for technical assistance. These two rights of overflight and stopping for technical reasons have been referred to as the first and second freedoms of the air since 1944. (The third and fourth freedoms are the rights of airlines to fly back and

Table 4.1 *The international air transport regime*

=====

Principles

Free movement of commerce: obligation of states to reduce impediments to the free movement of goods and services.

Free flow of information: obligation of states to allow the flow of information among peoples of different states.

Efficiency: obligation of states to provide goods and services to their populations at lowest possible cost.

Transnational damage control: obligation of states to prevent activities of their nationals from imposing damages on the nationals and property of other states and to provide compensation for any damages.

Internal political control: right of states to assert jurisdiction and control over activities within their territories.

Equity: obligation of states to provide all states with a reasonable share of resources and financial returns from international commerce.

Norms

Jurisdictional rights

State control over adjacent air space and airplane landings: right to exclude foreign aircraft from national air space and landings at airports.
* Relevant principles: internal political control
* Strength: strong

Open access to air space above the high seas: right of aircraft to have free access to airspace above the high seas.
* Relevant principles: free movement of commerce
* Strength: strong

Innocent passage: right of commercial aircraft to transit through the sovereign air space of other countries (to reduce distance of a route) and to land for technical service or emergencies as long as they do not violate the security or laws of the "host" states.

Table 4.1 (*cont.*)

- Relevant principles: free movement of commerce, internal political control
- Strength: medium (over 40 percent of ICAO members have not formally accepted the Transit Agreement, but even this group often grant overflight rights in bilateral accords)

Flag state sovereignty: right of flag states to exercise jurisdiction over the activities of and on their own aircraft while in international air space.
- Relevant principles: internal political control, free movement of commerce
- Strength: strong

Damage control problems

Accident prevention: obligation to prevent aircraft accidents.
- Relevant principles: transnational damage control, free movement of commerce, efficiency
- Strength: strong

Commercial crime control: obligation to prevent fraudulent practices against airlines and theft of goods carried by aircraft.
- Relevant principles: free movement of commerce, efficiency
- Strength: strong

Political crime control: obligation to prevent hijacking and sabotage against aircraft.
- Relevant principles: free movement of commerce, efficiency
- Strength: medium

Pollution prevention: obligation to prevent aircraft from despoiling the environment of other states (from fumes and noise).
- Relevant principles: transnational damage control, free movement of commerce
- Strength: moderately strong

Reasonable compensation: obligation to assure payment of reasonable compensation to foreign parties for damages that have been caused by their nationals.

Table 4.1 (*cont.*)

- Relevant principles: transnational damage control, free movement of commerce
- Strength: medium to moderately strong

Technical and procedural barriers

Technical interconnection: obligation to promote standardization of equipment and practices so as to permit the efficient intermeshing of planes and ground facilities.
- Relevant principles: free movement of commerce, efficiency
- Strength: strong

Facilitation: obligation of states to reduce barriers to the flow of passengers, baggage, and cargo.
- Relevant principles: free movement of commerce, efficiency
- Strength: moderately strong

Prices and market shares

Cartel: obligation to regulate plane fares and market shares so as to assure a division of passengers, cargo, and revenues in rough proportion to shares of the global market.
- Relevant principles: internal political control, equity
- Strength: weak in interwar period (when industry in nascent stage); moderately strong from 1946 through late 1970s; moderately strong for intraEuropean, African, Latin American, and some Asian routes from the late 1970s through the 1980s; but a distinct weakening in Europe and Latin America in the 1990s

Limited competition: obligation to promote competition in fares and to a limited extent in market shares.
- Relevant principles: efficiency, free movement of commerce, internal political control
- Strength: moderately strong for routes involving the USA, Southeast Asia, Australasia, and several European countries after late 1970s; growing adherence in Europe and some parts of Latin America in 1990s

---

forth between their home state and another state, and the fifth freedom is the right of an airline to fly between two foreign states on a route beginning or ending in the aircraft's home country.) Lastly, there is the *flag state jurisdiction norm*. It prescribes that flag states have jurisdiction over acts by their aircraft or in their aircraft when they are in international space over the high seas. This norm is not as important as it is with regard to international shipping, but it still does contribute to the order of international air transport.[15]

The first conference concerned with jurisdictional issues in international air transport was convened by France in 1910. The impetus for the conference came from private international lawyers, and they influenced the policies of France and a number of other continental European countries. These latter countries favored recognizing states' sovereignty over air space above their territories, but they supported liberal rights of access by foreign aircraft (i.e. innocent passage over the territory and right to land for non-commercial reasons) comparable to those rights enjoyed by ships in territorial seas. Britain and a number of other countries came down strongly on behalf of unqualified state sovereignty over adjacent air space. Consequently, the conference ended without an accord. In 1911 Britain declared sovereignty over its air space, and most European states soon passed comparable legislation so that by 1914 there was a *de facto* norm of state sovereignty over adjacent airspace.[16]

Experiences with air warfare in World War I settled any remaining doubts concerning the desirability of states' having sovereignty over their air space. At the Paris conference in 1919 states formulated the Paris Convention on the Regulation of Aerial Navigation that declared: "Every power has complete and exclusive sovereignty over the air space above its territory." It modified this by the provision that "Each contracting State undertakes in time of peace to accord freedom of innocent passage above its territory to the aircraft of the other contracting states, provided that the conditions laid down in the present Convention are observed." However, some ambivalence on this latter provision was exhibited by the participating states when they inserted the proviso: "The establishment of international airways shall be subject to the consent of the states flown over." This ambivalence was clarified by an amendment to the Paris Convention in 1929 that clearly gave states the right to suspend the right of innocent passage. It is, however, important to stress that most countries allowed the right of overflight or innocent passage in their bilateral agreements during the interwar period. Jurisdictional issues were considered again near the end of World War II at the 1944 Chicago conference that formulated the Convention on International Civil Aviation. It restated the doctrine of state sovereignty over adjacent air space. In addition, the convention made clear that states had free access to air space above the high seas and had jurisdiction over their aircraft while in international space.[17] Concerning the area over the high seas it has always been acknowledged that it is an "aerial highway open to all nations and not subject to the jurisdiction of any state."[18] These questions of sovereignty over adjacent air space and open access to international air space were basically non-controversial issues.

What was controversial in 1944 was the issue of innocent passage for civilian (not military) aviation which was framed in terms of the willingness of states to accept "the first two freedoms" – the right to travel through the air space of foreign countries in order to shorten routes and the right to stop for technical repairs and refueling. These two freedoms were included in Article 5 of the convention for non-scheduled (charter) services and in a special accord entitled the International Air Services Transit Agreement (the Transit Agreement) for scheduled services. About 60 percent of all members of the International Civil Aviation Organization have accepted the Transit Agreement, and many of the holdouts have accepted innocent passage in bilateral accords. Such holdouts sometimes do not accept the Transit Agreement because they find the granting of overflight rights a valuable bargaining chip in negotiating the terms of bilaterals. The major groups of states that have not ratified the Transit Agreement are the socialist and formerly socialist states, those African states that wanted to deny overflight rights to South African Airlines, and almost half of all Latin American and Caribbean states. Many of these states may reverse their policy in the near future as a result of the political revolution in Eastern Europe and the acceptance of majority rule in South Africa. Concerning broad international support for "innocent passage" for aircraft a recent study comments: "Perhaps because of its similarity to traditional maritime doctrines of navigational freedom and the right to enter foreign ports for nontraffic purposes, [the Transit Agreement] has been ratified by more than 100 nations."[19] A key reason for states' acceptance of innocent passage is that it can be suspended on very short notice should the need arise. This power of reversibility is important since it maintains state freedom to control air spaces when security, or even economic, threats loom.

Central to the jurisdictional aspect of the air transport regime is states' commitment to protect their national airlines. Because national airlines have been and still are regarded as symbols of national independence and prestige, the ability to determine who can and cannot carry passengers to and from a country is very important. Concerning the adoption of the principle of state sovereignty over adjacent air space after World War I a legal expert has written that "The implications of this principle were clear: if international aviation was to develop at all, it would have to proceed on the basis of agreements among states."[20] This is, of course, the central reason that states' support for the norm has remained so strong.

On the other hand, the broad international acceptance of the norms of freedom of flight over the high seas and innocent passage through national air space are indications that states are interested in facilitating the flow of commerce. They are not willing to push a concern for state autonomy to such a degree that it undermines the benefits they derive from participation in the world economy. From the perspective of controlling market failures these jurisdictional provisions most importantly reduce impediments to the international movement of goods and services and also reduce cost uncertainties and transaction costs that flow from an absence of uniform jurisdictional rules.

There is one development that may alter jurisdictional rights in the future, and it concerns the development of regional economic groupings that involve derogation of authority over international aviation to a common authority. Examples are the European Union and the 1992 agreement between Australia and New Zealand to establish a common aviation market. To quote a recent study on international aviation:

> If it [regionalization] develops as a characteristic of the future aviation scene then the price of exclusive sovereignty over a country's air space may need to be redefined. A common sovereignty principle shared by all member countries could replace the conventional understanding for commercial aviation purposes.[21]

Whether and how this trend will develop will depend a great deal on the future policies of the European Union, but it is also dependent on the liberalization of air transport services and the emergence of global carriers (discussed below). Groups of countries could form regional megacarriers and regional air transport markets as a strategy for participating in an internationally competitive carrier.

Damage control problems

In probably no other international industry is safety or the prevention of accidents a bigger issue than it is in air transport. The reasons are quite simple. Aviation accidents usually mean death for the passengers and a reluctance of the public to use air transport.[22]

From the earliest days of international civil aviation states have adhered to an *accident prevention norm* since the use of air transport depends on a strong safety record. In the Paris Convention of 1919 the signatory states required certificates of airworthiness of aircraft engaged in international flight, required aircraft personnel to hold certificates of competency, and prescribed rules on other matters such as procedures for landing and takeoff. The states at the Paris conference also created the International Commission for Air Navigation (ICAN) to develop rules to promote safety, although it did not come into operation until 1922. Over the course of the interwar years ICAN was very active in improving weather reporting, communications, and equipment and construction standards, although bilateral airworthiness agreements also played a major role in the evolution of equipment and construction standards. By the 1930s even non-members of ICAN such as the USA looked to it as the source of standards for airplane construction.[23]

A dramatic increase in international cooperation to prevent accidents occurred in the postwar period as a result of the dramatic expansion of air travel and aircraft size. The central international rules are embodied in the Standards and Recommended Practices (SARPs) in the annexes attached to the Convention on International Civil Aviation. These annexes flesh out in great detail those general obligations that appear in the articles of the 1944 Chicago Convention and its revised versions. Of the eighteen annexes fifteen are concerned for the most part with the prevention of accidents and the minimization of damage from accidents (the exceptions being those concerned with registration, facilitation, and security).[24] While the annexes are developed and approved within ICAO, other organizations such as IATA and the International Federation of Airline Pilots Association as well as the major airplane manufacturers are very active in the deliberations. ICAO bodies meet almost constantly on the revision of the annexes, and between the formal adoptions of amendments the ICAO committees and commissions approve recommendations that are generally followed by airlines and governments.[25]

The annexes concerned with accidents are listed in Table 4.2. They basically deal with: crew standards (1), navigation rules (2), information needed for safe navigation (3, 4, 5, 11, 15), technical equipment and construction standards and operating procedures (6, 8, 10), design and operation of airports (14), practices concerning carriage of dangerous goods (18), rescue in cases of accidents (12), and investigations of accidents (13). Related to the provision of adequate information to air crews, two accords have been formulated within ICAO for the provision and joint financing of radio aids and meteorological stations in Iceland and Greenland. States pay for the facilities proportional to their use.[26] The international aviation community has also arranged with the International Maritime Satellite Organization to obtain facilities on its satellites for aeronautical navigation, and it is looking into new satellite facilities.[27]

There have been some significant differences in how ICAO standards are made and in how states comply with these standards. Most writers on ICAO's decision-making indicate that evaluations of proposals are based on technical criteria and that decisions are for the most part consensual.[28] Occasionally someone points to a particular decision such as the choice of the US–Australian proposal for a Microwave Landing System in the late 1970s over a British alternative as indicating that competitive national industrial interests and power relations sometimes play an important role.[29] A forceful statement concerning the importance of power relations (but not really protectionism) is set forth in a recent study by Vicki Golich on the politics of international safety standards. Her basic position is that the dominance of the USA as an airplane manufacturer (80 percent of the global jet market in the 1980s) and its significance in the global air transport market (with about 40 percent of all international kilometers accounted for by flights to or from US cities) have given it tremendous leverage in establishing international safety rules – especially with regard to construction and equipment standards. However, Golich does indicate that, apart from US influence, a network of about twenty-four Bilateral Airworthiness Agreements among the key producers of aircraft and aircraft parts has had a central role in establishing technical standards. She also notes that the role of ICAO has been "substantial" in the development of standards.[30] Concerning the leverage of the United States Golich writes:

Both Bilateral Air Transport Agreements (BATAs) and Bilateral Airworthiness Agreements (BAWs) gave the US agency responsible for improving and maintaining aviation safety extraordinary power at the global level. Virtually every state wanted to participate in the largest, richest, and therefore most desirable air transport market. BATAs required all airlines to meet US safety standards in order to penetrate US air space or to land and take off from US airports. Similarly BAWs required all aircraft components to meet US quality standards. Thus when US standards changed, so did the world's. US agencies have long dominated international commercial aviation and virtually controlled its safety regime because nearly every state in the West subscribed to US Federal Aviation Regulations (FARS).[31]

Golich is certainly correct that the USA exerts a major influence on technical standards. However, given many writers' comments on the technical and consensual character of ICAO's safety decision-making it is important not to overstate the impact of the USA on the existence and character of the rules. An appropriate evaluation is probably that of a group of economists who concluded that while the USA had traditionally taken the lead on safety standards, "important roles" were performed by ICAO and IATA – that is to say, by multilateral deliberations.[32] Perhaps more importantly for the purposes of the analysis in this study, all states have been and still are committed to developing credible safety standards of one form or another. At one point in her analysis Golich comments: "Clearly the hegemon receives most benefits, but all participants gain some benefits."[33] At another point she remarks that most states "have found it to be more convenient and less costly to utilize US regulations than to create and implement their own."[34] These observations point to the centrality of states' commitment to have reliable safety standards and their realization of benefits from these standards.

Turning to compliance issues, there is a high degree of compliance with airplane equipment and construction regulations, but the record is not as good when it comes to regulations concerning provision of services that depend on state and airline actions. The biggest problems, needless to say, exist in the Third World. Both ICAO and IATA offer extensive assistance in the form of both publications and advisory services to member states and airlines in complying with regulations so that their overall compliance record is reasonably good. In some cases, such as the transport of nuclear materials, ICAO's and IATA's work is supplemented by organizations such as the International Atomic

Table 4.2 *Annexes of the International Convention on Civil Aviation concerned with safety*

1	Personnel Licensing (8th edn, 1988, 74 pp.)
2	Rules of the Air (9th edn, 1990, 41 pp.)
3	Meteorological Services for International Air Navigation (11th edn, 1992, 148 pp.)
4	Aeronautical Charts (8th edn, 1985, 120 pp. approx.)
5	Units of Measurement to be Used in Air and Ground Operations (4th edn, 1979, 33 pp.)
6	Operation of Aircraft (4th edn, 1990, 2 vols., 73 and 71 pp.)
8	Airworthiness of Aircraft (8th edn, 1988, 38 pp.)
10	Aeronautical Telecommunications: Equipment and Systems, Radio Frequencies, and Communications Procedures (4th edn, 1985, 2 vols., 283 and 81 pp.)
11	Air Traffic Services: Air Traffic Control Service, Flight Information Service, Alerting Service (9th edn, 1990, 52 pp.)
12	Search and Rescue (6th edn, 1975, 22 pp.)
13	Aircraft Accident Investigation (7th edn, 1988, 27 pp. approx.)
14	Aerodromes (1st edn, 1990, 159 pp.)
15	Aeronautical Information Services (8th edn, 1991, 38 pp.)
18	The Safe Transport of Dangerous Goods by Air (2nd edn, 1989, 15 pp.)

Note: The number of pages for each annex is included to provide some information on the extensiveness of the regulations.

Energy Agency which since 1961 has had its own rules and advisory services dealing with the transport of radioactive materials. One legal provision in the Convention on International Civil Aviation that helps ICAO and IATA identify problems is that states are supposed to inform ICAO of their inability or unwillingness to go along with particular regulations in the annexes following their approval by the Council. In addition, considerable information on states' non-compliance comes from the airlines that come in contact with practices of states and other airlines. Finally, of course, compliance is promoted by the effects of air safety records on the willingness of the public to travel by air.[35]

A unique issue of "accident prevention" arose in 1983 as a result of the shooting down of Korean Airlines flight 007 over Siberia by a Soviet plane. While no one denied that the Korean Airlines plane had strayed off course into Soviet air space, there was broad condemnation of the use of force in such a circumstance. Following an ICAO investigation and resolutions in 1983 the ICAO Assembly revised the convention's Article 3 (now Article 3bis) to the effect that states *inter alia* should not use force against commercial airliners in flight. Given the consensus among the 107 states at the meeting the new article should constitute a deterrent to such actions in the future.[36]

Airlines and states clearly recognize that "safety in all aspects of aviation is fundamental to the industry's ability to provide the reliable and efficient transportation network required in today's interdependent world."[37] States and airlines are literally consumed by the need to cooperate to develop sound safety standards throughout the world. They realize that the safety of their planes and citizens is affected by what other countries and airlines do and, in addition, all aircraft accidents create a bad reputation for the industry that can affect the willingness of people to travel by air. Uncertainty about safety is perhaps the worst development that could occur in such an industry.

In recent decades states have become increasingly concerned about the elimination of noise and gaseous emissions and have developed a moderately strong norm of pollution reduction as a part of the regime. However, everyone realizes that there are limits to what can be technologically accomplished. It was only in 1981 that the ICAO added an annex concerned with pollution to its convention, and in so doing it was responding to growing international environmental concerns of the 1970s. In many ways it basically codified what aircraft manufacturers had been developing as a result of the airlines' sensitivity to public pressure. More, in fact, has been accomplished with regard to noise pollution than air pollution. In the 1980s IATA also became increasingly involved in the issue and in 1990 created both an Environmental Task Force and an Environmental Coordinator. These actions indicate that the airlines were coming under increasing pressure in their own countries to respond to a number of environmental criticisms. The key point for our purposes is that the international industry wants the regulations so as to avoid political criticism, uncoordinated and varied national regulations, and a possible loss in business. Of central importance is that airlines want to avoid both the uncertainty of unilateral actions and a costly patchwork pattern of national regulations. International uniformity is their byword in the environmental regulatory field as it is in other fields where technical standards are at issue.[38]

There are a number of types of crime that concern the international airline industry. They include fraudulent practices involving tickets (theft, forgery, and failure to pay), theft of goods on planes, hijacking, and sabotage. Fraudulent practices are a traditional commercial problem, and in the mid-1980s they cost the airlines over $200 million a year.[39] Theft of luggage and goods in airports is also a problem with which airlines and airports have always had to deal. The importance of hijacking and sabotage, on the other hand, has varied quite a bit over the years. The first plane hijacking occurred in Peru in 1930, but hijacking did not become a major problem until after World War II. Until the late 1950s hijacking incidents were not frequent and generally involved citizens of communist states forcing pilots to fly to the West. Then, starting in the late 1950s, most hijacking involved planes being forced to fly from the West to Cuba or the Middle East. While there has been a decided decrease in the frequency of hijacking since the late 1960s and early 1970s, there is still a modest number. Also, the 1980s witnessed the worst incidents of aircraft sabotage.[40] With regard to the above problems there has been a *norm of commercial crime control*, which has been quite strong, and a *norm of political crime control*, which has had medium strength. A key problem has, of course, concerned the prosecution of individuals committing criminal acts.

States and airlines have always sought to control commercial crimes. By the 1960s the problem of fraudulent tickets had grown large enough that IATA created the Fraud Prevention Group, and since then it has provided advice to airlines and governments and has disseminated information on fraudulent tickets. The main activity of IATA's Revenue and Property Crime Subcommittee is to coordinate and disseminate information on stolen and fraudulent tickets, and it also organizes seminars on a worldwide basis that provide information to airline officials on how to detect and prevent commercial fraud. The subcommittee works closely with ICAO and the International Association of Airline Security Officers. It is, in fact, this latter association that is the central international body dealing with cargo security matters. Its annual seminar has become "the most important of the aviation security seminars."[41] With regard to the security of air mail the key international crime-control regulations are formulated by the Universal Postal Union (UPU), but there is considerable cooperation between the UPU and IATA in designing and monitoring the rules and procedures.[42]

Prior to addressing international cooperation to control the very contentious issue of the political crimes of hijacking and sabotage it is desirable to provide a brief description of recent historical developments. While hijackings occurred occasionally before the mid-1950s, a dramatic change occurred in the late 1950s when suddenly the major victims became the Western nations as opposed to the Soviet bloc states. In the case of hijackings from the USA to Cuba the hijackers tended to identify with the socialist revolution in Cuba, and in the case of the hijackings and acts of sabotage in Europe and the Middle East most were connected to support of the Palestinian cause. The late 1960s and early 1970s witnessed a marked increase in hijackings between the USA and Cuba and within Europe. Of particular note were the hijacking and destruction of four planes in Jordan and Egypt in September 1970. While the rate varied over the years, it saw a decided upsurge in the mid-1980s. Noteworthy were the mid-air explosions on an Air India plane over the Irish Sea in 1985, a Korean Airlines plane off Burma in 1987, a Pan Am plane over Scotland in 1988, and a UTA plane over Niger in 1989. Hijackings and sabotage have since decreased.[43]

With regard to the *prevention* of hijacking of planes and sabotage against aircraft ICAO and IATA issued some recommendations of security measures prior to the 1970s. However, it was not until the incidents of 1970 that states and airlines decided to take major steps beyond what they had been doing on their own. In 1970 the ICAO Assembly passed twenty-four resolutions on the subject. This was followed up in 1971 by ICAO's publication of the *Security Manual for the Prevention of Unlawful Acts Against Civil Aviation* which has been updated periodically. In 1974 ICAO then added to its convention an annex 17 entitled "Security: Safeguarding International Civil Aviation Against Acts of Unlawful Interference," and it has become the bedrock of international collaboration in this field.[44] IATA was also very active in the 1970s in promoting better security practices by airlines and airports. In 1970 it converted its Fraud Protection Group into the Security Advisory Committee (replaced by the Security Task Force in 1988) so as to encompass hijacking among the crimes it was considering. Since then IATA authorities have monitored security practices at airports and have traveled to countries to provide advice on measures to thwart hijackings and sabotage. IATA also distributes a great deal of information among airlines and governments concerning potential hijackers and means of prevention.[45] Overall the degree of international cooperation through ICAO and IATA to prevent political crimes is extensive, although some airports and airlines do not apply the lessons as rigorously as they might. However, the biggest sins of omission arise not so much with prevention as with *prosecution*.

International cooperation to deal with the prosecution of highjackers and individuals suspected of sabotaging aircraft began in earnest in the early 1960s. Three conventions were formulated in less than a decade: in Tokyo in 1963, in The Hague in 1970, and in Montreal in 1971. The central problem confronting the conferences concerned what state(s) should have jurisdiction to prosecute perpetrators of crimes on aircraft and what prosecutory obligations they should have. Both the Paris Convention of 1919 and the Chicago Convention of 1944 affirmed that when a criminal act such as hijacking occurred over a state, that state had jurisdiction, and when it occurred over the high seas, the state of registry had jurisdiction. However, problems exist because planes often fly over many countries and the oceans and because it is the state of landing that actually first has physical control over the hijacker. The ICAO Legal Committee considered the issue throughout the 1950s, but it took the escalation of hijacking starting late in the decade to pressure states to formulate a treaty. The 1963 Tokyo Convention on Offences and Certain Other Acts Committed on Board Aircraft provides that the country in which a hijacked plane lands should take custody of the hijacker and following an initial investigation should inform both the state of the plane's registry and the state of the hijacker's citizenship whether it plans to initiate criminal proceedings. If it does not choose to initiate proceedings, it may return the hijacker to the state of which he/she is a national or the state from which the plane started its journey. However, the convention did not obligate the landing state to extradite the hijacker if it chose not to do so. The reason was that a number of countries (particularly Cuba and Middle Eastern states) did not want to accept obligations to extradite individuals with whom they sympathized politically.[46]

The escalation of hijackings and the emergence of airplane sabotage in the late 1960s and early 1970s led to the approval of two conventions. The 1970 Hague Convention for the Suppression of Unlawful Seizure of Aircraft dealt solely with hijacking whereas the 1971 Montreal Convention for the Suppression of Unlawful Acts Against the Safety of Civil Aviation was concerned with sabotage and other acts against aircraft. In both conventions unlawful acts are spelled out in some detail, and states are obligated to impose "severe penalties." Both the state of a plane's registry as well as the state where an aircraft lands are given jurisdiction to prosecute. If the state where a plane lands does not extradite a hijacker soon after the hijacker arrives, it is obliged to submit the case to its own legal authorities to consider the desirability of prosecution. While extradition proceedings are made subservient to any existing bilateral agreements, states are allowed to use either of the two conventions as an extradition treaty if a bilateral agreement does not exist. Many Western countries wanted either mandatory prosecution or mandatory extradition and imposition of collective sanctions against states protecting hijackers or saboteurs, but there were too many states that were opposed as a result of their potential sympathy with the cause of the hijackers. In the years immediately following the signing of these accords the developed countries called for revisions to make them stronger (for example, forbidding landing rights to states protecting alleged hijackers), but it was impossible to reach a consensus.[47]

In 1978 the seven major Western economic powers (the G7) agreed that they would deprive airlines whose states refused to prosecute or extradite hijackers of landing rights and would cut off flights to those countries as well. And, in fact, they did exactly this to Afghanistan in 1982 following its failure to prosecute or extradite the hijackers of a Pakistan International Airlines plane to Afghanistan. They also successfully pressured South Africa into prosecuting some hijackers who had attempted a coup in the Seychelles in 1981.[48] A unique international accord relevant to the prosecution of individuals involved in hijackings occurred in 1990, and it is a treaty to "fingerprint" all semtex (the explosive used in most acts of sabotage) so that if it is used in the destruction of an aircraft, it will be easier to determine the purchaser and user. This agreement was possible because of the political changes in Eastern Europe and the Soviet Union.[49]

Writers on the international regulation of hijacking and aircraft sabotage tend to be rather pessimistic about the strength of the regime because approximately 15–20 percent of all states have not signed the existing conventions, some hijackers have not been prosecuted, the nature of penalties against convicted "criminals" has varied greatly, and it has been impossible to agree on collective sanctions (apart from what the G7 have done). Representative of this perspective is the comment that "there currently exists no uniform and universal enforcement system. It appears to be a formidable task to promulgate enforcement measures which would be adopted by a sufficient number of states to function effectively because of the wide spectrum of political ideologies."[50] The reality is, however, as these authors recognize, that the incidence of air crimes has gone down. The major reason certainly is the precautions that states are individually taking, but these precautions are often vetted by ICAO or IATA; and they are reinforced by the fear of international censure and possible sanctions from the Western community and a good number of Third World states. The explosions on the Air India and Korean Airlines planes and the hijacking of the Pakistan Airlines and Egypt Air planes in the mid-1980s had a definite impact on the thinking of many Third World states.

The motivations behind the concern of states to control hijacking and sabotage have been well stated by one writer:

> Recurring acts of unlawful seizure and interference with aircraft have threatened the lives and safety of thousands of passengers and crew. In more and more instances these unlawful acts have resulted in both injury and death. Financial interests have also been adversely affected by hijackings. Airline companies fear the loss of passenger revenues and the destruction or demise of aircraft. Insurance companies are concerned about the increase in the number of claims by airlines and by, or on behalf of, those passengers who sustain injuries or death. Banking concerns are wary of losing security interests in aircraft, and realize that a threat to the stability of international aviation would ultimately adversely affect their own financial interests.[51]

From the early years of the development of the international air transport industry there were negotiations on issues of airlines' liability for losses suffered by passengers and cargo owners from theft or accidents and by parties on the ground who suffered from plane crashes. While there has always been a commitment to a *norm of reasonable compensation for damages suffered from the activities of airlines*, there have been some important differences among countries since the 1950s over the magnitude and bases of liability. Because of these differences the international liability norm has only been of medium strength in recent decades.

The first major agreement on airline liability for damages suffered by passengers, luggage, and cargo was the 1929 Warsaw Convention for the Unification of Certain Rules Relating to International Carriage by Air. It established financial limits of liability for different damages, the basis of the liability (fault with a reversed burden of proof), and those types of states that could claim jurisdiction. Prior to World War II the Warsaw Convention was "an outstanding example of a successful and almost universal unification of an important sector of private law," and it still commanded very broad support for two decades after the war.[52] While important international differences have emerged since the 1960s, states still agree on aspects of the Warsaw system, and one writer has commented that it does create at least "a certain degree of uniformity in the rules governing the carrier's liability."[53]

In the 1950s the USA and several other countries exerted pressure for a liability regime that would be more favorable to passengers and cargo owners. The results were the Hague Protocol to the Warsaw Convention of 1955, which *inter alia* raised liability limits, and the Guadalaraja Protocol of 1961, which covers charter flights.[54] In 1963 the Hague Protocol entered into force after thirty states had ratified it. However, the USA continued to voice dissatisfaction with the protocol because the limits were viewed as too low. An important event was the rejection of the Hague Protocol by the US Senate in 1965. From this point "a disintegration of the system set in" and it "has progressively continued since then."[55] After long negotiations IATA offered a compromise (the Montreal Agreement) whereby the US proposals were accepted for all flights into and out of the USA, and the rest of the world stayed with the existing rules. In the words of one commentator, the agreement introduced "a situation of more or less 'regulated confusion'."[56] In 1971 a compromise proposal was approved, but this Guatemala City Protocol has been accepted by very few countries.[57] In 1975 an ICAO conference developed four protocols (the Montreal Protocols) dealing with the nature and limits of liability, but they too have not attracted sufficient backing. While the USA is the biggest obstacle to legitimizing the Warsaw system, it is by no means the only important state that would like higher limits.[58]

In 1991 109 states had accepted the Warsaw Convention as amended by the 1955 Hague Protocol, and twenty states had accepted just the 1929 Warsaw Convention. In addition, all airlines that fly into the USA are bound by the 1966 Montreal Agreement, and some states have imposed special liability plans on their own. In the words of one eminent legal expert:

> All this results in a rather chaotic situation, which with different passengers on the same aircraft may eventually be found to be under different liability regimes with different liability limits and different points of applicable national laws. Working out the legal situation of multiple claims after an accident is a very time-consuming effort.[59]

While this statement is correct because of the different levels of financial liability since the 1960s, the Warsaw system still provides considerable uniformity on many jurisdictional and procedural matters. To quote a recent study:

> Its attempts to unify and clarify the regulation of international carriage have, in many ways, been successful for many years. It has established a framework of regulations adopted by most countries involved in international aviation and many of its provisions have given organization and cohesion to vital areas such as the documentation of carriage and the fundamental principles of liability. Many of its provisions have provided a uniform practical framework for the carriage of passengers, baggage, and particularly cargo. Despite discrepancies and conversion of liability limits, many claims have been settled quickly, effectively and predictably without the need to resort to lengthy and expensive litigation.
>
> The system has provided one significant and often underestimated commodity – *predictability* which in itself provides stability and a degree of fairness.[60]

As is intimated by this comment, the present system whereby certain parts of the Warsaw system enjoy acceptance by significant groups of states does offer some stability for many claims. Still it would be misleading not to judge that the absence of agreement on liability limits does introduce significant problems in many litigations.

The important point for the purposes of this analysis is that while the lack of uniformity on certain important matters such as the limits of liability does create some additional transaction costs for airlines and states, it does not significantly hinder the operation of the international air transport system. To quote Diederiks-Verschoor: "The carriers are fully aware of their responsibilities, against which insurance can be arranged; the passengers know what to expect in cases of injury or damage. If they are not satisfied with the limits for compensation, they can take out their own additional insurance policy."[61] While this comment overstates the knowledge of most passengers, those who are knowledgeable and concerned can take out extra insurance. Also, to stress the more general point, national differences on insurance and compensation do not affect seriously the use and flow of air transport.[62]

There has never been a strong consensus with regard to some key liability issues in the air transport industry. More than anything else states' levels of economic development explain their differences on liability limits and the scope of damages to be covered. The lack of consensus has often meant multiple litigations and varied legal results in the case of individual accidents. The costs have, however, not been high enough to deter the growth of the air transport industry, and therefore the differences have been tolerated. As long as states can require that airlines have insurance coverage adequate to cover the obligations set forth in their laws, states feel secure.[63]

The promotion of aircraft safety has been quite successful over the years, and there has been a steady decline in the rate of accidents and deaths. While people tend to remember horrible disasters such as the crash of the Turkish Airlines DC-10 over France in 1974 (346 killed) and the explosion on the Pan Am Boeing 747 over Scotland in 1985 (259 killed), there have been marked improvements in airline accident records and incidences of hijacking. An indication of the steady progress is that in the years 1988–91 the number of deaths per million passenger kilometers was about a quarter of what it was in the period 1971–74.[64] A poor safety record would be a huge impediment to the use of international air transport services and the flow of commerce, and the damage-control regulations have removed this impediment. Also, an effective international framework of regulations means that states do not develop unique safety standards with individual or small groups of countries that increase transaction costs and reduce the efficiency of the international air transport system. International rules certainly have reduced the possibility that states would legislate national standards that would reduce the international mobility of aircraft. As noted, there are some weaknesses in parts of the regime dealing with damage control problems, but they do not concern issues where a lack of international rules would seriously undermine the use of air transport.

Technical and procedural barriers

The reduction of the multitude of technical and procedural barriers to the movement of aircraft, passengers, and cargo is a central dimension of the air transport regime. The major concerns of states and airlines are to increase the use of air transport and the flow of commerce. The coverage of this dimension is very descriptive, but it does provide an indication of the complex sets of rules and collaborative programs that exist.

The importance of the *norm of technical interconnection* is palpable from looking at all of the annexes to the ICAO Convention which were discussed in the section on damage control. Virtually all of the annexes are concerned in some way with ensuring that planes can interconnect efficiently with airport and navigation facilities. It would be superfluous to review the technical provisions again.

The *facilitation norm* concerns the obligation of states and airlines to remove impediments to the flow of aircraft, passengers, and cargo. While many of the impediments are in airports, they exist in various aspects of the air transport industry. Probably the most important step that has been taken to facilitate air transport is the development of single tickets and waybills that allow passengers and cargo to be carried by several airlines on a single trip. This makes international travel much easier than it would be if a traveler had to purchase separate tickets from each airline. In order to make the system work IATA operates a clearing house in Geneva which arranges for the settlement of debts among airlines (90 percent of the debts are actually offsetting and therefore do not have to be paid).[65] Relevant to this point a recent book comments:

> IATA's greatest contribution to the internationalisation of air transport, in the most practical sense of the term, is in the field of standardization of airline documents, of procedures for the exchange of tickets, and quick settlement of interline accounts. That a passenger can move around the world on one ticket and change airlines according to his needs without additional charges or bureaucracy is obviously a crucial achievement.[66]

IATA's facilitation of air transport goes beyond the establishment of single passenger tickets and cargo waybills. There are also IATA-originated systems for settling accounts between travel agents and airlines (the Bank Settlement Plan) and between cargo agents and airlines (the Cargo Accounts Settlement System).[67]

There are also a host of arrangements and agreements that deal with technical or physical impediments to the flow of traffic. The IATA Multilateral Interline Traffic Agreement provides for a uniform system of handling, transfer, rerouteing, and related procedures for all passengers, baggage, and cargo moving between participating carriers. There are also regular passenger and cargo conferences that deal with obstacles to the expeditious flow of travelers and their luggage. More recently, non-airline elements of the travel industry, such as airports, the suppliers of ground handling services and equipment, computer companies, car hire agencies, railways, and hotels have been given access to IATA's standard-setting process through the Registered Suppliers and Travel Partners Programmes. It is of interest that over the years many airlines that did not belong to IATA, in fact joined various IATA schemes that reduce a host of impediments to efficient air travel and consequently enhance consumer demand.[68] Proof of the great strides toward uniformity that have occurred are revealed in a recent study by economists that found "great similarity" in the non-flight operations and maintenance practices of airlines. It also noted that international treaties exist for many of these issues.[69]

Another area where both ICAO and IATA have done a tremendous amount of work is in expediting the movement of passengers, luggage, and freight into and out of airports. This may not appear to be a particularly important issue, but the airlines certainly view these matters as salient to people's willingness to use the airlines. A very important annex to the Convention on International Civil Aviation concerns "facilitation," and this basically refers to reducing the multitude of obstacles that extend the time people and cargo must spend in airports. Apart from the constant revision of standards and procedures concerning customs, immigration, health regulations, agricultural products, checking-in, baggage handling, and a host of documentary matters, ICAO holds conferences on these issues to educate airline and airport personnel, and IATA does a great deal in developing supplementary accords, monitoring compliance at airports, and sending out teams to assist airport authorities.[70]

Some of the impediments to the movement of aircraft, passengers, and cargo within the international air transport system are created by governments to protect or enhance the market shares of their national airlines. Such barriers include user charges in airports, taxes, takeoff and landing slots, ground handling operations, and computer reservation systems. Both ICAO and IATA have been active in preventing governments' discriminatory practices, but some obstacles remain. A major problem that has developed since the 1970s is the use of computer reservation systems used by travel agents that encourage the use of certain airlines rather than others. The problem started in a serious manner in the USA with the development by United Airlines and American Airlines of their own systems (called Apollo and Sabre respectively). The US government acted to assure access by the other airlines to these systems, and in 1989 the European Union adopted its own code to assure access for all airlines. ICAO and IATA have also become involved in developing international policies on these issues, and for the most part discrimination by the big airlines that own the computer reservation systems has been eliminated.[71]

Expediting the flow of passengers and cargo and preventing states from erecting protectionist barriers have been and still are central aspects of the international air transport regime. ICAO has tended to focus on technical matters and IATA on commercial questions, although the line is difficult to draw between the two. Most air passengers do not realize it, but when they fly, a host of international rules affect the purchase of their tickets, their activities in airports, and the flight itself. Making the wheels of international commerce run smoothly is a very complex matter in the air transport industry.

Prices and market shares

In the period following World War I international civil aviation grew gradually, but it was for the most part limited to particular regions. Only late in the interwar period did transoceanic travel become possible – with commercial transatlantic flights first occurring in the late 1930s. There were diplomatic negotiations in the 1920s about allowing an "open port" regime whereby airlines could service any foreign airport, but they came to naught because of states' desire to protect their nascent air transport industries.[72] During the interwar period there were no large international bodies concerned with rate-setting or the distribution of market shares, although informal coordination of airline policies sometimes took place at meetings of the International Air Traffic Association. Virtually all bilateral agreements on the award of routes, market shares, fares, and revenues were based on the principle of reciprocity. Usually the agreements were concluded between the largely state-owned carriers.

Most bilateral agreements within the industrialized world gave rough equality of privileges to the carriers of each country. They sometimes fixed frequencies, and often they were supplemented by secret interairline agreements that set rates, regulated quality of service, and pooled revenues. Overall one must conclude that there was little in the way of a formal commercial regime during the interwar period, and this was due in part to the very nascent stage of the industry and its confinement for the most part to regional routes. At most one can say that there was an informal accord in the industrialized world on an approximate equal sharing of passengers and revenue between national airlines.[73] Hence the *cartel norm*, which was formally institutionalized after World War II, had clear roots in the interwar period.

The evolution of the IATA cartel regime

During World War II it was evident that there would be a burgeoning of international air transport after the war as a result of the marked increase in the carrying capacity and range of aircraft. A major conference to discuss various aspects of international civil aviation was convened in Chicago in November 1944. It succeeded in settling the key substantive and procedural issues concerning jurisdictional rights, the control of accidental and intentional damage, and technical interconnection. However, despite many negotiating sessions concerning the regulation of fares and market shares, the participating states could not reach agreement.

There were a number of proposals concerning the regulation of market shares, fares, and the sharing of revenues, and some were very ambitious in the powers proposed for an international authority. However, ultimately the debate centered on several key issues that divided the USA and Britain. While both sides basically accepted that the granting of rights to fly particular routes would be settled in bilateral intergovernmental agreements (albeit with some ambiguity in the US stance), they differed on whether there should be any restrictions on frequency, market shares, and tariffs. The USA with by far the largest and most technologically advanced air transport industry favored no restrictions on market shares and passenger fares. On the other hand, most of the other countries, led by Britain, feared that open competition would mean the demise of their airlines and the eventual dominance of the American carriers. They wanted a regulatory system that protected their national airlines and minimized the need for government subsidies. The Americans were not completely hostile to some international regulation of fares, but they wanted rules that afforded significant leeway for the airlines. After the failure of the 1944 Chicago conference to reach agreement on the central commercial issues, sixty airlines established the International Air Transport Association (IATA) in 1945 in order to provide a negotiating setting for commercial and non-commercial issues that might concern them in the future.[74]

In the year and a half after the Chicago conference many states made bilateral agreements, and there were significant variations in their character. However, it was clear that a greater degree of uniformity was desirable.[75] In 1946 the USA and Britain met in Bermuda to negotiate a bilateral accord, and the result (known as the Bermuda Agreement) became the model for most bilateral agreements. Each side formally compromised one of its positions, although in reality the British won on both key issues. On the matter of fares it was agreed that IATA would set tariffs through its Traffic Conferences, and this of course was an important concession by the USA. As part of the Bermuda Agreement the USA's Civil Aviation Board agreed to grant antitrust immunity to IATA's multilateral tariff-setting conferences. On the other key issue of market shares or "capacity" it was agreed that while there would be no predetermination of the percentage of total passengers that could be carried by the two countries' airlines, there would be *ex post facto* reviews of figures. This last proviso opened the door to the regulation of market shares. While the market share provisions were publicized as a British concession little, in fact, was conceded. According to Anthony Sampson, the Europeans "never accepted the flexibility of the Bermuda agreement: they insisted on fixing frequencies and fares rigidly beforehand." They also "successfully limited their competition through the 'pools' which shared the profits between the two ends of the route."[76] It was soon clear that virtually all countries were committed to a roughly equal division of passengers although the USA never explicitly admitted this. The British also successfully resisted US demands for extensive "fifth freedom" rights – or the ability to fly from the initial foreign landing spot to a third country. These were to be bargained for in the same way as "third and fourth freedom" rights (the rights to fly back and forth between the two countries making the agreement) were negotiated.[77]

In the years immediately after the Bermuda conference the procedures and rules for the airline cartel developed very quickly. IATA developed its procedures for setting fares at its regional and interregional Traffic Conferences. A unanimity rule was accepted, and this ensured that the states of departure and landing states and potentially affected regional states approved a fare. In other words, in negotiations on a fare for a particular route, both the state preferring a very high rate for revenue-raising purposes and neighboring states fearing that low rates might deflect traffic from them were given significant leverage over the setting of the fare. A recent study has commented that central to IATA's multilateral process for establishing fares was the concern to prevent competition and competitive price wars among carriers on similar routes.[78] On the matter of market shares, most bilateral accords not involving the USA established provisions for an equal sharing of passengers and revenues (pooling), and even the USA did not veer significantly from the guideline that a state's airlines should carry approximately half of the passengers and receive half of the revenues from the traffic involving their country. The USA was, in fact, quite generous in bilateral accords because of political concerns for its allies and the pressures of its own aircraft industry that sold planes to foreign airlines. One provision that was included in most bilateral accords strengthened the positions of the state-owned airlines and hence the cartel, i.e. that only a single airline would be allowed to assume the rights given to a particular state.[79]

There were a variety of reasons for both the policies adopted during the 1944–46 negotiations and the bargaining outcome. On the matter of policies of the two sides they were influenced in part by different views of interwar commercial developments. The USA saw the interwar years as a period of inefficient collusion among carriers, whereas the British saw them as ones of excessive competition, burdensome subsidies, and rate wars. It should be noted that the dominant US international carrier, Pan American, was supportive of market sharing along interwar lines since it feared competition from subsidized foreign airlines, but its voice did not prevail in US decision-making.[80] The main reason, however, for the policy split was that Britain and most other states feared that US airlines would drive them out of business as a result of their size and technological advancement and the power base provided by the huge US domestic market.[81]

The assertion that most states supported a tariff-setting and market-sharing cartel to protect their national airline begs the question as to why they were all dedicated to preserving a national airline. Some of the reasons concerned a desire to have a military air transport reserve, a desire to shape their international commercial and political ties, the need to earn foreign exchange, and the possibility of having a reliable buyer for a domestic plane manufacturing industry.[82] These reasons should not be discounted in the immediate postwar years, or now, although they have probably declined in importance over time. However, they do not identify what is the most important reason – namely, states' view that a national airline is a crucial symbol of independence and political autonomy. To quote a British airline executive:

> Airlines have mainly been founded and expanded as a clone of the government – an unassailable symbol of prestige and sovereign virility . . . The intimacy of these airlines with their governments developed a longstanding acknowledgement that consumer and commercial considerations have been subordinated to national interest and political interference.[83]

For countries of reasonable size it has almost been inconceivable that they would not have a national airline or that that airline would be foreign-owned. A nationally owned flag airline has simply been a hallmark of being "a real state." It is significant that almost all countries require that their airlines be owned by nationals or that only a small percentage can be owned by foreigners. Even the USA limits foreign ownership to 25 percent of voting control, although ownership of shares can be as high as 49 percent.[84] There is, however, another way that governments ensure national ownership of airlines, and that is that they stipulate in their bilateral agreements that all designated airlines must be nationally owned and registered.

There are two basic reasons why Britain (supported by most other states) won out against the overriding economic power of the USA in the immediate postwar years. First, international air transport requires landing rights, and this gives states with modest economic wealth considerable leverage. Britain, in particular, had significant leverage in the late 1940s because of its extensive network of colonies.[85] Second, one consideration that had a profound effect on the American acceptance of the IATA cartel was the perception that economic concessions were necessary in order to assist the economic recovery of America's allies and to knit together an anti-communist alliance. To quote an excellent political analysis of US international air transport policy:

> US policy called for maintenance of non-communist governments in all states not already communist. This required strong, economically healthy governments throughout the world . . . Thus when a foreign government begged for favorable treatment from the United States government for their airline, the United States, fearful of weakening a friendly government or of restricting the foreign exchange earning power of the weaker, felt obliged to assist.[86]

Of course, under the Bermuda system the US government could bargain for slightly more liberal provisions concerning market shares than those adopted in most bilateral accords and its airlines could bargain for reasonable rates in IATA. The agreements negotiated by the USA and its airlines did not, however, differ significantly from those negotiated by most other countries.[87]

The 1950s were a period of rapid expansion in the international airline industry as the number of passengers went up by over 15 percent per year. In the 1940s the USA and some other countries allowed the introduction of modest charter services on some routes, and pressure soon developed for allowing additional charter flights.[88] In 1953 IATA took several steps that responded to the argument that tourist traffic could increase significantly if fares were lowered. First of all, it created special tourist fares and, secondly, it permitted non-scheduled or charter flights if the passengers were associated with certain types of groups. In the late 1950s the USA began to come into conflict with other states over the level of fares, but the opposition of high-cost airlines (whose numbers were being augmented by the creation of new Third World airlines "operating chiefly for reasons of politics and pride")[89] prevented any significant decrease in IATA fares. The USA gave in to the demands of non-American airlines since, in the words of a State Department official, it had little choice "but to be liberal with other members of the free world alliance."[90]

The 1960s witnessed the large-scale introduction of jet aircraft, and this led to a situation of reduced costs and overcapacity. The USA began to exert greater pressure for lower fares, and following a serious conflict in 1962–63 when it was forced to back down from its demand for greater liberalization in IATA tariffs, the US government began to promote charter airlines which were not members of IATA. Also, US airlines pursued additional strategies for evading the strictures of IATA Traffic Conferences and the Bermuda Agreement. The impact of US policy on charter flights is indicated by the fact that, whereas in 1959 charters accounted for 12 percent of all international miles flown, in 1971 the figure was 32 percent. Overall violations of cartel norms increased during this period because of overcapacity and US dissatisfaction with high IATA tariffs. In looking back at this period the former IATA Secretary-General has written that "It was not until the early and mid-60s that substantial changes – the beginnings of the fragmentation – began to occur in the regulatory structure."[91]

In the early 1970s the scheduled airlines responded to the growing role of charter airlines by offering discounted fares. The US government responded by authorizing Advanced Booking Charters (ABC) on the North Atlantic. Still, the non-American airlines were able to reverse the growth in charters – with a decline from 32 to 25 percent between 1971 and 1975. Despite this struggle over the charters and new types of fares and an excess supply of seats caused by the oil crisis, the introduction of wide-bodied jets, and the expansion of some non-IATA airlines (particularly from Asia),[92] most airlines continued to support an equal division of passengers in their bilaterals, and IATA Traffic Conferences continued to set fares on most routes. It appeared that the cartel would continue to control most of the industry since the state-owned airlines (sixty-eight out of eighty-two IATA members in 1970) controlled IATA and most bilaterals. Also, most private airlines such as the major US carriers were reasonably happy with the prevailing regime since they received good profits on scheduled flights and were able to compete for the tourist market through charters.[93] An indication of the apparent resilience of the regime in the mid-1970s was the fact that the USA and Britain renegotiated a new bilateral (Bermuda II) in 1976, and it contained stricter rules to assure an equal division of the passenger market.[94]

The fracturing of the cartel and the movement toward competition

While Bermuda II gave the appearance of a relatively stable status quo, major forces of change were welling up in the USA. Fundamental to this change was the growth of a body of economics research in the 1960s and early 1970s that indicated that consumers were paying much more for their airline fares than they would pay under a system of open competition. The research attacked inter alia claims that there were economies of scale or possibilities of "destructive competition" in the industry that justified a cartel.[95] The political salience of these findings was raised by the Kennedy Congressional hearings of 1975–77 on the civil aviation industry which provoked increasing demands by consumer interests and politicians for reform.[96] A crucial step in the reformulation of US policy occurred in 1977 when President Carter appointed Alfred Kahn, a Cornell economics professor (referred to as "the high-priest of deregulation") as the chairman of the Civil Aviation Board.[97] Another important development that year was the commencement of transatlantic service by Laker Airways which offered dramatically reduced fares.[98] It was clear in 1977 that some major changes were occurring in the international air transport market, but no one knew how far they would go. The situation with regard to international fares was chaotic over the year. As the *ICAO Bulletin* noted: "Passenger fares were open for all or most of the year in more than half of the international conference negotiating areas despite a long series of conferences and meetings and various other attempts to achieve closed situations."[99] Within ICAO the developing countries sensed that the air transport cartel that allowed them to charge high fares and hence avoid large subsidies for their airlines was disappearing. They convened an

ICAO conference to try to strengthen the cartel, but it had little impact.[100]

In 1977 and 1978 the USA embarked on a campaign to undermine the air transport cartel and to establish an international commercial regime based on increased liberalization of passenger fares and market shares. Its motivations were both a desire to reduce rates and a desire to increase US airlines' share of the market. There was, however, another factor that spurred the change in US policy, and that was that it no longer feared that it had to be so protective of the economic interests of its political allies since they were prosperous and the danger of war had declined. Relevant to this issue Richard Thornton was very prescient in 1970 when he wrote: "We can suspect that the prosperity of the United States international airlines and the quality of airline service will become high priority US objectives once the previously overriding defense needs have disappeared."[101] There were two key strategies that the USA employed to restructure the international airline industry. First, it stated that it would remove the antitrust immunity from IATA if it and its member airlines could not provide a good justification why the immunity should be preserved. Second, it set about to negotiate a large number of "liberal bilaterals" with the following stipulations: no limitations on market shares; ability to designate multiple airlines to an individual route; minimal fare controls; the need for both states of origin and destination to disapprove of a fare negotiated between two airlines in order for it to be overturned (double disapproval); expansion of charter flights into more routes; and the jurisdiction of states of origin over charter fares.[102]

The central tactic it used in promoting liberalization of the crucial transatlantic routes was to sign liberal bilaterals with several states that aspired to be hubs for transatlantic traffic (particularly the Netherlands and Belgium). This then pressured states like Britain and Germany that did not want to lose business to accept some liberalization in existing arrangements. Between 1978 and 1981 the USA signed twenty liberal bilaterals whose key provisions were broad "zones of reasonableness" for fares, the requirement of double disapproval to force a revision of fares, designation of multiple airlines, introduction of charters on more routes, and country-of-origin pricing for charter flights. While some bilaterals had flexibility on market shares, the implicit rule was still a roughly equal sharing of business. In a few cases like the US–Netherlands relationship, the new accords led to quite uneven sharing of the passenger market. By 1981–82 the USA realized that a strident liberalization policy would seriously alienate many other states and, in addition, some of its own airlines were complaining that the liberal bilaterals were often undermining their market shares and overall financial positions. As parts of a more flexible civil aviation policy the USA accepted "zones of reasonableness" for fares in an agreement with the European Civil Aviation Conference and dropped its threat to withdraw antitrust immunity from IATA. US negotiators also became tougher in bargaining over market share or capacity clauses in new bilateral accords. It is, however, important to recognize that a great deal of liberalization in fares on North Atlantic and select Asian routes occurred in the late 1970s and early 1980s. In fact, the recognition that the air transport world was evolving toward a bifurcation of liberal and protectionist states led IATA in 1978 to permit airlines to join solely for the purpose of participating in technical coordination activities – abjuring tariff coordination. Of course, this recognition was influenced significantly by US pressure and the success of the non-IATA Asian airlines.[103]

As part of the movement toward liberalization in the late 1970s certain changes occurred in IATA's role in setting tariffs. IATA Traffic Conferences in certain regions lost a great deal of their authority and were at most information-exchange sessions. Also, airlines generally were more prone to revise previous accords without multilateral approval. In the area of enforcement major changes occurred. From the late 1940s through to the early 1970s two IATA bodies (the Breaches Commission for airlines and the Arbitration Board for travel agents) dealt with complaints concerning violations of IATA tariff rules. They imposed fines in cases of some infractions although there were not a large number of violations of rules when the IATA-based cartel was working well. The whole enforcement system began to fall apart in the early 1970s because of overcapacity and rate-cutting, and with the US drive toward liberalization in the latter part of the decade the system collapsed. In 1981 IATA replaced the former arrangements with the Fair Deal Monitoring Program, and some regional groupings created their own restraint and monitoring programs. It has, in fact, only been in some Third World areas where any real discipline in rate-setting and compliance has continued, and there compliance does not rest for the most part on a sanctioning system.[104]

One thing that became clear in the early and mid-1980s was that virtually all states were committed to maintaining the financial viability and existence of their national airlines. And this meant that their national airlines had to carry about half of the passengers flying between their territory and other states. Relevant to this point a report of the European Economic Committee on the Aviation Industry stated that it was "inconceivable that a European government would accept the elimination its flag carrier" for reasons of prestige, foreign exchange, and political considerations.[105] The power of these airlines in defending themselves was indicated by the demise of Laker Airways in 1982. It was driven out of the market by price-cutting and legal actions.[106] It is still the case that most national airlines control close to half of the business going into and out of their countries although there is a little more variation on individual routes as well as for particular airlines than there used to be. Even the great protagonist of liberalization, the USA has only managed to increase the control by its airlines over traffic going into and out of the country from 50.9 to 53.8 percent over the decade 1982–1991.[107]

While the traditional division of market shares between pairs of countries continued for most routes in the 1980s, there were some routes where open competition and changes in market shares did emerge. Also, there was significant competition with regard to fares on many routes, and the liberalization of cargo rates was even more significant than in the case of passenger fares. The gradual process of liberalization was promoted by the privatization or partial privatization of many airlines starting in the late 1980s. The financial success of British Airways after its privatization in 1987 had a marked effect on the withdrawal of many governments from their financial involvement in national airlines.[108]

With regard to Europe some dramatic movements toward deregulation started in the mid-1980s although some European states certainly resisted the trend. A very liberal bilateral between Britain and the Netherlands in 1984 encouraged some other states to take steps in the same direction.[109] In 1985 the European Commission developed a proposal for a dramatic abolition of internal barriers to trade, and the following year the Council approved the Single European Act with a 1992 target for the implementation of internal liberalization. Of perhaps even greater importance for air transport, in 1986 the European Court of Justice judged that air transport was subject to the jurisdiction of the Community's competition rules. Then, in 1987 the Council decided that there should be a competitive common market for air transport by 1992 – the same schedule as for other sectors of the European economy. At this point European airlines recognized that significant steps toward liberalization would be required, and at 1987 and 1989 meetings of the European Civil Aviation Commission they accepted greater flexibility with regard to both fares and market shares. In 1990 the Council approved further liberal regulations to take effect in 1993 – including freedom of airlines to fly any routes between Community states and the need for double disapproval to prevent adoption of fares negotiated between two airlines. Also, the Community regulations assured new airlines access to airport landing and takeoff slots and computer reservation systems – something that was not provided in US deregulation. It will not be until near the end of the decade that the European Union has a true open market for air transport, but it is coming. Also, it may provide impetus for liberalization agreements with foreign countries – particularly the USA.[110]

In the midst of all the changes in Europe since the mid-1980s and more limited movements toward liberalization elsewhere there were negotiations on international services in the GATT Uruguay Round. With regard to air transport, the only areas where the accord promotes liberalization are aircraft repair and maintenance, the marketing of air transport services, and computer reservation systems. Nothing was accomplished as to the liberalization of fare-setting and market shares because the adoption of the GATT non-discrimination and national treatment norms would solely benefit protectionist states in the markets of the liberalized states, and the latter countries will not permit that. It is also unlikely in the short run that many states are going to accept a high degree of liberalization because it would mean the demise of their national airlines.[111] This places limits at least for a while on what GATT or another international body could do to promote liberalization. The air transport economist Michael Tretheway has grasped this problem in his comparison of the US and European situations, and the European situation could be generalized to many other countries.

> The US started deregulation with 11 trunk air carriers and an additional eight local service carriers. None of these embodied the ego of the US presence in the world airline community. Therefore, culturally, it was possible for the US to let one or several of those carriers go out of business. Such is not the case in Europe. Most countries have a single national airline. The flag carrier embodies the entire ego of that country in the world airline community. Further, most of these carriers are either wholly government owned or have substantial government interests.[112]

And it must be stressed, many national airlines would disappear if there were broad multilateral moves toward liberalization.

Daniel Kasper has written that the bases for multilateral liberalization lie with states' acceptance of a number of policies: privatization; abolition of subsidies; assurance of access to computer reservation systems; liberal regulatory policies concerning fares and market shares; and binding dispute settlement.[113] These points, however, beg the question of states' attachment to a national airline as a symbol of national independence and international status. If states do not accept the possible demise of their national airline or participation in a multinational carrier, the prospects for liberalization are limited. It is quite possible that states will judge that the economic costs of a national airline are too great and that such symbols of independence and status are less important in our interdependent world. However, the transition is likely to be a gradual one. In the short run we are likely to see liberalization within certain regions and the increasing emergence of some megacarriers that will represent a number of flags. This is highly likely in Europe, and it could spread to other areas.[114] Daniel Kasper could well be correct that the industry is moving toward the dominance of a modest number of global megacarriers,[115] but this situation is unlikely to emerge quickly. On the other hand, the fact that the world airlines lost $16 billion between 1990 and 1992 (because of increasing competition and a reduction in the growth of demand) is bound to provoke some serious reevaluation of the costs and benefits of national airlines.[116]

Some of the indications that the air transport industry is evolving toward the emergence of multinational megacarriers are the share purchases, merger discussions, and possibilities for outright purchase among airlines that have emerged in the 1990s. British Airways bought 25 percent of USAir and Quantas (with the likelihood of further purchases), and it has bought small airlines in Germany and France. KLM has bought 49 percent of Northwest. Air France has purchased 30 percent of Sabena. Lufthansa has joint marketing and seat-sharing arrangements with United Airlines, and British Airways and United Airlines cooperate in feeding traffic into each other's network. In 1993 SAS, KLM, Austrian Airlines, and Swissair were close to merging into a firm called Alcazar, and while the talks broke down over which US airline to affiliate with, negotiations are likely to recommence. Swissair has swapped shares with Delta and Singapore Airlines. Within North America, American Airlines has purchased 25 percent of Canadian

Airlines International, and Air Canada has purchased a share of Continental. A number of other airlines are known to be looking for partners. Still, it is difficult to predict the long-term significance of the proliferation of alliances. To cite an excellent study on the international aviation industry: "What remains uncertain is whether alliances are a short term precursor to globalization, or whether they will be a long term strategy of international airlines."[117] A former chairman of Lufthansa has predicted that by the end of the 1990s there will be solely three or four major airlines in Europe,[118] and while one can make a good case for this vision of accelerated consolidation in the international industry, it is difficult to be confident about particular evolutionary patterns. He is probably correct in his projections concerning the movement toward multinational carriers and greater competition, but there are a lot of obstacles to overcome – most of them embedded in states' concern to protect national airlines.[119]

International regulatory arrangements governing fares and market shares have undergone some marked changes since the 1920s. In the interwar years the international industry was separated into regional networks because of the limited range of aircraft. However, in the European region the cartel norm began to develop in that states accepted a roughly equal sharing of the passenger market and revenues in bilateral relationships and also negotiated fares for many routes. Between the late 1940s and the mid-1970s there was a strong cartel in place. Most states accepted an equal sharing of the passenger market, multilateral determination of fares, and a discouragement of competition among national airlines. To quote one study: "One of the principal functions of IATA has been to develop a fare structure that minimized the threat of traffic diversion."[120] In fact, not only did international fare structures prevent competition among airlines, the fares were also high enough such that government subsidies for national airlines could generally be avoided or at least kept at reasonable levels.[121]

Prior to the 1970s there were some signs of weakening of the cartel – particularly the growth of charter airlines. Also, cheating on tariff accords occurred at times because of overcapacity. Then, starting in the 1970s, some airlines that had stayed out of IATA (particularly Asian airlines such as Singapore International, Malaysia, Cathay Pacific, and Korean) were able to expand their market shares steadily. It should be recalled that the Asia–Pacific region's share of global traffic increased from 14 to 29 percent between 1973 and 1988.[122] These weaknesses in the cartel *might* have been contained if it had not been for the decision by the USA to press for liberalization. Starting with the late 1970s the international civil aviation world basically split in two although there were differences within each group. On the North Atlantic and some Pacific routes fares were liberalized, although only minor progress occurred in weakening restrictions on market shares. While there was some modest progress toward liberalization in the early 1980s, the next major step did not come until the move toward reducing restrictions within Europe in the late 1980s and early 1990s. In fact, there is some promise of a reduction in market share restrictions in Europe that has not occurred elsewhere. While liberalization has a clear momentum at the moment, there are definite limits to its progress in that certain states and areas will insist on maintaining a national or regional flag carrier. Rigas Doganis has stated that as long as states are committed to maintaining national airlines, some market share and price regulation will be necessary, and on this issue he is almost certainly correct.[123] The big question concerning the future is whether we are on the verge of an era when states will no longer require a national airline or at least will be satisfied with participating in a joint venture of some kind.

In explaining the existence of the cartel regime for many years and the subsequent bifurcation of the civil aviation world, it is first important to explore whether the cartel regime was based on mutual interests and, if so, what mutual interests? One thing that is quite clear from the preceding analysis is that the cartel did not rest on a perception that a natural monopoly (or increasing economies of scale or scope) existed. This argument seldom emerged in the relevant literature. The dominant view in the 1960s and early 1970s was that increasing economies of scale or scope did not exist and that the costs of national and international cartels had been high. In the words of one writer:

> Scale economies are not large; entry into, and exit from both the industry and the individual markets are relatively easy; capital-output ratios are low; most costs are variable; and there is some opportunity for product competition. All of these conditions are inconsistent with predatory price cutting that would drive out competitors and create monopoly positions.[124]

Most economists today believe that there may be economies of scale or scope over certain routes or route networks, but not over significant segments of the international industry. To quote a recent OECD study that reviewed economics studies and recent experiences with

122

deregulation: "the air transport sector has some economies of scale and scope so that there will never be room for numerous airlines competing on each route but that even with some sunk costs, new entry can be a significant competitive force so that an incumbent airline is not generally able to reap monopoly profits for a non-transitory period unless regulation distorts the market."[125] It is also noteworthy that the airline business does not earn a great deal for government treasuries since its profits are quite low in comparison to other industries. Hence, the argument that the cartel promoted great financial gains for revenue-starved governments does not hold.[126]

What the air transport cartel provided was the ability of almost all states to sustain their own national airlines. Equal division of passengers flying between two countries and multilateral fare-setting quite simply promoted states' mutual interest in sustaining an important symbol of national autonomy. To quote Anthony Sampson's study on the international air transport industry:

> most governments outside America were determined to have their own flag-carrier on which they could rely . . . The planes painted in their national colours and the glossy showrooms and advertising in foreign capitals were becoming more visible representatives than embassies or sports teams.[127]

Here is a perfect example of where a concern for state autonomy can be a basis for international collaboration – more particularly, a cartel.

Of course, the USA as well as several small states finally sought to undermine the cartel, and they had the power to divide the world along the lines of two different commercial models. The question now arises as to whether a new global regime based on a limited competition norm will evolve. As intimated above, it is possible that states are gradually losing their identification with a national airline as economic globalization progresses. However, states are likely at least for some time to be associated with a regional airline or even an interregional airline, and therefore some supports for the financial viability of these new multi-airline megacarriers will be required. The shape of the air transport regime will probably reflect developments in the overall global economy. If regional blocs do not become too strong and self-sufficient, a new international liberal regime may emerge. On the other hand, if economic regionalism progresses in terms of growing protectionism and self-sufficiency, international civil aviation arrangements are likely to reflect this regional pattern.

Until the late 1970s states' perception that state independence required possession of a national airline basically dictated the shape of the IATA cartel. While competition weakened the cartel, it was also undermined by a greater acceptance of liberal economic values and a decline in states' willingness to subsidize national airlines. Under these conditions states' concerns to control market failures have grown. Former collusive practices of the IATA cartel have been eliminated for many routes, and some countries have at least reduced their barriers to entry which were linked to a managed division of market shares. This liberalization trend is likely to continue to grow.

Conclusion

The regulatory arrangements pertaining to jurisdictional rights, damage control problems, and technical barriers in the international air transport industry have been and still are quite strong although there are certainly some areas of weakness. These areas of weakness concern liability limits, political crimes, and some protectionist practices at airports. However, they are not major weaknesses that impose serious impediments to the flow of airline services. The industry can cope with different national liability limits; states are operating on their own and in small groups to reduce hijackings and sabotage; and the remaining protectionist barriers at airports generally have rather modest impacts on market shares. With regard to prices and market shares there was a strong cartel norm until the 1970s. Since then there has been movement toward a more competitive environment, but one can only describe the present situation as one of diverse international orders linking groups of states. Whether a new global regime based on a limited competition norm is going to emerge is difficult to judge. There are movements in that direction, but there is still considerable uncertainty as to what will emerge.

It is clear that important elements of strength in the air transport regime were built on states' mutual interests in protecting their policy autonomy in preserving a national airline. The regime components that facilitated states' maintenance of a national airline include the jurisdictional rights to exclude foreign aircraft and to grant permission to land and the cartel norm. Even now the concern of states to maintain a national airline constrains the degree of liberalization that most countries are willing to contemplate. If a new international consensus emerges that replaces the old accord underlying the IATA cartel, it is likely to be partially shaped by the insistence of a good number of countries that they do not lose their flag carriers (even if the carrier is a component of an international consortium).

Many aspects of the air transport regime that govern jurisdictional rights, damage control, and technical interconnection and facilitation are based on the concern of states and airlines to promote the rapid and safe international movement of goods and people. The flow of commerce is promoted not just by the reduction of barriers imposed by the policies of airlines and governments, but also by the reduction of uncertainty in the costs that they face and of the resources that they expend on negotiating accords. In the area of jurisdictional rights the key provisions promoting commercial openness are the right of free access to air space above the high seas and the right of innocent passage. There are good prospects that the minority of countries that have opposed this latter right will soon support it.

The regime's multifaceted provisions concerning damage control and facilitation are based even more firmly on the desire of states and industry to mitigate any impediments to the movement and growth of air transport. The value placed on safety by the regime because of its impacts on the use of air transport and hence the expansion of international commerce was placed in good perspective by Golich:

> Aviation safety . . . has been considered important because unsafe airways, airlines or airports diminish the potential of the industry to serve political and economic ends. To serve these functions, the general public and business must be convinced of air transport's reliability, and that requires safe operations. Thus, safety generally has been subsumed within the broader context of the industry's vital role in the future development of communication and transportation systems.[128]

A comparable point was made by Charles Perrow in his well-known study *Normal Accidents*:

> [There is] an enormous incentive to make commercial aviation safe. Airline travel drops after large accidents; airframe companies suffer if one of their models appears to have more than its share of accidents. Public reaction appears to be strong when identifiable, rather than random, victims are produced in an accident. There are passenger lists in airline accidents.[129]

The efforts of ICAO and IATA in standardizing safety, navigation, and transit regulations have had a major impact in removing barriers to the international movement of aircraft and promoting economic efficiency in air and ground operations. On this matter one writer has remarked that

> one of the great services which IATA has succeeded in performing, in both the technical and the commercial fields, has been a high degree of standardization. While this success has received little publicity, it is one of the achievements which has made it possible for air transport to expand throughout the world with a minimum of complication and expense.[130]

Those aspects of the regime that are not often analyzed in the academic or popular literature are, in fact, of great international economic and hence political import.

An important issue in reflecting on mutual interests underlying the air transport regime is whether the significant weakening of the international airline cartel has also been a product of a concern to make international air transport more efficient, or whether it is simply a product of attempts by certain countries to gain larger market shares. It is interesting because it may provide an indication as to whether a new regime based on a basically open system of competition will emerge. In looking back over recent decades it appears that the policies of the USA and the airlines of the small Asian countries to expand their market shares *and* to provide consumers with cheaper services were crucial to the fracturing of the cartel, but it is unclear whether their policies may have reflected a growing trend in thinking in favor of more open competition that was bound to occur as economic knowledge and liberal economic values grew and as states began to accept a loss of control over certain domestic policy sectors. As noted previously, evolution toward a very different commercial world of air transport is emerging based on new notions of mutual interest. However, the new consensus is likely to contain some protection for national or regional carriers as well as more open competition in fares and market shares.

5   The international telecommunications regime

International telecommunications services and the regulatory framework

Telecommunications refers to the transmission of verbal messages, numeric data, and pictures by wire and by the electromagnetic spectrum. For the past century and a half there have been revolutionary developments in the technology of telecommunications, and these changes have been central to the growth of the global economy. In reviewing the technological changes it is useful to divide the years between those from the mid-nineteenth century to 1945, and those after 1945 and to focus on the three interrelated and even overlapping forms of telecommunications – telegraph, telephone, and radio.

Telegraphy refers to the sending of information by codes over wires or through the radio spectrum, and it was the dominant form of international telecommunications from the mid-nineteenth century until after World War I when telephony assumed a more important role. In the 1830s and 1840s wired telegraph networks grew rapidly in Europe and North America. Efforts were soon made to link adjacent countries, and by the 1860s telegraph cables had been laid across both the English Channel and the Atlantic. Important technological developments in the early twentieth century were the emergence of radio telegraphy (used especially by ships) and significant increases in the transmission capabilities of cables.[1]

Telephony originated with the transmission of speech over wires by Alexander Graham Bell in 1876, and by the end of the century it was possible to transmit voices over wired networks over long distances. Then in the early decades of the twentieth century radio began to be used for the transmission of some telephone calls. In 1927 telephone services across the Atlantic were inaugurated by radio phone. It was not possible to transmit voices on transatlantic cables until 1956 because the repeaters that boosted the sound signal were not sufficiently powerful.[2]

The third traditional form of telecommunications is radio or the transmission of messages through the frequency spectrum. As mentioned above it was used quite soon after its invention in the late nineteenth century for certain types of telegraphy and telephony. In the early twentieth century radio was used largely for communications between ships and between ships and shore stations. It was not until the 1920s that public radio broadcasting mushroomed and also that radio was used for transoceanic telephone service.[3]

An important engineering development in telecommunications in the 1940s was the introduction of microwave communications. Microwave communication is the sending of transmissions at very high frequencies between relay stations (terrestrial towers and satellites), and it is used by both the broadcasting and telephone industries. It was the later development of communication satellites that made microwave transmissions very important for international telecommunications. A technological change in the telecommunications and electronics industries that followed soon on the heels of microwave communications was the replacement of vacuum tubes by transistors (as transmitters of electrons) during the 1950s. It meant that the repeaters in cables could be much more powerful; and this enabled the use of cables for transoceanic telephone traffic – the first one being TAT-1 across the Atlantic in 1956. In the 1960s and 1970s transistors were replaced by circuit boards and then integrated circuits ("chips"), and this meant a dramatic increase in the power of repeaters and the capabilities of switches – and hence the transmission capabilities of a single cable.

Of course, a revolutionary development that affected telecommunications in the 1950s was the dramatic improvement of computers and the introduction of digitalization, or the sending of transmissions in codes of binary digits instead of by the analogue or the electrical waves mode.

The services that have been greatly expanded or introduced with the advent of digitalization are *inter alia* data transmission, facsimile, electronic mail, electronic data interchange (EDI), videoconferencing, and videotext (which together are often referred to as non-basic or enhanced services). One way that digitalization has improved all of these services is by allowing "compression" or the transmission of a much greater volume of data in a set amount of time.[4]

Two of the most important advances in telecommunications technology in the 1960s were the introduction of communication satellites and fibre optic cables. The first communications satellite was launched by the USA in 1962 (Telstar). The increase in transmission capacity has been dramatic – with the mid-1960s generation of INTELSAT I satellites having 240 channels and the INTELSAT VI series in the late 1980s having 120,000 circuits. Satellites now carry about two-thirds of all transoceanic telephone traffic and almost all TV transmissions. In the near future, low earth-orbiting satellites for cellular phone communication will be introduced.[5] Turning to the introduction of fibre optic cables they, in fact, are more important to the long-run development of telecommunications than are communication satellites. Fibre optic cables carry transmissions of light as opposed to electrical impulses, and their development was made possible by the invention of new types of glass and lasers. They were only introduced on a large scale in the 1980s, but they will replace most paired-wire and coaxial cables in the future. The advantages of fibre optic cables are that they have a much larger capacity, are excellent for digital transmissions, and are less subject to corrosion and interference. The dramatic increase in capacity due to fibre optics is indicated by the fact that the last coaxial transatlantic cable laid in 1983 (TAT-7) has 4,200 circuits; the first fibre optic cable (TAT-8) laid in 1988 has 40,000; and TAT-12 laid in 1995 has 120,000. An interesting figure recently cited by the ITU Secretary-General is that the increase in the rate of transmission from the founding of the ITU in l865 to the present has been 500 million fold.[6]

During the 1980s the demand for national and international telephone services grew at over 7 percent per year whereas that for the new services expanded by over 20 percent. However, telephone calls still accounted for close to 90 percent of traffic. One projection of future developments is that early in the next century the demand for the old and the new services will be approximately equal.[7] With regard to increase in the use of phone lines, there was a six-fold rise in world traffic by minutes in the 1980s, and there is a five-fold projection for the 1990s. During the 1980s the increase for most Western countries was between three- and four-fold, and figures for some of the industrializing Third World states were remarkably higher.[8] One implication of the developments in the variety and capabilities of telecommunications services is that such services and their costs are becoming much more important to competition among firms. In the words of several authors, telecommunications is a major "competitive weapon" in the contemporary commercial world. An indication of this trend is that 5 percent of all users account for over 50 percent of all long-distance traffic.[9]

The technological changes have also had some marked effects on costs and prices. The typical cost of a voice message was $3 per minute in 1970, and today it is just a few cents. The cost of leasing a channel on a transoceanic cable is now about a fifteenth of what it was in 1956. And in the case of a satellite circuit rented from INTELSAT the price is now about an eighth of what it was in 1965. Overall the cost of international telecommunications services has fallen on average 8 percent per year from the late 1960s to the early 1990s.[10] Currently the international global telecommunications industry is one of the fastest growing industrial sectors in the world. In 1992 it generated $415 billion in revenue, and approximately 10 percent of this came from international services.[11]

Important international bodies

The roles of different organizations, conferences, and committees in the regulation of international telecommunications is quite complex. Therefore, before describing the evolution of the most important organization (namely, the International Telecommunications Union or ITU) the roles of the key bodies in different policy sectors since 1947 are outlined.

Jurisdictional rights

International Telecommunications Union (implicitly through the regulation of radio interference)

United Nations Committee on the Peaceful Uses of Outer Space, United Nations General Assembly

United Nations Education, Social, and Cultural Organization (UNESCO) (confined basically to "prior consent" for foreign transmissions, especially from satellites)

Damage control problems (i.e. interference with radio transmissions)

International Frequency Registration Board (IFRB) of the ITU (since 1993, the Radio Regulation Board and the Radiocommunication Sector)

Consultative Committee on Radio (CCIR) of the ITU (since 1993, the relevant parts integrated into the Radiocommunication Sector)

World Administrative Radio Conferences (WARCs) and Regional Administrative Radio Conferences (RARCs) of the ITU (since 1993, the World Radio Conferences)

Technical and procedural barriers

Consultative Committee on Telephone and Telegraph (CCITT) of the ITU (since 1993, integrated into the Telecommunication Standardization Sector)

Consultative Committee on Radio (CCIR) of the ITU (since 1993, integrated into the Telecommunication Standardization Sector)

Conference of European Postal and Telegraph Administrations (CEPT)

European Telecommunications Standards Institute, the American National Standards Association's T1 Committee, and Japanese Telecommunications Advisory Council (formed in late 1980s) (members of the Global Standards Cooperation Group since 1992)[12]

International Standards Organization (focus on enlarging markets for products) and International Electrotechnical Commission (focus on safety and technical efficiency)

Prices and market shares

Study Group 3 of the ITU's CCITT (since 1993, Study Group 3 of the Telecommunication Standardization Sector)

World Administrative Telephone and Telegraph Conferences (WATTCs) of the ITU (since 1993, the World Conference on International Communications)

International Satellite Communications Organization (INTELSAT) (since 1965)

General Agreement on Tariffs and Trade (GATT) (from the beginning of the Uruguay Round in 1986 through the signing of the General Agreement on Trade in Services or GATS in 1994) (since 1995, the World Trade Organization)

Given the centrality of the International Telecommunications Union, it is important to have an understanding of its development – including its predecessors. Its origins can be traced back to the first international public union, the International Telegraph Union, which was formed in Paris in 1865. Three years after its founding, member states decided to add a permanent administrative arm, the International Bureau of Telegraph Administrations (known as the Berne Bureau). Its role was to gather and publish information on international telegraphic matters. In 1883 the regulation of international telephone communications was placed under the International Telegraph Union. However, with the advent of international telegraph communications by radio at the beginning of the twentieth century, it was decided in 1906 to form a separate International Radiotelegraph Union (IRU) to deal with all radiocommunications issues.[13]

The 1920s and 1930s saw some important changes in the structure of international telecommunications bodies. In the mid-1920s three committees were formed to establish technical standards for telegraph, telephone, and radio since communications required increasing standardization of equipment.[14] Then, in 1932 the International Telegraph Union and the International Radiotelegraph Union were amalgamated into the International Telecommunications Union. At this time the telephone, telegraph, and radio regulations, which contained rules on rates, were separated from the convention so that states could belong to the ITU without formally subscribing to the regulations. The reason for this was that up until this time the USA and Canada had not belonged to the International Telegraph Union because the convention included regulations for rates, and the two North American countries refused to impose rates on their private companies.[15]

In 1947 the International Telecommunications Union and its regulations were reconstituted at three conferences in Atlantic City in 1947, and the ITU was made a specialized agency of the United Nations. The major changes at the structural level were that the three committees concerned with technical standards were integrated more tightly into the ITU, and a new body concerned with managing the radio spectrum – the International Frequency Registration Board (IFRB) – was created. As in the past, it was agreed that the Administrative Council would provide ongoing policy direction for the ITU although the most important ongoing work would occur in the key committees and periodic conferences. The titles and mandates of the committees were altered in 1992 (outlined above).[16]

The most important conferences for the regulation of international radio communications until 1993 were the World Administrative Radio

Conferences (WARCs), and they were divided into general conferences and specialized ones which dealt with matters such as maritime, space, and high-frequency issues. Since 1993 they have been superseded by the biannual World Radio Conferences (WRCs) although some specialized conferences will still be held. The WARCs (superseded by the WRCs) have been responsible for formulating the Radio Regulations that are attached to the ITU convention.

Until 1989 telecommunications equipment standards were approved as recommendations by the plenary assemblies of the CCITT and the CCIR every four years. Since then there have been procedures for polling states to secure formal approval of standards immediately after their approval in study groups of the CCIR or CCITT (or now the new Telecommunication Standardization Sector) – a process that takes about five months. This assists the ITU in maintaining a preeminent position in standard-setting in the face of increased activity by regional and national bodies.[17] Private industry organizations as well as firms play important roles in the standardization activities of the ITU.

In the case of commercial regulations for telephone and telegraph they are formulated less frequently by World Administrative Telephone and Telegraph Conferences (WATTCs) (superseded by World Conferences on International Communications). The last three WATTCs were in 1958, 1973, and 1988. Since 1973 the regulations have been shortened and deal with very general commercial guidelines on rates. The body that has played a much more central role in shaping the commercial environment has been Study Group 3 of the CCITT (now the Telecommunication Standardization Sector) since it meets several times a year.

Technical background information

In order to understand the politics of managing the frequency spectrum it is first necessary to understand what the radio frequency spectrum is. In the atmosphere there are electromagnetic waves whose magnetic and electrical polarities vary at fixed rates per second. The range of these electromagnetic waves is called the frequency spectrum, and those frequencies on which radio signals can be transmitted comprise the radio frequency spectrum. Radio transmissions are emissions of electromagnetic energy of varying power at certain frequencies or certain rates of variation per second. The frequencies that can be used for radio transmissions as well as the spacings between frequencies that must be respected to avoid harmful interference are influenced by technological changes. Over time the amount of the spectrum that can be used has increased a great deal. In addition it has been possible to transmit on narrower portions of frequency bands. The radio frequency spectrum is thus both a limited and expandable resource.[18]

The many varied services provided over the radio frequency spectrum can often only operate at certain wavelengths or frequencies. The frequency bands are classified as follows: very low or VLF (3–30 kHz or kiloHertz), low or LF (30–300 kHz), medium or MF (300–3000 kHz), high or HF (3–30 mHz or megaHertz), very high or VHF (30–300 mHz), ultra-high or UHF (300–3000 mHz), super high or SHF (30–300 gHz or gigaHertz), and extremely-high or EHF (300–3000 gHz).

The one zone of outer space that is most crucial for international telecommunications is the *geostationary orbit* (GSO). It is an area that rings the earth approximately 36,000 kilometers above the equator. It is in this zone that most present communications satellites are located. When placed in the geostationary orbit, satellites rotate around the earth in twenty-four hours and hence have fixed locations in relation to different spots on the earth. The advantages of such a geostationary location are that satellite tracking devices are not necessary, and that three satellites positioned at equal distances around the earth permit transmissions between any two spots on earth (excluding the polar regions). The number of satellites that can be accommodated in the GSO is open to dispute because estimates are dependent on evolving technology. Until the 1990s there were not any serious overcrowding problems, but recently some problems have developed over the Pacific. One development that is likely to decrease the importance of the geostationary orbit is the launching of a large number of low earth-orbiting (LEO) satellites which will travel in a polar orbit and which will be particularly useful for cellular phones. The best known system is the Iridium system by Motorola, and it should be in use by the late 1990s.[19]

Following the launching of Sputnik by the Soviet Union in 1957 it was recognized that satellites could have a revolutionary effect on international telecommunications. And since the launching of the first commercial communications satellites, the INTELSAT I series in 1965, it certainly has had this impact. INTELSAT presently has thirteen satellites and close to 800 earth stations. It is, however, important to recognize that telecommunications satellites are not revolutionary devices *per se*. They are merely relay stations in earth orbit. Over time the key changes in satellites have related to the number of messages that they can simultaneously transmit and their power. As the transmitting power of satellites increases, the size of the antennae or "dishes" that are necessary to receive transmissions goes down.[20]

Overview of the international telecommunications regime

There has been considerable stability in most dimensions of the international telecommunications regime (outlined in Table 5.1). The implicit norms concerning the jurisdictional status of the airwaves and outer space have promoted the principles of the free movement of commerce and information while giving states the ultimate right to curtail foreign transmissions when they threaten domestic order. The norms with regard to damage control encourage the free flow of goods and services and the efficient use of the spectrum while offering a measure of equity for all countries. With respect to issues of technical barriers there has always been a consensus that there should be technical standards that permit the international flow of information.

The major change in the telecommunications regime has occurred with regard to the sector of prices and market shares. From support for an intergovernmental cartel that promoted both efficiency and states' ability to control their domestic telecommunications system, states have moved gradually since 1980 toward support of greater competition that reduces the costs of communications. The principle of internal political control is being gradually traded off in favor of a stronger priority for the principles of efficiency and the free flow of commerce.

Several characteristics of the telecommunications regime deserve stressing at this point. First, in several areas of the regime the norms and/or the rules are not highly formalized, and they must be deduced from a variety of specific accords, statements, and state and industry behavior. This is particularly the case with regard to jurisdictional questions and issues of prices and market shares. Second, despite tremendous technological change the normative content of the regime has remained remarkably stable. The one exception to this stability is the sphere of prices and market shares where the mutuality of interests in a cartel began to break down in the 1970s.

Jurisdictional rights

Of all the international service industries that are examined in this study, the one where there is some uncertainty with regard to

Table 5.1 *Outline of the international telecommunications regime*

Principles

Free movement of commerce: obligation of states to reduce impediments to the free movement of goods and services.

Free flow of information: obligation of states to allow the flow of information among peoples of different states.

Efficiency: obligation of states to provide goods and services to their populations at lowest possible cost.

Transnational damage control: obligation of states to prevent activities of their nationals from imposing damages on the nationals and property of other states and to provide compensation for any damages.

Internal political control: right of states to assert jurisdiction and control over activities within their territories.

Equity: obligation of states to provide all states with a reasonable share of resources and financial returns from international commerce.

Norms

Jurisdictional rights

State control over entry of foreign firms: right of states to exclude foreign telecommunications firms from offering services within their own territories.
- Relevant principles: internal political control
- Strength: strong

Qualified open access to international spaces: right to use frequencies and orbital slots in international air space and outer space and to lay cables under the high seas, but an obligation to accept limited international planning to promote efficient use of resources, avoid interference, promote safety of commerce, and assure a measure of equity.
- Relevant principles: free movement of commerce, transnational damage control, equity
- Strength: moderately strong (some weakness in relation to importance of equity in planning)

Table 5.1 (*cont.*)

Qualified open access to national air spaces (or right of innocent passage): right to use frequencies in foreign air spaces and to jam hostile transmissions on own air space, but an obligation to accept limited international planning.
- Relevant principles: free flow of commerce and information, internal political control
- Strength: moderately strong (weakness largely in relation to conditions justifying deliberate interference)

Damage control problems

Prior use: obligation to respect frequencies in use and registered by other states.
- Relevant principles: free movement of commerce, transnational damage control, equity
- Strength: strong

Necessary planning: obligation to allocate spectrum bands to different services and to allot individual frequencies to states when it is crucial for safety of planes and ships and when there is very high demand in certain bands.
- Relevant principles: free movement of commerce, transnational damage control, equity
- Strength: moderately strong
(* Prior use and necessary planning norms are equivalent to the accident prevention norm in the regimes of the other issue areas.)

Physical damage compensation: obligation to pay compensation if satellites inflict damage on the territories or satellites of other states.
- Relevant principles: transnational damage control, free flow of commerce
- Strength: moderately strong

Restricted intentional interference: obligation not to jam foreign transmissions unless transmissions are seen as serious threats to states' political control and values.

Table 5.1 (*cont.*)

- Relevant principles: free flow of information, internal political control
- Strength: medium
  (* Restricted intentional interference norm is equivalent to the crime prevention norm in the regimes of the other issue areas.)

Technical and procedural barriers

Interconnection: obligation to develop technical standards that permit interconnection among national telecommunications systems.
- Relevant principles: free movement of commerce, free flow of information
- Strength: strong

Equipment standardization: obligation to agree on international equipment standards that will promote lower costs.
- Relevant principles: efficiency, free movement of commerce, internal political/economic control
- Strength: weak in past, but moving toward moderate strength

Prices and market shares

Cartel: obligation to establish market shares commensurate with share of international telecommunications, co-finance infrastructure projects, set prices (rates), and divide revenues.
- Relevant principles: internal political/economic control, efficiency, free movement of commerce
- Strength: moderately strong (except on rates) *until 1980s*; weak to medium in most of developed world and moderately strong in developing world by mid-1990s

General rules for cartel norm:
(1) Anti-competition rule: obligation not to pursue competitive strategies to take business from other telecommunications administrations.
  - do not establish transit rates that differ from those of other states
  - do not offer collection rates that are significantly lower than those of other states so as to encourage "sourcing" of trans-

Table 5.1 (*cont.*)

missions in own state (parties will often arrange to have the party in the country with the cheaper rates initiate a phone conversation or will bypass domestic networks via "call-back" services and private networks)
- do not allow differences in accounting rates for different international carriers involved in a particular bilateral transmission (i.e. maintain universal accounting rates)

(2) State monopoly defense rule: obligation to prevent the development of rival telecommunications firms outside the cartel.
- do not allow subleasing or selling of lines
- do not allow interconnection of leased lines
- maintain joint ownership of the means of transmission (satellites, cables) by state telecommunications administrations so as to enable exclusion of rivals

(3) Anti-defection rule: obligation to pursue strategies that provide incentives for loyalty to the cartel and not to pursue strategies that provide incentives for defection.
- establish minimum returns for all transmissions (the setting and division of accounting rates)
- allow equitable ownership of transmission links (cables, satellites) and remunerative returns from investment
- do not allow rates to differ by route so as to discourage states from offering different transit charges.

Limited competition: obligation to allow competition in international telecommunications services (especially in non-basic services) while allowing state administrations to maintain financial viability through control of most domestic services and some international services.
- Relevant principles: efficiency, free movement of commerce
- Strength: medium in developed world and weak in developing world in mid-1990s

139

jurisdictional rights is telecommunications. The *norm allowing states to exclude foreign firms* has never been in doubt, and it provided a legal basis for the long-standing dominance of national telecommunications monopolies. Also, in the case of cable communications across the oceans the rights are clear. States have a right to lay cables under the high seas although they must accept some planning with coastal states with regard to cables across the continental shelf to avoid interference with seabed mining.[21] However, the jurisdictional situation is not as clear with regard to airwaves – with the exception of outer space.

In the case of outer space it is clearly stated in the 1967 Outer Space Treaty that it is an area belonging to all and open to all. The treaty stipulates that outer space should "be free for exploration and use by all states" and should "not [be] subject to national appropriation by claim or sovereignty."[22] Turning to air space (reaching to about 100,000 feet above the earth) it is valuable to start with jurisdictional accords concerning air transport which establish that air space above the high seas is a common property resource and air space above states' territories is a zone of state sovereignty. These rights that were developed with regard to air transport, however, beg the question: What jurisdictional rights have states accepted *de facto* with regard to radio transmissions in these zones? In particular, it is necessary to determine what have been the weightings that they have assigned to the jurisdictional concepts of free access, common heritage planning, and national enclosure (or state control).

With regard to both international and national air space states have accepted hybrid arrangements that contain certain mixes of open access, common heritage planning, and national enclosure, but in both areas open access is, in fact, given precedence. The two key norms are: (1) qualified open access to international spaces and (2) qualified open access to national air spaces (or a right of innocent passage). The "qualified open access" proscription is that states can use any frequency unless it is being used by another state and as long as they comply with limited bodies of community rules promoting efficient use, damage control, and a measure of equity. In the case of national air spaces it also provides that states can jam transmissions in their air spaces if they constitute serious threats to their internal political order. One point that is evident from this discussion is that the key jurisdictional issues concerning the airwaves are the extents to which national enclosure and common heritage planning have impinged on states' right of open access to the airwaves. These issues are now considered in succession.

National enclosure and open access

The analysis of both states' freedom of access to the world's airwaves and their limited jurisdiction over the airwaves in their national air spaces must start with the signing of the first International Radio-telegraph Convention in 1906. The Convention established the right of states to transmit on unused frequencies throughout air space. The Convention stated that in choosing frequencies for radio transmissions all contracting parties should "not disturb the services of other radio stations."[23] This basic proviso has been continued in international radiocommunications conventions over the twentieth century. On several occasions in the interwar and postwar periods some states sought to gain acceptance of claims to frequencies in perpetuity regardless of whether they ceased using them, but these proposals never gained significant support because of their obviously inefficient effects.[24] Very importantly there was no change in states' acceptance of open access to all airwaves after states' jurisdiction over adjacent or national air space was recognized in the Convention on Air Transport in 1919. States continued to assume that they not only had the right to transmit through international air space but also that they had a comparable right to transmit through the air spaces of other countries. The debate over states' powers to block transmissions into their air spaces began in the 1930s, and it has taken place in two contexts since then. One concerned the right to jam foreign radio broadcasts, and the other concerned the right of states to demand "prior consent" before satellite TV signals (DBS-TV) were transmitted to their populations.

The debate over the right to jam foreign transmissions originated with the expansion of foreign broadcasting in Europe in the mid-1930s and the jamming of the broadcasts by some states. By the late 1930s all countries in Europe except for Britain were involved in jamming foreign broadcasts.[25] A major study on international broadcasting in the late 1930s commented: "There is little reason to hope that radio broadcasting as a political weapon of the state, will be the subject of serious general international regulation within the immediate future."[26] In other words, states reserve for themselves the right to exclude information from their societies when it is judged to have very deleterious impacts on security and domestic politics. During the postwar period the Soviet Union, its allies, and a few other states regularly jammed foreign broadcasts.[27] Then in the mid-1960s the developing countries emerged as supporters of the right of states to jam foreign broadcasting.[28] Of course, the amount of jamming outside of the socialist world was quite limited because of the cost.

It is true that since the 1980s the criticism of jamming by many states at the conference on the use of the high-frequency spectrum,[29] the political transformation in Eastern Europe, and the increasing inability of states to monitor and control the multiple transmissions by satellites and cables all point to a weakening of the right of states to deliberately interfere with foreign broadcasts. However, it is unlikely that the great majority of states will completely renounce the prerogative. On this matter a recent study of international telecommunications politics by James Savage makes a number of pertinent comments. First, virtually all states regard acts taken within a state's territory to restrict access to foreign telecommunications as being "within the limits of what are viewed as acceptable sovereign controls over domestic telecommunications." Second, "The ITU can . . . only involve itself in a deliberate harmful interference dispute when attempts to restrict incoming signals affect other countries' use of the radio frequency spectrum." Third, after noting that Third World states continue to reserve the right to control incoming transmissions, Savage remarks: "Jamming and other forms of deliberate interference, no matter how antithetical to the spirit and role of the ITU or lofty free flow principles, will continue to exist and may, as information exchanges increase, multiply in form, severity, and technological complexity."[30] This last statement may be incorrect as a result of the increasing permeability of states to foreign communications, but at the same time Savage is correct that many states will continue to maintain a right to block transmissions.[31]

In more than fifty years of debate over jamming of radio transmissions, states have only occasionally stated that foreign broadcasting from terrestrial transmitters into their air spaces is illegal. They just claimed that they had the right to interfere with it if they judged the content to be "hostile" or "non-innocent." There has, however, been one major controversy where the great majority of states have wanted to establish an obligation on the part of transmitting states to seek the "prior consent" of the receiving countries. It concerns TV transmissions from direct broadcasting satellites (DBS-TV), and it started in the early 1970s when the prospect of satellites transmitting TV broadcasts directly to homes with receiving "dishes" was first mooted. The developing and Soviet bloc states were most concerned by the prospect, but many developed countries also thought that some controls were called for. In 1971 and 1972 the ITU, UNESCO, and the United Nations all passed resolutions that explicitly or implicitly required that states obtain the "prior consent" of other states for DBS-TV transmissions. The USA and a few other developed countries opposed the resolutions, but most industrialized states either abstained or supported the resolutions.[32] Then, in 1977 an ITU conference stated that "all technical means shall be used to reduce, to the maximum extent practicable, the radiation [of DBS-TV] over the territory of other countries."[33] Finally, after eight years of inconclusive negotiations in the UN Committee on the Peaceful Uses of Outer Space the Third World and Soviet bloc states secured the passage of a General Assembly resolution calling for prior consent. The developed countries, however, either opposed the resolution or abstained in the voting because the resolution did not give adequate weight to the free flow of information. A few, like the USA, were unwilling to contemplate prior consent under any conditions.[34]

Some international legal scholars might argue that the many resolutions on prior consent established a legal norm. This position, however, is somewhat difficult to support because the Western nations with launch capabilities are generally opposed. Also, the power of states to prevent TV transmissions from reaching their populations has been hindered by the decreasing size and cost of satellite dishes and by the fact that once a satellite is launched to transmit to one state in a region, other countries in the region can pick up the transmissions. A very good example is AsiaSat which is registered in Hong Kong and whose satellite broadcasts can be received throughout most of Asia.[35]

International planning and open access

The incursion of rights of national enclosure into the basic open access regime for the airwaves has remained very modest over the years and, in fact, the powers of states in their own air spaces may have declined. Where more limitations on open access to the spectrum have developed is with regard to how international planning should impinge on free access. The basic guidelines for international planning, in fact, developed quite early in the history of radiocommunications.

While international planning is generally viewed in terms of the allotment of frequencies to individual states, the first, and perhaps the most important, form of international planning is the allocation or the reserving of particular bands of the spectrum for particular services. It started with the allocation of one band to maritime communications in 1906; by 1927 there were seven services; and now there are approximately thirty-five different services to which particular bands are allocated by periodic ITU conferences. There are a lot of conflicts over these allocations, but virtually no one challenges either the right of international conferences to regulate in this area or the allocations once they have been approved.

There has also been a consensus that planning should be given precedence over free access in the allotment of particular frequencies for maritime and aeronautical services so as to promote carrier safety. This started in 1919 with aeronautical services. Since then frequency planning or allotment for safety reasons has held a sacrosanct role in radiocommunications. Another long-standing area of allotment planning is the prevention of interference among broadcasting stations (largely MF and LF) in regions where there is a large number of stations. This began in Europe in the late 1920s, and while regional planning in ITU-sponsored conferences is still much more highly developed in Europe than in other regions, it has increasingly grown in several other areas as well.[36] The final form of international planning that has developed in the last two decades is the allotment of frequencies and satellite orbital slots for equity reasons – particularly to reserve certain resources for Third World states. The developing countries succeeded in obtaining statements in conventions (including the Outer Space Treaty of 1967) and resolutions from international organizations favoring an equitable distribution of orbital slots and frequencies for space communications,[37] and at conferences in 1977, 1983, and 1987 they obtained modest allotments of orbital slots and associated frequencies.[38] It is, however, important to realize that equity considerations still have a rather modest role in strengthening international planning.

The key point to realize is that states have *implicitly* accepted a general obligation to plan aspects of spectrum use – especially the allocation of bands for particular services and the allotment of specific frequencies to assure minimal interference in maritime and aeronautical communications. An interesting historical note concerning the role of the common heritage planning principle in the jurisdictional regime is that the USA in both 1921 and 1947 tried to obtain acceptance of a regime based solely on this principle (then called a priori planning). Other states feared that they might not fare very well in international planning meetings, and they defeated the proposals at international conferences.[39] Eventually the USA lost interest in a completely planned spectrum – in part because it feared that Third World states would dominate decision-making in the relevant international organizations. Still, planning is regarded by all states as having at least limited a role in the implicit jurisdictional understandings.

On the whole there has been considerable consensus on the jurisdictional aspects of the telecommunications regime. States have been interested in assuring the flow of international communications, adequate access to the spectrum and the GSO, and their right to block communications if they threatened their political order. In pursuing these goals they have given varied weight to free access, common heritage planning, and national enclosure in different circumstances. As a recent US study noted: "Over the last 75 years one or the other approach has been advocated or used by nearly all nations to allocate spectrum, both nationally and internationally."[40] In fact, the head of the US delegation to the 1979 WARC, where the USA was a major opponent of a priori planning, noted that his government "does not oppose all planning" but that the case for it "must be carefully weighed in each instance based on distinctive efficiency and equity considerations."[41]

A central underlying point of these comments is that states find that a regime based in varying degrees on these three legal concepts is in their mutual interests. Their preferences vary somewhat, but they have more common than conflicting interests with regard to the basic shape of the jurisdictional guidelines. With the exception of states' ability to control certain communications entering their territories (i.e. jamming of foreign broadcasts and prior consent for DBS-TV), politically competitive or even hostile states have generally backed the jurisdictional norms over this century, and with perhaps the exception of prior consent for DBS-TV there are no signs that major groups of states find present guidelines and practices inimical to their interests. The keys to their continuing support are concerns with the facilitation of international communications and commerce and states' freedom to block hostile foreign transmissions.

Damage control problems

The two key damage control problems in telecommunications are unintentional interference between transmissions and the intentional jamming of transmissions, although the former has certainly been a more central issue. The damage control facet of the telecommunications regime reflects the same principles as are embedded in the jurisdictional norms. This is to be expected given the previous observation that jurisdictional consensuses have generally been worked out implicitly in the context of dealing with concrete damage control problems.

The central norm relating to damage control is the *prior use norm* which is closely tied to the jurisdictional norm of qualified open access. It posits that states must respect other states' use of particular frequencies and not transmit on them. The norm is seen as furthering both the mitigation of interference among radio transmissions and the free movement of commerce by encouraging maximum use of the spectrum. It even promotes equity to an extent in that all states have a right to transmit on an unused frequency. Related closely to the above norm is the *necessary planning norm* which circumscribes on what frequencies states can transmit, and its main purpose is the reduction of mutual interference. It prescribes that there should be certain areas of the spectrum reserved for certain services and a limited number of frequencies allotted to individual states for specific purposes. These purposes include assuring that interference with maritime and aeronautical transmissions do not place the safety of carriers and their passengers at risk and that states' transmissions do not interfere with each other in heavy traffic areas (e.g. AM broadcasting in Europe). Without a measure of planning a pure first-come, first-served system could evolve into chaos.

The *physical compensation norm* is a relatively minor one in that it refers to compensation from accidents involving satellites. The *restricted intentional interference norm* is more important in that it deals with the very important political matter of jamming. It stipulates that states should refrain from jamming unless foreign transmissions are regarded as seriously threatening the peace, good order, and security of the state.

The centrality of the *prior use norm* was established at the time of the formulation of the first International Radiotelegraph Convention in 1906 which prescribed that states have the responsibility "not to disturb the services of other radio stations" and that they should send information on their use of particular frequencies to the Berne Bureau for publication.[42] Since the late 1940s the legal status of the prior use norm has actually been strengthened in the ITU Radio Regulations. States now must send information on their use of a particular frequency to the Radio Registration Board (RRB) (the successor to the Berne Bureau and the International Frequency Registration Board); the RRB then "notifies" all ITU members of it; and finally it "registers" the frequency on the Master Register if no states object and if it finds that there is no interference with users of other frequencies. Once it is listed on the Master Register, a state enjoys the somewhat ambiguous "right of international protection from harmful interference."[43] The language is due in part to a conflict in 1947 between some European states who believed that states should have a long-term priority right to frequencies that they first used and the majority of countries that opposed giving states rights to frequencies that they no longer used.[44] In fact, states have maintained claims to a good number of frequencies that they have ceased to use, although in recent decades the IFRB had some success in identifying unused frequencies and having them deleted from the Master Register. The scope of the task is clear from the figures that in the late 1980s the IFRB received: there were about 1,200 requests for registration each week, and the number of frequency registrations on the Master Register went up from 500,000 to one million between 1978 and 1988.[45]

On the whole, the main challenge to the prior use norm before World War II was some states' support for permanent jurisdiction over frequencies. Since 1945 the central challenge has come from some states' (particularly the developing states') interest in a priori or common heritage planning. A key defense for the prior use norm has been that it provides a very good balance among the goals of minimizing harmful interference, giving reasonable opportunities to developed and developing states to secure frequencies, minimizing the number of unused frequencies, and finally pressuring states into adjusting to technological change.

The one frequency band where a rather unique manifestation of the prior use norm exists is the high-frequency spectrum. It has generally had the worst interference problems since transmissions can carry throughout a region or even over most of the globe if the transmitter is very powerful. Also, the usable frequencies in the spectrum change over the four seasons of the year because of alterations in ionospheric conditions, and therefore stations have to change their frequencies from season to season. At the 1959 WARC, states developed a new system (now called the Article 17 system). Four months prior to the beginning of a season states send their intended frequency assignments to the RRB. The RRB then distributes this information to all countries. States then send revised assignments to the RRB, and these are included in the High Frequency Broadcasting Schedule for that season.

Sometimes states assign stations to several frequencies. Strictly speaking the prior use norm does not apply to HF broadcasting, but in fact states tend to respect each other's use of particular frequencies from year to year.[46]

The second norm relating to damage control can be labeled the necessary planning norm, and it modifies the prior use norm. It basically stipulates that states have an obligation to coordinate their use of the spectrum with other states for reasons of efficiency and equity. More specifically, it prescribes that states (a) should allocate adequate frequency and orbital space to different services; (b) should allot frequencies among states when there is very high demand in a particular spectrum band or when interference could affect maritime and aeronautical safety; and (c) should generally promote mutual adjustment in the utilization of frequencies. Like the prior use norm it serves the principles of free flow, efficient exploitation, and equitable access – and hence the reduction of cost uncertainty and of impediments to international commerce.

A first type of international planning – the allocation of particular bands for certain services – originated in the early days of radio-communications. Because the use of particular bands for several services can cause a great deal of interference and because it is sometimes crucial that there be no interference with particular services, states soon realized that they would have to allocate at least some frequency bands. The first allocation in the International Radio-telegraph Convention of 1906 established a band for maritime communications.[47] Now the Table of Allocations in the Radio Regulations contains over thirty services (for example, broadcasting, space satellite communications, radar, and cellular phones). There have been long and conflictual negotiations at World and Regional Administrative Radio conferences over how different bands should be used, and it is unquestionably the case that the major users exert considerable influence in these deliberations.[48] However, all states recognize that certain general rules of the road are necessary in order to minimize interference and promote efficient use of the spectrum. And, in fact, there have been very few violations of the Table of Allocations.

The second form of community planning concerns the allotment (and assignment) of frequencies respectively to states (and stations) for the purpose of assuring safety of maritime and aeronautical communications. The first allotments to states started with the 1919 International Convention on Air Navigation,[49] and they have grown dramatically since then.[50] It is obvious that states' willingness to support these exceptions to the first-come, first-served procedure is based on the recognition that the growth of international shipping and air transport depends on excellent safety records. There has never been any question that community planning is desirable for these services.

The third and last type of situation where there is widespread acceptance of international planning concerns situations where there is a high level of demand for frequencies in relation to supply. The major problem area has been radio broadcasting. On the whole, there have not been serious objections to the development of regional allotment plans for crowded broadcasting bands since they were first developed in Europe in the mid-1920s. Two reasons for the general lack of controversy are that most broadcasters are harmed when there is overcrowding and that regional plans are not legally binding.[51] Several technological developments have occurred recently that greatly decrease the problem of overcrowding. A number of services are moving to fibre optic cables and, in addition, it is possible to accommodate many more transmissions in a frequency band because of digital transmission and bandwidth compression. Planning will still be necessary, but there will not be the same resource constraints and hence political conflict.

There have also been very ambitious plans for avoiding overcrowding through the planned use of the spectrum that did not come to fruition. In the aftermath of the two world wars, proposals for a priori planning or an "engineered spectrum" were submitted by the USA. They were, however, rebuffed on both occasions because many states feared that they would lose registered frequencies and/or be deprived of future needs.[52] Demands for international planning came from the developing countries beginning in the 1960s. They focused on allotments in the high-frequency spectrum and the geostationary orbit. The developing countries were rebuffed on their demands for planning of the high-frequency spectrum at the 1979 WARC and the 1984/87 HF-WARC because the superpowers, as well as a number of both developed and developing countries, did not want to sacrifice their existing frequencies. It is, however, important to point out that most developing countries are successful in obtaining frequencies in the HF band to meet most of their needs.[53]

There is one manifestation of planning that exists with respect to space services and is directed at preventing mutual interference. Beginning at the Space WARC in 1963 and then going on through the

1971 Space WARC and the 1985/88 ORB-WARC, ITU members developed three-stage procedures for publication of plans, coordination, and registration of their space satellite systems before they were actually launched. Several years before a satellite is launched, the launching state initiates discussions with other potentially affected states and often with ITU officials as well. The basic result is an informal planning system that has prevented interference problems from arising. Both the USA and the Soviet Union opposed formal planning schemes at the 1985/88 ORB-WARC since they did not want other states dictating what they could and could not do, but they find informal coordination very beneficial. In the past such informal planning worked very well, but there are signs in the 1990s that increased demands for orbital slots and space frequencies could lead to more formal arrangements.[54]

In reviewing the planning activities of the ITU it is clear that any portrayal of the spectrum/GSO management system as "first-come, first-served" is inaccurate because it "does not reflect the importance of accommodation that is essential if the Radio Regulations are to work." Also, "The existing Radio Regulations have been working because most administrations accept that newcomers must be accommodated."[55] Mutual coordination and planning permeates the utilization of the frequency spectrum and the geostationary orbit.

A third norm is the *physical damage compensation norm* which prescribes that if satellites cause physical damage to parties on earth or to other satellites, the states that launched them will pay compensation. The regime arrangements for damage caused by satellites started with the Outer Space Treaty of 1967 which included some general provisions. The obligations of the states possessing the satellites were then spelled out in considerable detail in the 1972 International Convention on Liability for Damages Caused by Space Objects. An indication of the acceptance of the basic purposes of the treaty was the willingness of the Soviet Union to settle a claim with Canada concerning the crash of Cosmos 954 in Canada in 1978. The key to the acceptance of the norm by the space powers is that they do not want any diplomatic or physical interference with their satellite systems, and an acceptance of occasional compensation for damages is a small price to pay for avoiding attempts by foreign states to discredit or interfere with their commercial or military enterprises.[56]

There has never been a major attempt to require compensation for damages to transmissions since everyone accepts that a part of the system of trying to maximize the use of the spectrum is that there will be some interference. The accepted goal of spectrum management is the minimization of interference, not its elimination. A potential problem in designing compensation provisions relating to harmful interference is that it would be very difficult to evaluate the financial value of the damages.

It is interesting that a subject on which a norm has not developed is the theft of broadcasts – in particular the taping of TV programs for sale or rebroadcasting. The Berne Convention and the Universal Copyright Convention do not provide protection for the authors or broadcasters of TV broadcasts, and hence in 1971 UNESCO and the World Intellectual Property Organization convened a conference to formulate a treaty. A rather weak Convention Relating to the Distribution of Program-Carrying Signals Transmitted by Satellite was accepted in 1974, but a very small number of states have ratified it. The key problem is that certain countries, especially the USA, tend to be pirated, and others tend to be pirates. (The pirating occurs because the "footprints" of transmissions fall outside the boundaries of the transmitting states or the intended receiving state.) A few countries would benefit greatly from strong regulations against pirating, but a much larger number would lose. Countries that have faced problems of having their transmissions pirated have largely had to deal with them on a bilateral basis. They have, however, achieved increasing success since they make pirating countries' accession to bodies such as the GATT/World Trade Organization or the North American Free Trade Area contingent on acceptance of multilateral norms concerning copyright. A number of Asian and Latin American countries have accepted constraints on pirating by their citizens because of a desire to join multilateral trade organizations.[57]

The final norm is titled the *restricted intentional interference norm*. It prescribes that a state should allow the flow of radio transmissions into its air space unless the transmissions undermine its political order – in which case jamming is permissible. This legal guideline has certainly not been formally adopted, but it is implicit in the actions and statements of most states. First of all, in the 1930s virtually all European countries engaged in jamming broadcasts, and while a few countries and groups of lawyers decried the practice as illegal, it was accepted practice.[58] Then, in the postwar period the Soviet Union and most other members of the socialist bloc jammed Western broadcasts regularly. While the Western countries decried such activities, the great majority of Third World states starting in the 1960s refused to support UN resolutions condemning jamming by the socialist states.[59]

One development that did strengthen the right to jam in "threatening" circumstances was the evolution of the consensus among many countries in the 1970s that states should only be allowed to transmit DBS-TV signals into other countries with the permission of the latter. It is, however, important to stress that all Western countries and many developing states as well thought that states had an obligation to allow the free flow of information except in circumstances where political order or economic interests are severely affected.[60]

The damage control norms, like the jurisdiction norms with which they are so closely interrelated, are clearly built on the foundation of states' mutuality of interests in furthering the free movement of commerce. From the perspective of reducing market failures the regulations reduce impediments to the flow of international goods and services, uncertainty of costs, and transnational damages. States have differences on how the spectrum and geostationary orbit should be divided, but they have found that the central norm of prior use supplemented by some limited moves toward international planning promotes both the flow of international information and commerce and a reasonable distribution of resources. Almost all countries are active supporters and participants in the regime – regardless of their political differences. With regard to the issue of the jamming of foreign transmissions there are differences among states on the circumstances under which the jamming is permissible, but most countries agree that it is a prerogative that they must maintain. They want to hang on to their right to control the entry of foreign information into their societies even if they recognize that their ability to do so is seriously limited by international commerce and communications.

Technical and procedural barriers

A central aspect of the work of the ITU is the establishment of standards that permit interconnection among parties in different countries. The present ITU Secretary-General remarked recently that "Standards making has clearly become the dominant collective activity in the telecommunications-information world today."[61] This is correct, but it ignores the fact that it has always been central to the international regulatory regime. A recent study observed that "from its inception, the main purpose of the ITU proved to be the promotion of compatible telecommunication interconnection between nations."[62] Today the ITU's activities to promote interconnection are not only interlinked with the International Standards Organization and the International Electrotechnical Commission, but also with a group of national and regional standard-setting bodies which in 1992 formed the Global Standards Cooperation Group. There is a good chance that the ITU Standardization Sector will maintain the ITU's preeminence in standard-setting, but it is also possible that the ITU will become a mere rubber stamp for the outcomes of deliberations within the Global Standards Cooperation Group.[63]

In the general field of standardization there are really two separate issues. First, there is the issue of interconnection between telecommunications systems in different states and, second, there is the issue of reducing the cost of this interconnection and telecommunications services generally through standardization of the equipment used in different states. The main obstacle to international equipment standardization has been a desire on the part of governments to protect national equipment manufacturers from foreign competition.

As is implied above, the two key prescriptions relating to market access are the *interconnection norm* and the *equipment standardization norm*. The interconnection norm has always been very strong since it is central to the free movement of commerce. The equipment standardization norm has grown gradually in strength because of states' concern for promoting low prices for telecommunications equipment and services, but its strength has been limited by states' protection of national manufacturers. The central point that is made in the following discussions of technical standards is that states and industries almost always reach accords when interconnection between commercial enterprises is at stake, but that when technical standards concern consumer electronics equipment, agreement is often elusive. In the following analysis of telecommunications standards the politics of interconnection standards and equipment standardization are discussed together since they are so closely interrelated.

Radio standards did not generally cause a great deal of conflict prior to World War II. The standards dealt largely with station call letters, certain transmission practices, procedures for using distress frequencies, the qualifications of radio operators, and a few equipment specifications. Even with the expansion of radio standards after the *Titanic* disaster of 1912 their economic implications were not very extensive.[64] With the establishment of transatlantic radio communications between

Europe and North America in the 1920s certain technical adjustments had to be made, but even here the required regulations did "not involve extensive economic interests."[65]

The most interesting conflict regarding technical interconnection standards prior to World War II concerned an attempt by an individual company to impose certain interconnection procedures and hence certain telecommunications equipment on the world. Shortly after the turn of the century the Marconi company sought to bar all land and ship stations using its equipment from communicating with stations using the equipment of other firms. Most states reacted against this attempt because its success would have given Marconi a virtual monopoly over equipment sales and threatened the safety of ships that were not properly equipped with Marconi transmitters. Hence the participants at the early International Radiotelegraph Conferences forbade radio stations from refusing to interconnect because the manufacturer of another station's equipment was different from its own. In so doing they overrode the two main supporters of Marconi – the UK and Italy.[66]

Since 1945 there has been a burgeoning of ITU technical regulations for radio equipment. In some cases disagreements among states have led to the acceptance of multiple standards, but generally states have been able to formulate global standards. Within the CCIR states have been very successful in reaching accords on equipment used for point-to-point communications (e.g. microwave) since it is generally crucial for commercial linkages: businesses demand reliability in their communications. Standards have also been relatively strong in satellite communications since only a few states are involved and because the financial costs of not interconnecting are very large. For the most part CCIR interconnection standards are accepted throughout the international industry since almost all buyers insist on them.[67]

While the incentives for supporting interconnection standards for radio telecommunications equipment have generally been very strong, there have been some failures to reach accords when the products had large consumer markets. On these occasions states refused to diverge from their national industry standard in order to protect a market for their national manufacturer. The key conflict over the past two decades has concerned color TV standards, and recently serious differences have emerged over high definition television (HDTV) and transmitting systems and dishes for direct broadcasting satellites (DBS).

The failure to develop a single color TV standard goes back to the decade from the mid-1950s to the mid-1960s when three countries developed their own technological system. One system was American (NTSC); a second was French (SECAM); and a third was German/Dutch/English (PAL). Each had an international coalition behind it. All three countries tried to get the CCIR to approve its technological system since they wanted to protect their national manufacturers. In the end the CCIR deliberations ended in a stalemate in the mid-1960s, and three different standards were accepted. This has meant that particular national manufacturers have tended to dominate the markets of the three groupings of states.[68]

A similar conflict to that over color TV (if not a continuation of it) has been the dispute over HDTV since the 1980s. In the early part of the decade the Japanese announced that they had developed a HDTV system that would provide a much clearer picture, and they sought CCIR approval. Because approval by the CCIR would have given the Japanese the possibility of capturing a large segment of the European TV market, the Europeans refused to accept the Japanese proposal and began to develop their own standard. The Americans, after initially supporting the Japanese, also launched an effort to develop their own technological version of HDTV. In 1990 a US firm invented a way of transmitting TV signals in digital, as opposed to analogue, code, and this gave US manufacturers an advantage in the commercial competition. After eight years of discussion in the ITU the chance for an accord in 1994 looks better than it has in the past because of the recognition of the technological superiority of the American alternative. On the other hand, new technologies are eclipsing it, and its use may be quite different and more limited than first envisaged.[69]

In the case of transmitting systems and dishes for DBS, several European countries have developed different standards, but because of the lure of a large consumer market they have been unable to agree on a single standard. The short-run prospects for an agreement are not good.[70] With regard to cellular phones there are quite a few standards throughout the world as a result of states' protection of national manufacturers. At the moment this situation has made cellular phones more expensive and has required that business officials use different phones in different countries; but it has not produced serious interconnection problems because cellular phones connect with local telephone networks. There is a good chance that the European states will develop a regional standard, but there is presently a low probability that all ITU member states will be able to agree on a global standard.[71] There is, however, a chance that pressure for a global standard may become very strong when polar or low earth-orbiting satellites (e.g. Motorola's Iridium system) come into operation. Then cellular phones will be linked through a satellite or satellites rather than through physical networks. There is one point that should be stressed with regard to the above-mentioned technologies where ITU members have not been able to agree on a global standard, and that is that, with the exception of cellular radio telephones, they are not used to link businesses involved in international commerce. They are basically consumer products. Hence the lack of a single standard does not undermine the operation of the international commercial system. In the case of cellular phones the existence of different standards does not block commercial communications. Some business officials will be able to use a single phone if they work in "compatible" countries, and others will have to buy several phones if they work in "non-compatible" countries.

International standards for telegraph networks date back to the mid-nineteenth century, and in the case of telephone standards they first emerged around the turn of the century. In the case of telegraph networks the biggest interconnection problem in the nineteenth century related to telegraph codes. Complete agreement on codes was never realized as a result of states' commitments to their own systems, but there was sufficient agreement to allow international telegraphic communications to grow rapidly.[72] With the addition of the telephone regulations to the International Telegraph Convention in 1903 new problems arose. At first a modest number of issues relating to procedures and technical network standards had to be negotiated, but with the increasing demand for international telephone communication (especially in Europe) the interconnection problems and standards multiplied. It was for this reason that international consultative committees to develop standards for telephone and telegraph were created in 1925. The major accomplishment of the telephone committee in the interwar period was the solution of the interconnection problems among the European telephone systems which had developed along distinct national lines. International connection standards were finally accepted despite the protectionist policies of the European states, and a key reason was that most of the compatibility problems related to limited aspects of transmissions plants and switching/signaling systems at borders (network gateways).[73]

In the postwar period the problems of interconnection grew

considerably. With the advent of transatlantic cables in 1956 certain interconnection problems between European and North American telephone systems had to be resolved. However, what really began to change the scope of the interconnection problems about this time was the advent of direct dialing. Direct dialing was eventually introduced on transatlantic circuits in the 1960s, and this forced Europe and North America to standardize more of their equipment. As the recent director of the CCITT has noted: "The national networks became integral characteristics of the international networks and consequently standardization had to be expanded, thus broadening the field considerably."[74]

The 1950s also saw the beginnings of what is the most important technological development in recent decades, and that is the integration of computers and telecommunications systems. This phenomenal development really marked a watershed in the evolution of tele-communications standards. As one recent study has noted: "The work of the ITU for the past 117 years has assured world-wide telecommunications in telegraphy and telephony, most often against tremendous odds. During the first 100 pre-digital years, recommendations were: slow to come about; often polished and refined over several study periods, if needed; written 'after the fact,' following the establishment of physical plants; and written primarily (if not exclusively) to ensure interconnectibility of national networks (largely European). As a result, recommendations were slow to change." It then went on to note that the speed and nature of technological change beginning in the 1950s brought about a need for a much quicker and more extensive standard-setting process.[75]

A key impact of the integration of computers and telecommunications is that it created a need to standardize more aspects of national telecommunication systems – blurring the line between national and international systems. That is to say, it became increasingly necessary to develop international standards for domestic networks and terminals, and not just switching equipment at "gateways." Thus the CCITT had to address a much wider range of technical issues, and this is reflected in the fact that its books on technical standards have grown from 3,400 to 20,000 pages over the last two decades. On the other hand, complete homogenization of equipment is by no means necessary, and, in fact, computers have allowed the CCITT to deal with many interconnection problems through software standards. Approximately 70 percent of the CCITT's standards today are software as opposed to hardware standards.[76] Also, ITU recommendations are sometimes framed so as to allow the existence of considerable variation in national equipment standards – which, of course, protect national manufacturers.[77]

The CCITT has achieved accords on many specific technologies in recent years. An agreement on a standard for facsimile in 1968 opened the door for the explosion in the use of that technology.[78] In the late 1970s there was an agreement on a French proposal for a crucial packet switch (X-25) that facilitated the expansion of many services. And that accord was very much a product of pressure by commercial users.[79] More recently, in 1988, the CCITT approved a standard for video conferencing after several years of negotiations during which different national industries sought to have their technology accepted. On that decision one industry official remarked: "Business today operates on a global scale. Videoconferencing's ability to allow instant face-to-face communication anywhere in the world provides significant strategic advantages, improves utilization of human resources, and reduces travel costs for the companies that use it."[80] On the other hand, there have been occasions when agreement eluded states and industries. One was the case of videotext, which is a system for the transmission of various types of information to monitors in homes or businesses. France, Canada, and the UK each developed its own standard, and each had a number of allies. In the end the three competitors would not bend, and there is presently no global standard.[81] It is, however, important to note that videotext, like color TV and HDTV, is a consumer product, and the absence of agreement on standards does not undermine international communication among commercial enterprises. There is one technology of some importance to international commerce where standardization has not been possible, and that is electronic mail (e-mail). However, a multiplicity of standards has not made communication between different e-mail systems impossible since software innovations have made interconnection between different systems feasible – if somewhat expensive. It is, in fact, probable that in the long run the lack of a global standard will be seen as desirable since it has allowed creative innovation in a very rapidly changing area.[82]

In concluding this discussion on standard-setting, one rule pertaining to patents of both the CCIR and the CCITT (and now merged into the Standardization Sector) should be mentioned. It is that, in order for an equipment standard of a particular company to be approved, the company must either waive exclusive right to the patent for the equipment or must indicate a willingness to negotiate licences "with applicants throughout the world on reasonable terms and conditions."[83] This policy greatly reduces the obstacle to agreement that would result if CCITT or CCIR approval of a standard gave the company with the patent a virtual monopoly in the international market.

Past studies of standardization in the telecommunications industry have commented on a variety of factors that have promoted international accords: the dominance of a particular country or firm in the international industry;[84] the concentration of buyers in a single state or small group of states;[85] very gradual technological change;[86] requirement of a large investment or economies of scale;[87] and an absence of a commitment to protect national manufacturers.[88] These are valid observations, but they leave out the most central factor – and that is the salience of the technology for international communication or interconnection. As a recent study of the international politics of telecommunications points out, "In the nature of telecommunications technology there exists a strong imperative for technical homogeneity. Only in a very few instances can that imperative be overcome by domestic economic, social, and political concerns."[89]

Governments have been very effective over the years in assuring interconnection among international businesses. And the reason, of course, is that telecommunications users or customers demand interconnection. Telecommunications is, after all, a service industry, and most businesses involved in international commerce depend on it. Relevant to this point one observer has noted that "companies and countries can no longer afford to use a multitude of electronic machines in order to be able to talk to each other."[90] The most serious failures in assuring interconnection have concerned communications to end users or consumers where a larger consumer market was at stake (e.g. color TV, HDTV, and videotext). For reasons of commercial gain "Industries . . . have always attempted to limit connectivity to secure market advantages."[91]

There is a decided movement toward greater standardization of a wide range of equipment – not just technologies relevant to interconnection – because users want to benefit from cheaper goods and services and manufacturers want to be assured of markets for their goods.[92] In part, this is due to an acceptance of greater competition in the international telecommunications service industry. The providers of telecommunications services are obviously anxious to lower the cost of equipment in order to better compete with each other in international markets. To quote a French telecommunications expert, "The restructuring currently underway has given the industry an international dimension that is incompatible with national standardization and approval practices."[93]

A recent indication of growing support for standardization is the prospect that thirty of the world's largest telecommunications and computer standards organizations will become linked by a global electronic network.[94] Telecommunications is seen as the central nervous system of the international economy, and not only are incompatibilities among various parts seen as intolerable, but protectionism in equipment and service markets is increasingly regarded in the same way. Some protectionism is unquestionably going to continue in both telecommunications services and equipment markets, but the trend seems to be in the direction of global standards. It is noteworthy that the CCITT recently adopted a procedure for speeding formal approval of recommendations (support by 70 percent of the members in a mail ballot) because of the rapidity of technological change and the growing importance of standardization in all areas of international telecommunications.

There have never been serious differences on states' mutualities of interest in interconnection, and there is movement toward perceived mutualities of interest in more pervasive standardization of equipment because of a greater concern for economic efficiency. States have always been committed to assuring the technical feasibility of international telecommunications. Now they are becoming more concerned with the cost of communications and are more willing to accept common standards for equipment throughout the system. This contemporary development indicates growing support for further reductions in the costs involved in conducting international commerce.

Prices and market shares

The issue of prices and market shares in the telecommunications industry is complex and has changed over the years. The key pricing issues until fairly recently were confined to rates for telephone calls and telegraph/telex messages and the division of the revenues among states of origin, transit states, and terminal states. With the increase in the number of new services, such as data transmission and facsimile, issues relating to prices and revenues have multiplied dramatically.

Until very recently there was not a market share problem; it was simply assumed that state telecommunications monopolies would control all traffic originating in their countries. However, since the multiplication of services and the moves toward deregulation and privatization in the 1980s, market share issues have become quite controversial.

There are two major opportunities for joint gains in the regulation of prices and market shares.[95] First, a regulatory regime can assist states in maintaining control of a national industry that is viewed as crucial to the management of their economies and political orders. This function has certainly been central to the telecommunications regime since the middle of the nineteenth century although the situation has been changing in recent years. Second, mutual economic gains can be realized through either price regulation in circumstances of increasing economies of scale (i.e. existence of a natural monopoly) or liberalization of trade. The existence of a natural monopoly certainly was an important justification for the cartel arrangement that existed in international telecommunications until very recently, although the actual existence of a natural monopoly has certainly been problematic.

An international cartel dominated the prices and market shares policy sector from the mid-nineteenth century through to the 1970s, and it is still supported by most Third World states and in varying degrees by a number of developed states as well. The traditional cartel norm prescribed that all state telecommunications administrations should cooperate in determining market shares, setting rates, and dividing revenues.[96] Since the 1980s the developed capitalist states have moved gradually toward a regime, which at least applies to relations among themselves, that prescribes open competition in the provision of non-basic services (i.e. services other than telephone and telex); and some are moving toward competition in telephone and telex as well. There is, however, broad acceptance of the position that state administrations can maintain control of basic services within their borders. This emergent regime for the industrial world can be viewed as reflecting a limited or qualified competition norm. Such a regime, which resembles the economic regimes based on "embedded liberalism" described by John Ruggie,[97] could be consolidated in the developed world in the 1990s, but it could take some time for it to take hold in the developing world. Third World countries are not yet willing to make the same tradeoff between openness and domestic control that the First World countries are increasingly willing to make.

The intergovernmental cartel, 1860s–1970s

In describing the traditional cartel regime, the analysis focuses on three general rules that sustained the cartel: the *anti-competition rule*, the *state monopoly defense rule*, and the *anti-defection rule*. However, before looking at the three general rules, the shape of the traditional cartel and its historical development will be reviewed.[98] In the nineteenth century telegraph and telephone services were defined as public services in Europe and were placed under state administrations. Often they were joined to the administration of the postal services – hence the term PTTs (post, telephone, and telegraph administrations). Prior to World War II the telecommunications industries in most Third World countries were owned by multinational corporations such as Cable and Wireless and ITT, but after 1945 most were purchased by the state.[99] At the international level it was accepted that state telecommunications administrations should regulate rates, revenues, and market shares and should jointly own international infrastructure facilities such as cables and satellites. Because of states' commitment to control their communications systems, telecommunications until very recently was "one of the most protected, insulated, and monopolized industries in the economies of virtually all nations."[100]

Key to understanding the early years of international telecommunications is the division of the world into three quite distinct systems. The members of each region operated a *de facto* cartel, and the limited relations among the three tended to follow the rules of one regional system. First, there was the British-controlled network linking the countries and colonies of the empire as well as some other non-European countries. The dominant firm in this network through the early twentieth century was the Eastern and Associated Companies, which then merged with the Marconi Company to become Cable and Wireless in 1927. Second, there was the US-centered network in the Western Hemisphere. Lastly, there were the European PTTs who were the main participants in the International Telegraph Union and the International Radiotelegraph Union. Members of the British and American-dominated systems set their own rates for communications between members, but they tended to follow the European (or ITU) rules in interconnecting with countries in other systems.[101]

A telecommunications cartel began to develop in Europe in the mid-nineteenth century. In the 1850s there were some regional accords among European telegraph administrations to facilitate international communications, and then in 1865 the International Telegraph Union was formed by twenty states. Its central tasks were the establishment of rates and the division of revenues among states of origin, transit, and destination, and the rules were placed in the Telegraph Regulations attached to the ITU Convention. States' key concerns were to promote a sense of financial certainty in the incipient industry and to assure adequate financial returns for the PTTs. At times such as in the 1880s, cohesion within the cartel declined because of an oversupply of transatlantic cable lines, but such periods were the exception.[102] In 1903 the Telephone Regulations with their rules concerning international rates were added to the International Telegraph Convention. Between 1906 and 1932 the rules governing radiotelegraph rates were placed in the International Radiotelegraph Convention. Then in 1932 the regulations for telegraph, telephone, and radiotelegraph were attached to the Convention for the new International Telecommunications Union. On the whole, the distribution of revenues and to a lesser extent the setting of rates were regulated reasonably well for the European states. As noted above, rates and division of revenues within the British and American networks were managed quite autonomously.[103] After World War II the ITU-centered cartel arrangements were embraced enthusiastically by most developed and developing countries, and even as late as the mid-1980s a German telecommunications official was correct in writing that since the nineteenth century international regulatory arrangements "have remained relatively unchanged."[104]

Prior to World War II the one country that stood out at times as a challenger to an intergovernmental cartel was the USA. The USA only agreed to join the International Radiotelegraph Union in 1927 and the International Telecommunications Union in 1932 when the rate regulations were placed in annexes – and hence it could refrain from formally adhering to the regulations. However, despite a general ideological stand against intergovernmental rate-setting, the USA adhered to the cartel regulations in its dealings with other telecommunications administrations and even backed the common rationale for state monopolies. In fact, in 1934 the American government created the Federal Communications Commission (FCC), and it accepted the natural monopoly justification for national telephone monopolies (in the US case – AT&T). As Jeffrey Hart comments: "Although the US network was privately owned, regulation of AT&T created a national monopoly in telecommunications as effectively as the publicly owned and operated monopolies in Europe."[105] Then, in 1943 the FCC was given the task of managing the involvement of international record carriers with foreign PTTs.[106] The USA was basically a very cooperative partner in the cartel until around 1980.

Turning to the general rules of the telecommunications cartel, the first one is that of *anti-competition*, or the prescription that telecommunications administrations should not pursue competitive strategies to take business from each other. By definition, such strategies could lead to an unraveling of the cartel. One of the most important ITU rules, designed to proscribe competition, was the rule that states should charge uniform transit rates for "refiling" transmissions through their territories. This was meant to discourage attempts by states to take transit business from each other by lowering their transit rates. State administrations followed the rule closely until very recently, but violations are now common. An important rule that still survives is that there must be a single or universal accounting rate between two states. That is to say, if there are several carriers in two countries, they are not able to negotiate lower accounting rates as a way of attracting more business. This rule is, however, likely to disappear in the near future.[107] Another guideline that some state administrations supported to discourage competition was that all administrations should charge roughly equal "collection rates" (what is charged to senders) so as to discourage businesses from "sourcing" their communications in the lower-cost country. However, these attempts to promote roughly comparable collection rates have never had much of an impact outside Europe. And even in Europe there have been some significant disparities.[108]

The second of the three general rules is the *state monopoly defense rule* that all cartel members should not pursue policies that would promote the development of rivals to foreign monopolies. One specific cartel strategy was that the PTTs should not interconnect with any companies other than state administrations or designated monopolies (e.g. AT&T). An exception was made with regard to international record carriers (traditionally telegraph/telex) in the USA and Canada where there were respectively three and five carriers. However, those cases were exceptions that could be tolerated as long as there were not multiple carriers in other states, and as long as the USA and Canada coordinated their carriers' international linkages so that they would not challenge the international cartel.[109]

A related strategy was that the cartel members should maintain joint ownership of all international means of transmission so as to give them the ability to exclude rivals. In the case of oceanic cables there has always been a sharing of ownership among the state administrations and designated monopolies such that the parties on each side owned a share to a hypothetical mid-way point (the "half-circuit arrangement").[110] When satellites came along, state telecommunications administrations and designated authorities (e.g. COMSAT in the USA) formed the International Telecommunications Satellite Organization (INTELSAT) in 1965 so as to maintain intergovernmental control of that new medium. They also gave INTELSAT a veto power over the launching of any satellites with telephone circuits.[111] When a special satellite system for maritime traffic (International Maritime Satellite Organization or INMARSAT) was formed in 1975, the traditional pattern of ownership was maintained despite attempts by a number of firms to have it owned by a private consortium.[112] As one writer has noted, it has been through cable and satellite ownership arrangements that "the national monopoly structure has been extended to international markets."[113]

With the integration of computers and telecommunications and the expansion of new telecommunications services beginning in the mid-1950s, challenges arose to the traditional practices of the PTTs and the international cartel. Multinational businesses began to lease lines from the PTTs in order to link their branches, and some soon tried to interconnect their systems and to sublease excess capacity on their lines. Both interconnections between leased lines and the subleasing of lines created *de facto* rivals to the PTTs – and certainly undermined the PTTs' revenue-earning capabilities. Therefore, the PTTs soon promoted the adoption of rules by the ITU against the subleasing, sharing, or connecting of leased lines.[114]

Another strategy that implicitly sought to control the growth of rivals to the PTTs was the prescription that the rates for leased lines be "volume-sensitive." That is to say, the rates for transmissions on leased lines should not be so different from those paid by users of the PTTs' lines that there would be a wholesale movement away from the use of the normal PTT services. In the last decade violations of this rule have become common in countries committed to deregulation.[115]

A third general rule of the traditional cartel is the *anti-defection rule*, or the obligation to pursue strategies that provide incentives to states to maintain loyalty to the cartel. One specific strategy used to discourage defection was to assure that all states receive reasonable financial returns from the operation of the cartel. This was done by establishing that all pairs of states set "accounting rates" for communications between their two countries and that they and any "transit states" receive prescribed percentages of the accounting rate. (In the case of direct communications the prescribed division of accounting rates between transmitting and receiving states was generally 50–50.) States of origin were also given the option of setting collection rates (i.e. charges to users) higher than the accounting rates – and hence giving them a financial return above the 50 percent of the accounting rate.[116] Linked to these procedures is the general understanding that states or PTTs should be able to purchase international transmission facilities such as cables in rough proportion to their use of them. This gave them the opportunity to benefit from the investments and not to pay charges to other telecommunications authorities. Again, the system was designed to provide strong financial incentives for loyalty to the cartel.[117]

This international cartel operated very well from the nineteenth century through to the 1970s. It assured all PTTs high profits from their international telecommunications services so that they could subsidize their domestic telecommunications systems and even other government services (particularly the postal service). It has been estimated that in the late 1980s (when most states still clung to cartel practices) the world's telecommunications users were paying at least $10 billion over costs each year for international transmissions, and that international calls were on average three times cost.[118] States' profits from international telecommunications gave them greater resources to shape their economies and to provide universal telephone services. Aronson and Cowhey have appropriately labeled this traditional system the "cash cow model" of international telecommunications management.[119] Of course, some obvious losers from this particular cartel arrangement were users, and especially large international businesses. However, other important losers in recent years have been the group of states that decided to embark on a course of liberalization, and more particularly to lower collection charges to their users. They have lost in terms of the balance of "outpayments" between pairs of states because a high percentage of calls between two countries originate in the country with the lower collection rate – a trend that has been accentuated recently because of the growth of country-direct and call-back services. The countries from which most calls are made clearly have to pay the countries of destination more than vice versa. (The settlement rate per minute between carriers in two states is generally half of the accounting rate, and total outpayments equal the total number of minutes times the settlement rate.) An example of the problem is that US carriers presently pay out more than $2 billion more each year than they receive. The USA and some other states are, however, promoting change in this situation through negotiations in the ITU, OECD, and GATT, but progress requires a significant decrease in the collection rates of many states – something that a good number of them strongly resist.[120]

Demise of the intergovernmental cartel: post-1980

The international telecommunications cartel, and more specifically the rules discussed above, suffered a serious weakening in the 1980s, but the roots of the decline can be traced back several decades. An analysis of the decline must look not just at international developments but also a number of national developments – especially in the USA. The USA's importance is based on the fact that it has been ahead of other countries in adopting more liberalized practices, has pressed other countries to move in similar directions, and has the largest market for telecommunications services and equipment.

The move toward liberalization and a gradual acceptance of a *limited competition norm* among the industrialized countries can be traced back to a 1959 decision by the FCC in the USA that firms should be allowed to create their own microwave networks independent of the monopoly carrier, AT&T.[121] In the 1960s telecommunications monopolies in the USA and other Western states began to lease lines to government agencies and national and multinational businesses so that they could fashion systems suited to their particular needs.[122] Also, in the late 1960s and early 1970s the USA first allowed telecommunications firms other than AT&T to establish alternative networks between certain cities and also to offer new telecommunications services.[123] It is, however, important to note that the USA at this time was by no means trying to undermine the basic structures of the traditional national telephone monopoly and the international cartel. In fact, in 1968 a presidential taskforce concluded that the international cartel remained in the USA's interest both because of economies of scale in the industry and the foreign political repercussions of any attempt to undermine the cartel.[124]

The early 1980s were a period of very rapid change in the telecommunications industry. In the USA the government allowed additional entrants into the telecommunications market and permitted firms that had leased lines to resell capacity. Also, AT&T was broken up, and AT&T itself was limited to long-distance and international traffic so as to create the conditions for liberalization of international markets. That is because it could no longer use its control over domestic networks to exclude other providers of long-distance and international services (i.e. Sprint and MCI). The US government also moved to promote competition among record (non-voice) carriers in both national and international markets.[125]

Several other countries also began to move toward liberalization of telecommunications markets. Britain allowed the creation of a rival (Mercury) to the traditional monopolist British Telecom. Mercury, which soon became a subsidiary of Cable and Wireless, began to establish links with foreign carriers – notably with the US firm Tel-Optik for the purpose of building a transatlantic cable service to serve private firms.[126] British Telecom also moved in a competitive direction in that it set up a satellite communications system that circumvented PTT networks, and it established links with several US companies to create new transatlantic cable networks. British Telecom also began to offer low transit rates so as to become an entrepot for transatlantic communications, and it allowed private companies that had leased lines to resell capacity. The British role in promoting liberalization of international telecommunications services can be attributed in part to the communications interests that it inherited from its colonial past.[127] Japan followed Britain toward greater liberalization. It eliminated the monopolies of the two companies that had controlled domestic and international telecommunications traffic, and it allowed the establishment of an international network with a private US company.[128] There are certainly differences in the policies of the USA, Britain, and Japan, but they all moved in comparable ways in permitting the liberalization of both basic and non-basic services, the reselling of capacity on leased lines, the interconnection of leased lines, and introduction of private international firms in international cable and satellite markets.[129]

In the late 1980s and early 1990s the liberalization trend began to spread to several European states, the European Community, Canada, Australia, and New Zealand. While there are some important differences among these countries, the basic trend is toward allowing competition in all aspects of telecommunications. Britain, Australia, and New Zealand have full competition in basic services ("the local loop"), and this is likely to come to the USA and other countries soon.[130] While there have been some movements toward privatization of national telecommunications administrations as a part of the encouragement of liberalization, there are no clear signs that most states will allow the demise of their national carrier.[131] As *The Economist* noted in 1991: "Most governments, especially in Europe, guard their PTT's national status as jealously as that of their flag-carrying national airline – indeed, more so."[132] Still major changes seem to be in the wind as a result particularly of a decision by the European Commission in 1993 to require full liberalization of all telecommunications services by 1998. This could mean not only open competition among European firms, but free entry of foreign firms and privatization of European telecommunications administrations as well.[133] Another indication of the kind of telecommunications world that is emerging in Europe is that by 1993 several international consortia centered on AT&T, the British Telecom/MCI alliance, and the France Telecom/Deutsche Telekom alliance had established new entities to provide international services. The new commercial entities will eventually include other telecommunications administrations and will act basically as competitive multinational firms.[134]

Any discussion of the movement toward liberalization of international telecommunications services in the 1980s must highlight the growing use of leased lines by multinational corporations and the reactions of state administrations to this growing use.[135] What states and their PTTs found increasingly in the 1980s was that international businesses threatened to move elsewhere if they were not given telecommunications deals comparable to what they could find in other countries. PTTs had to choose between violating ITU rules or losing business to other states, and consequently there were increasing violations of ITU guidelines on reselling of capacity on leased lines, the interconnection of leased lines, the uniformity of transit rates, and volume-sensitive rates.[136]

Another very important development in the late 1980s and early 1990s is that national telephone companies began to compete in each other's markets. This started when AT&T launched what are known as "country-direct" services. Such services provide a caller an opportunity to phone the USA from many foreign states by placing a call to a local number abroad that is then interconnected with an AT&T cable or satellite channel to the USA. Such services require the cooperation of local telephone companies in that they must allow local numbers for AT&T. According to AT&T such country-direct services accounted for 10 percent of US settlement minutes in 1991, so it is clearly a growing phenomenon.[137] Other systems of providing cheaper rates that have been developed by AT&T as well as a few other companies are "call-back" and "third-country calling." The call-back system requires that a person in a foreign country call a special number in the USA, and hang up after the first ring. The central office returns the call to the customer who hears a US dial tone upon answering. The customer then dials the desired number "from" a location in the USA using a US international carrier. The call is then charged as a call from the USA to the foreign country at the US collection rate. Third-country calling routes transmissions between two countries through another (e.g. the USA or Britain) when the rates for these two legs are cheaper than a direct call between the states of origin and destination. This is frequently the case.[138]

While country-direct, ring-back, and third-country calling services have allowed some telecommunications companies to enter foreign markets, they have been confined to voice communication, and their growth has been limited by various barriers. More adventuresome forays into international competition have developed in the realms of international commercial communications and enhanced (or non-basic) services. In the 1990s AT&T established WorldSource to offer services to international firms, and it has been joined in this venture by KDD (Japan), Unitel (Canada), Telstra (Australia), and Singapore Telecom as well as Unisource which is itself a joint venture of the national carriers in Sweden, the Netherlands, and Switzerland. Then, in June 1993 British Telecom and the American firm MCI formed a joint venture to provide international communications services. This was then followed in late 1993 by the establishment of a joint venture between Deutsche Telekom and France Telecom which provides services to multinational firms. Also, in 1993 British Telecom and AT&T took steps to gain access into each other's national markets for all international services and for domestic enhanced services. As of 1994 AT&T is a licensed full domestic carrier in the UK. These developments are additional indications that the telecommunications world may be on the verge of very different commercial arrangements in comparison to those that existed in the past. One commonly projected model is the development of a first tier of global firms that offer a wide range of services and a second tier of national firms that provide some local services which interconnect with the global firms in order to provide other services.[139]

A recent and ongoing development that will have major impacts on international telecommunications and will promote competition is the growth of wireless technology – specifically the expansion of cellular phone systems at the national level and the imminent introduction of low earth-orbiting satellites that will allow wireless phone communications between any two spots on earth. This will, of course, allow the telecommunications companies controlling this wireless technology to be free of dependence on local wired networks that are usually controlled by state monopolies. It is precisely because of these developments that telephone companies are increasingly moving into the cellular field (for example, AT&T's purchase of McCaw Cellular). It is, however, almost impossible for state telecommunications administrations to control the new wireless systems and all of the other means of international communication. In fact, there is now considerable competition among telephone companies, cable companies, TV networks, computer companies, consumer electronic companies, publishing companies, and film studios over their future roles in the telecommunications industry, and this enhances the movement toward liberalization that has been occurring.[140]

There were a number of international meetings that confronted the liberalization issue in the late 1980s and early 1990s. Some European PTTs and almost all developing states tried to shore up the cartel at the World Administrative Telephone and Telegraph Conference (WATTC) in 1988 by trying to gain acceptance of rules obligating all states to comply with traditional ITU strictures, but they did not succeed. In the end the refusal particularly of the USA, Britain, and Japan to revert to cartel practices led to the acceptance of a laissez-faire approach. In particular, states were allowed to enter into bilateral commercial arrangements that do not comply with ITU rules (the "consenting adults" clause).[141] For the multinational corporations that are the dominant users of telecommunications, the central message of the WATTC was that they would be given a great deal of latitude in adjusting to international technological and commercial changes.[142]

In the early 1990s the ITU officially backtracked on its restrictions against the reselling of channels on leased lines as a result of pressure from the major industrialized powers and their multinational firms. This opened the door to the development of competitors to the PTTs, and it could prove very significant to international deregulation. An ITU committee in 1992 also called for international accounting rates to be established on the basis of cost.[143] In addition, INTELSAT finally agreed, following pressure by the USA, that the launching of rival satellite systems was acceptable; that INTELSAT should not have a veto over satellites with under 100 telephone circuits; and that states should not be required to give INTELSAT a certain percentage of their international business. There are now several rival satellite ventures, and more will be launched in the 1990s. In addition, the USA is now pressing for the privatization of both INTELSAT and INMARSAT. One interesting venture is Tongasat which was launched when an American firm purchased from Tonga the GSO slot it had been allotted at the 1988 ORB-WARC. There is still resistance to the liberalization trend (especially from the developing world), but the die is probably cast. A 1992 survey of thirty-two countries by IBM reported steady movement toward liberalization in various facets of telecommunications, and an important industry journal reported that "Movement toward competitive provision of basic telecommunications services and network infrastructure is gradually, stubbornly building momentum."[144]

One of the most important developments in the international politics of telecommunications services was the introduction of trade in services into the GATT Uruguay Round and the inclusion of a General Agreement in Trade in Services (GATS) and a Telecommunications Annex into the series of accords that were approved at the end of the round in April 1994. The accords constitute the culmination of a trend in thinking among many commercial firms and governments, which started in the early 1970s, that telecommunications flows should be seen not as "jointly provided services" but as "trade in services." There are a number of key aspects of the accords. States undertake to promote progressive liberalization and to establish their own schedule of commitments to open their market. With regard to those policy areas where states make commitments, they are obligated to treat foreign firms in the same way that they treat national firms, although certain restrictions are permitted where issues of public order and morals are concerned. As a result of the insistence by the USA and some other countries, some exemptions to non-discrimination (or the most-favored nation clause) are permitted in order to avoid certain countries' taking advantage of open markets in other states while erecting protectionist barriers around their own markets. These exemptions are limited to ten years, but they can, of course, be extended in a subsequent agreement. What, in fact, is likely to occur is the development of open markets among groups of states (largely from the industrialized world), but over the long run an increasing number of countries will be integrated into a more deregulated commercial environment. Of great importance is that adherents to the 1994 GATT agreements established a Negotiating Group on Basic Telecommunications within the newly created World Trade Organization, and it is within that body that the most important international deliberations on telecommunications markets are likely to take place. What is occurring is a migration of political authority from the PTT-dominated ITU to the liberalization-oriented World Trade Organization. This migration of authority is still being resisted by some European and many developing countries, but the pattern is basically set as a result of the agreement within the European Union to move toward an open market by 1998.[145]

Sources of cartel development and decline

For the purposes of this study there are two key questions with regard to regulatory developments since the mid-nineteenth century. First, did the traditional international cartel develop in order to take advantage of economies of scale (a natural monopoly) or to assure states' control of their economies or for both reasons? Second, has the partial demise of the cartel been due to a decline of mutual interests because of technological and domestic political changes or to the opposition of powerful states with interests at variance from those of the majority of countries?

With regard to the reasons for the strength of the traditional cartel, the key issue is not whether the cartel was imposed or based on mutual advantage, but whether the mutual advantage was an increase in economic efficiency or an enhancement of state autonomy. There is no indication that any major group of states felt that the regime was imposed on them. If any state objected to the system, it was the USA; and its objection to governments' regulation of the international market seems rather hollow in the light of the monopoly or managed cartel arrangements that existed in different parts of the US telecommunications industry.

Virtually all analyses of the traditional international telecommunications cartel note that the key justification for the cartel was the existence of a natural monopoly.[146] In fact, an economist has commented that "by far the most common defence of monopoly in any public utility is the alleged presence of natural monopoly."[147] The argument has been clearly stated by one author: "Given two fully competing companies the opportunity to supply local connections in one region would almost double the cost because each would need a complete infrastructure to reach its market."[148] As recently as 1968 a US presidential taskforce came down clearly in favor of the economies of scale in the international telecommunications industry, and this thinking basically continued over the 1970s.[149] Most experts and officials thought that domestic monopolies and an international cartel bestowed economic benefits on virtually everyone. The change in thinking can be traced in part to a number of studies done in the USA in the mid-1970s that indicated that natural monopolies did not exist in various facets of the industry.[150] These studies, however, were part of a larger body of economics literature on deregulation that had been growing for several decades and that had dramatic impacts on a variety of issue areas. To quote Alan Altschuler, "It is . . . one of the clearest examples ever of the power of intellectual analysis to overturn a deeply entrenched political regime."[151]

There is, however, another sphere in which states recognized a mutual advantage in supporting the cartel, and that is with regard to protection of their own policy autonomy. Telecommunications are so crucial to the operation of an economy and touch on so many important political interests that states are very reluctant to release control of them. States' desire to maintain control over the industry is probably just as important as the existence of a natural monopoly to any explanation of why telecommunications has been "one of the most protected, insulated, and monopolized industries in the economies of virtually all nations" and why "the national monopoly structure has been extended to international markets."[152] In the 1980s the best defenses of the traditional system came from officials of the Deutsche Bundespost, and central to their defense was the system's facilitating the realization of various social and political goals – in particular, the provision of basic services for virtually all citizens, the subsidization of local calls by long-distance ones, and the subsidization of the postal service by the telephone and telegraph services.[153] There is, of course, a concern among many states that they be able to control and monitor communications coming into and leaving their countries, and government monopolies and an intergovernmental cartel facilitate this. These rationales are summarized by the statement of one telecommunications expert that "The straightforward proposition that a telecommunications provider operating as a legal entity in one country should be able to provide its service directly into another country, i.e. on an end-to-end basis, has traditionally been viewed as deeply offensive to national sovereignty and security."[154]

It is clear that states saw both economic and political advantages in

174

the traditional cartel. The crucial question about the recent weakening of the cartel is whether it is due to technological and economic changes that have reduced economies of scale, to new economics knowledge about natural monopolies, to domestic changes that reduced the importance of state control over telecommunications, and/or to the leverage of certain powerful states that thought they would benefit from a deregulated system. It is not easy to answer this question.

The first point to mention is that there are often disputes among economists on the existence of a natural monopoly.[155] With regard to telecommunications two authors have noted that "there is vigorous debate but no consensus about which telecommunications services are or are not natural monopolies."[156] This, however, overstates the degree of discord. There is, in fact, a general consensus that a natural monopoly does exist with respect to local physical networks, although the growing use of cellular phones and the declining costs of installing wired networks could undermine this consensus. On the other hand, with regard to interregional (trunk) and international communications, it is judged that competition among a number of firms yields greater economic efficiency.[157] Even one of the most prominent individuals in the deregulation politics in the USA, Judge Harold Greene, who presided over the break-up of AT&T, has corroborated this under-standing of economies of scale in telecommunications networks.[158] Unquestionably, changing economics knowledge did influence the decline of the international cartel.

Changes in the technological and economic character of the inter-national telecommunications industry have been fundamental to the weakening of the cartel, but there have also been changes in thinking concerning what should fall under state control. In the words of Peter Cowhey we are witnessing "a redefinition of the public sector" that is a product of "a shift in political economic interests and a transformation of the epistemic community."[159] What this fundamentally refers to is a growing perception that in order to reap certain economic gains states have to give up some control over their communications networks and their economies more generally. It points to a general willingness on the part of states to sacrifice a degree of autonomy for the sake of greater economic welfare. However, while many states are willing to accept significant loss of control of business communications, they will not accept such a loss with regard to a basic public telephone service. This reality is reflected in the observation that "The United States and its supporters now seem to grudgingly accept that other governments have legitimate socioeconomic objectives that may not be fully satisfied by a solely trade-oriented solution."[160] As is clear in recent trends in telecommunications regulation, there is a willingness to entertain a greater sacrifice of state policy autonomy, but there are also real limits to the extent of the loss that states and their publics are willing to tolerate.

In analyzing the economic developments that have led to the serious weakening of the cartel, one point that deserves stressing is that telecommunications have become crucial to all international service industries (while being a service industry itself) and that service industries now account for over 50 percent of the economies of the industrialized countries. This has meant that states have become increasingly receptive to demands of service companies and investors for liberalization. The new thinking about telecommunications has become part of a larger reconceptualization of international trade in services.[161]

The last issue to address in examining recent changes in international regulations for prices and market shares is the extent to which they are due to pressure by the USA and more recently the UK and Japan. These states have certainly had an influence, but it is quite likely that even without their pressure liberalization would have eventually developed as a result of the multiplication of telecommunications services and their increased economic salience. Firms want the reduced rates and special services that they know are possible, and they are pressuring governments to accept greater deregulation. This type of pressure was crucial to the Japanese decision to allow competitors to the traditional monopoly carrier of international telecommunications (KDD).[162] Having stated that liberalization would probably have come even without the prodding and example of the USA, the UK and Japan, it is still important to recognize that these countries did apply some effective pressure that expedited the process.[163]

In reviewing the factors that affected the fracturing of the cartel and the move toward liberalization it is important to highlight the impact of technological change. Relevant to its impact a government official commented that

> Technological advances . . . have led to the multiplication of potential channels for transmitting telecommunications signals (copper cable, fiber optic cable, satellite, microwave), for switching signals (electromechanical switches versus advanced computer

switches), and for transforming a client's message into an electric signal (phones, fax machines, modems). This has made it possible to offer varied services by linking together different facilities and equipment. The range of these services is so broad that a single organization no longer can be expected to meet all the specialized customer needs.[164]

Elaborating on these developments *The Economist* observed that by the early 1980s "technology, particularly satellite and microwave communications, had frustrated the arguments for a natural monopoly in making distant connections." It then went on to note that "There is no longer a single, universal public network. There is a mosaic of competing networks, a plethora of services to sell over them, and plenty of competitors."[165] Given the above trends the old cartel arrangement was bound to be viewed as a straitjacket by competitive multinational corporations. A consolidation or reconsolidation of the telecommunications cartel was probably never an option.

In conclusion, the traditional cartel regime was based on states' perceptions of mutual benefits at the economic level (exploitation of a natural monopoly) and at the political level (protection of policy autonomy). There now seems to be a new commercial arrangement emerging which is based on different notions of mutual interests and which is captured by the term "the limited competition norm." States (especially in the industrial world) are shifting the relative weight they assign to economic welfare and policy autonomy in favor of the former. Even their former commitment to maintain control by a single national carrier over basic services is beginning to crumble, as recent moves by the UK, Australia, and New Zealand indicate. A new conception of a strongly liberal regime has not been uniformly embraced among the developed states, but the trend is in that direction. There are even signs that it is beginning to catch hold in the Third World.

The principle of the free flow of commerce has definitely been given greater weight in relation to internal political control over recent decades, and the trend is likely to accelerate. In keeping with this movement, the mutual interests undergirding the emergent regime are related more to the correction of market failures such as reducing impediments to the flow of goods and services and reducing collusion among commercial enterprises than to protecting states' control over their economies. However, states' concern to retain at least a modest amount of control over domestic telecommunications is likely to be integrated into future regime arrangements.

Conclusion

There has been a reasonably strong regime for international telecom-munications for more than a century although there have been some elements of weakness. With regard to jurisdictional rights there are not formal accords – with the exception of outer space – but there are strong implicit consensuses that states will not interfere with transmissions in international space or, except in unusual circumstances, in national airspace. In a sense the ITU regulations concerning avoidance of radio interference establish implicit jurisdictional understandings. Without states' acceptance of and compliance with these understandings, there would be a high level of uncertainty with regard to the costs of telecom-munications services and significant impediments to the flow of communications and commerce. Differences over whether satellite firms should have to acquire the prior consent of states to which they are beaming DBS-TV signals do constitute an element of weakness in the dimension of the regime concerned with jurisdictional rights, but the *force majeure* of technological change may impose an acceptance of openness which eventually could receive a legal sanction.

A central aspect of the telecommunications regime and hence the work of the ITU concerns the prevention of interference among radio transmissions – or in other terminology, the management of damage control problems. ITU members have knit together certain rights for states to establish claims to radio frequencies and orbital slots with certain obligations to accept particular forms of planning such that interference is generally avoided. More specifically, they have adopted the first-come, first-served practice but combined it with the obligation of states to allocate bands of the spectrum to different services and to allot particular frequencies to particular countries in order to promote safety, efficient use, and equity. There are definitely conflicts among states with regard to how they should be able to establish claims to particular frequencies and what bands should be allocated for different services, but they virtually always agree on solutions. States and their industries do not want to risk uncertainty with regard to the flow of radio communications, and they want to reduce the absolute costs of communications by reducing impediments to the flow of communi-cations.

The dimension of the telecommunications regime relating to technical and procedural barriers has always been quite strong. The central reason is that states and industries have insisted on reliable interconnection. In the early years of the telegraph the central issue was telegraph codes, but over the years the major issue with regard to telephone and radio has been equipment standards. Also, until the 1950s standardization of equipment was confined largely to gateways, but since then standards have been required throughout the network to assure efficient communication. It is often possible for states to retain significant differences in equipment without impeding communications, and these possibilities for retaining differences have been used to protect national manufacturers. It is, however, important to recall that the only important failures in standard-setting have related to standards for consumer electronics, and these failures have not constituted significant blockages in the network of international commercial communications. The vast array of procedural and technical standards have promoted stability and a reduction in barriers in international communications, and in so doing they have opened the arteries of global commerce.

The regulation of prices and market shares was governed by a well-organized cartel of national PTTs from the mid-nineteenth century until the 1980s. The cartel was based on both *perceived* economies of scale in the industry as well as the importance of telecommunications to states' control of their economies and societies. There has been a weakening of the cartel as a result of the multiplication of telecommunications services and their increasing importance for international businesses. The old cartel is now seen as an impediment to the flow of international commerce, not a facilitator of international exchanges. Pertinent to this point a British telecommunications expert wrote recently that while international telephone users were being charged £10 billion over cost, "The real damage by the cartel is that it restricts the flow of information across frontiers and so hampers world trade and the globalization of industry."[166] What governments are finding is that the costs of maintaining a high degree of governmental control over international telecommunications is too great, and they are gradually having to trade-off internal policy control in order to realize economic gains from international commerce. And as the former Chief Executive Officer of Citibank, Walter Wriston, has noted, governments only accept such losses of control in a grudging fashion.

> The world, for better or for worse, is now bound together by an electronic infrastructure that carries news, money and data anywhere on the planet with the speed of light. This is a truly new phenomenon in the world. It is causing a fundamental shift of power [from

governments to multinational businesses]. Governments do not welcome this information standard any more than absolute monarchs embraced universal suffrage.[167]

In a period of rapid technological change when states are altering the priorities that they attach to key values, there are unlikely to be strong regime injunctions on central commercial issues. However, new consensuses favorable to liberalization may be emerging. Most industrialized states now agree that enhanced services should be subject to open competition, and a smaller but still significant group may soon agree on new rules for basic services. With regard to basic services many states do not want to open their markets to foreign competition, but even here there are indications that many countries will move significantly down the path of liberalization over the long term.

Pertinent to the above overview of the telecommunications regime there have been some comments by US sources that highlight the importance of open communications to the global economy and the importance of the regime to open communications. Relevant to the salience of effective telecommunications networks to international commerce one government report noted that "The global flow of information is essential to the sustenance of the currrent level and pattern of the world's collective intelligence and economic production, development and growth."[168] Concerning the role of the regime a US industry official testifying before Congress stressed the salience of the ITU regulations to reducing uncertainty and impediments to the flow of goods and services:

> The ITU is an organization where decisions can have substantial, practical impact on our communications services, on our industry, and on our economy. The ITU does not deal simply in political exhortations; it deals with the critical issues of ensuring that our telecommunications systems can work together with the greatest possible efficiency and without harmful interference. As the world's largest user of radio spectrum, the United States relies very heavily on international rules which establish a predictable and reliable environment for the operation of our systems.[169]

These comments of American government and industry officials are reflective of a much larger consensus of why international telecommunications regulations are important. Quite simply they facilitate the flow of international communications and commerce and hence increase the welfare of all or most countries.

6   The international postal regime

International postal services and the regulatory framework

Prior to the sixteenth century international postal communications were controlled by a variety of private and state enterprises. Often the mails were carried across foreign territories by nationals of the states of origin or destination. During the sixteenth and seventeenth centuries the sovereign states of Europe took over almost all postal services and formed Royal Posts and began to bar foreigners from carrying international mails on their territories. These moves were due to governments' perceptions that it was politically important to control the flow of information within their territories and that significant revenues could be earned from the posts. On these matters one author has written that the decision to create royal postal monopolies was "primarily political and designed to prevent secret communication of the King's enemies at home and abroad."[1] However, a desire to raise revenues for state treasuries was also an important motivation.[2]

During the seventeenth century states began to enter into bilateral postal agreements that dealt not only with bilateral flows but also with situations in which letters and parcels were carried across their territories to third countries. Central features of these accords were that mail was only carried across states' territories by their own postal authorities, fees were paid to transit states, and states assumed liability for damages to or loss of mail items carried by their postal authorities. All states were concerned to assert their sovereign control over the flow of information in their societies and to obtain maximum revenue for their services.[3]

Throughout the eighteenth century the number of bilateral

agreements proliferated as a result of the expansion of international commerce. They specified that mail was to be handed over to the authorities of other states when it reached the border, and they also spelled out the shares of postal charges that should go to the state of origin, transit states, and the state of destination (or the terminal state). These international agreements generated significant government revenues which were then often used to subsidize domestic mail services. The accords did facilitate the flow of international mail, but the overall system tended to be rather chaotic and expensive. The fee for each piece of mail had to be computed separately (differing according to the route); differences in weight standards and currencies complicated computations; payments had to be collected at the places of origin and destination; and debts to transit states had to be recorded and later paid. There were, in fact, significant differences among the bilateral agreements.[4] It is noteworthy that in the eighteenth century, but even more in the nineteenth century, another consideration arose that strengthened states' commitment to control postal monopolies. This was the desire to use mail service to promote national integration – and more particularly the integration of rural and urban areas. In fact, governments soon found it extremely difficult for political reasons even to contemplate the withdrawal of regular and subsidized mail service to rural areas.[5]

By the middle of the nineteenth century there were pressures for change in the international postal system. First, many European countries as well as the USA had instituted internal postal systems based on a single payment by the sender (i.e. through the purchase of a stamp) and uniform rates by weight, and this eliminated a lot of the expense attendant on the levying of charges on different parties and the time-consuming calculation of postal rates. It was inevitable that demands would emerge for the implementation of a comparable system for international mails. In the middle of the nineteenth century commercial interests increasingly voiced their displeasure with high transit fees, the cost of calculating the charges for each piece of mail and collecting fees from both senders and recipients, the variation in charges by route, and the complications of determining postal rates because of differences in weight standards and currency values. The many bilateral agreements had reduced some of these problems, but they were still serious enough to generate growing demands for reform.[6]

Given these pressures, the major industrialized states met in Paris in

1863 to consider revision of international postal arrangements. The efforts of most major states were directed at getting all countries to standardize their practices – including persuading the major transit states to lower their charges. Thirty-one principles were accepted as recommendations for the renegotiation of new bilateral agreements, and they included limits on transit rates, standard weight categories, prepayment of all charges, and procedures for the determination of international charges and the settlement of accounts. These recommendations did have an impact on the negotiation of new bilateral accords in subsequent years, but a great deal of variation in state practices remained. These variations led to continued dissatisfaction with the international postal system, and states therefore launched a new effort to reform the system in the 1870s.[7]

The framework of the modern international postal system was created in 1874 at a conference that formulated the Universal Postal Convention and established the Universal Postal Union (UPU) in Berne. The accords contained a number of key changes in the former system. Of central importance was that states accepted that the state of origin would collect and keep the entire postal charge – with the proviso that fees for the services of transit states would eventually have to be paid. States accepted that there was a rough symmetry in the flow of mail between particular pairs of states and hence that the payment of "terminal dues" would not be necessary. Some countries wanted to do away with transit fees, but important transit countries such as France and Russia insisted on their retention. Also, criteria for the setting of transit fees and ranges for international postal rates were accepted. One important development was the creation of the International Bureau of the UPU which was to collect and disseminate information on postal practices and to maintain accounts concerning transit fees that states owed each other. There were also quite a few technical regulations to assure uniformity of practices. One author has noted that "The Universal Postal Convention was not the result of the development of an international outlook so much as that of a more realistic conception of national interest."[8] This judgment is correct, and the national interests that were shared were a desire to reduce international postal charges, uncertainty as to the nature of the charges, and the costs of negotiating accords with other countries (by substituting multilateral for bilateral agreements).[9]

The character of international mail services remained quite stable for almost a century after the formation of the UPU in 1874. Mail was carried between countries largely by train and ship until after World War II. In the 1920s and 1930s limited amounts of mail were carried by truck and then airplane, but the dramatic expansion in the transport of mail by air did not occur until after the war. Of even greater importance to the evolution of international postal services than the changes in mail transportation methods have been the post-1960s revolution in telecommunications services and the emergence of private delivery firms. The new telecommunications services are e-mail (between computers), teletext (between typewriters), facsimile (remote photo-copying), and videotext (accessing data banks on TV screens). A recent study noted that e-mail could be substituted for one-half of postal deliveries over the next several decades.[10] Telephone costs have, of course, also dropped considerably, and for some purposes telephone is a substitute for the posts. On top of this there is the expansion of inter-national private courier services such as Federal Express and DHL since the late 1960s.[11] One impact of the growth of new carriers and telecom-munications services in the USA is that the volume of international mail carried by the US Postal Service declined by almost 30 percent over the 1980s.[12]

Some states have responded to the emergence of new message delivery firms that offer both old and new services by transforming their postal administrations into independent government corpor-ations, contracting out work to private firms, and developing new ventures for particular services (courier delivery and e-mail). On the other hand, almost all state postal administrations still maintain virtual monopoly control over lettermail (recent exceptions being Argentina and Sweden). At this point national and international postal industries are in the early stages of profound changes.[13]

Despite the challenges to governmental postal services the industry is still quite important. In 1991 there were well over 400 billion items delivered by national mail services (40 percent of it being mailed in the USA), and of these close to ten billion items flowed between states. Of all international mail around 70 percent originates in the developed countries. However, international mail as a percentage of total mail for most large industrialized states is in the 1.5–4 percent range while for many small developing countries it is in the 10–20 percent range. Also, in the case of many developing states the volume of incoming inter-national mail is much larger than is the volume of outgoing mail (for example, for Ghana and Zambia it is four times larger).[14] An indication of the importance of postal services in the industrialized states is that they account for a little more than 1 percent of GDP.[15] A conservative estimate of annual postal revenues throughout the world is about $90 billion.[16]

Important international bodies

Since its founding in 1874 the Universal Postal Union (UPU) has had several key legal instruments. Originally these instruments were the Universal Postal Convention which contained the constitution of the organization and some general rules concerning international postal services, Detailed Regulations which spelled out postal regulations (especially procedures for handling mail and technical standards), and specific agreements concerning services such as parcel post and money orders. Since 1964 the institutional provisions of the UPU have been included in its Constitution and parts of the attached General Regulations of the UPU, and the Convention now includes just general postal regulations.[17]

The two main deliberative organs in the UPU are the Congress, which meets every five years, and the Executive Council. Another important body is the International Bureau which is the organization's secretariat. Until 1969 it was headed by a Swiss national, but since then the Director-General has been elected by the Congress. It collects and disseminates information among the members concerning matters such as postal rates, customs regulations, shipping routes, and transit routes. It also provides technical assistance and keeps accounting records for most states on what they owe each other as a result of transit fees and imbalances in mail flows. The International Bureau also mediates disputes between members over the interpretation of various regulations.[18]

Some states on occasion do not ratify UPU agreements, but almost all states comply with the regulations. States basically accept that once the main postal regulations have been approved, they are binding on everyone. Concerning compliance George Codding noted that "nations are scrupulous in carrying out their obligations for fear of losing the benefits that accrue to them from this form of international cooperation."[19] On the other hand, the majority of member states are flexible in their expectations of what standards certain developing countries can meet in some areas.

There are a number of other international organizations with which the UPU cooperates that deserve mention. First, there are some organizations with which the UPU works on the development of specific types of regulations. It cooperates with the International Civil Aviation Organization and the International Air Transport Association on airmail issues; with the International Standards Organization on technical packaging and equipment standards; with the Customs Cooperation Council on customs issues; with the International Telecommunication Union on electronic services; and with the World Health Organization and the International Atomic Energy Agency on the shipment of dangerous substances.[20] Second, it cooperates with a number of regional postal organizations. These organizations deal with the facilitation of mail flows at a regional level, but they also sometimes prescribe standards that are more stringent than those adopted by the UPU. UPU regulations, however, prescribe minimum standards below which regional groupings cannot fall.[21]

Overview of the international postal regime

Within the international postal regime (outlined in Table 6.1) the norms relating to jurisdictional rights have been based significantly on states' commitment to the principle of internal political control, although some weight is given to the free movement of information and commerce – especially as it relates to the mail's movement through transit states. Those pertinent to damage control and technical barriers are based largely on the principles of free movement of commerce and transnational damage control, and the second principle could be seen as a derivative of the first.

In the case of prices and market shares, states' concern to maintain a high level of policy autonomy sustained broad support for an intergovernmental cartel norm for many decades, although the cartel was also seen by many as promoting economic efficiency. In the past two decades technological changes and competition from new companies and services have exerted pressure on the traditional cartel arrangement. There are signs that a new commercial regime based on a norm of "a limited competition norm" may emerge.

Jurisdictional rights

The jurisdictional norms relating to international postal services are few in number and were established in their basic forms several centuries ago. First, there is the *within-state carriage norm* or the right of states of origin, transit, and destination to carry all mails within their territories – and hence to exclude foreign carriers. As was stated in the introductory section of this chapter, the issue arose in the seventeenth century over the insistence of "transit states" that they carry mail through their territories. It was regarded as a natural prerogative of sovereign statehood and of states' right to control the flow of information within their borders. The right was recognized in the 1874 Convention which read: "The stipulations of the present treaty do not involve any alteration of the interior postal legislation of any country."[22] Some states now allow foreign postal administrations to carry some mail through their territories (for example, by truck within Europe), but states are still fully committed to the right of exclusion.

Another norm, which like the previous one is grounded in states' commitment to internal political control, is the *internal surveillance norm*. This refers to the right of states of origin and destination to open and impede delivery of international mail in keeping with their national legislation. The right is recognized in the International Postal Convention which states that "A postal item shall remain the property of the sender until it is delivered to the rightful owner except when it has been seized in pursuance of the legislation of the country of destination."[23] In order to deter states from seizing letters governments cite the provision in the UN Declaration on Human Rights that "every person has a right to look for, receive and spread without any limitation of frontiers, information and ideas by any means of expression whatever."[24] However, there has never been any serious movement to prevent states from asserting a right of surveillance over mails within their borders.

Since the founding of the UPU there has been a strong commitment to the *transit passage (or innocent passage) norm* or the obligation of transit states to allow passage of foreign mail through their territories. In the words of a former director of the UPU International Bureau, "the organization of the circulation of the international mail is based on the freedom of transit, which allows the utilization of the enormous world net of communications with all the means which science and modern techniques offer for its use."[25] The obligation not to impede transit is clearly spelled out in the Constitution of the UPU: "Freedom of transit shall be guaranteed throughout the entire territory of the Union."[26] There are, however, some limited exceptions to the right. One which is spelled out in the Convention is when a state suspects that an

Table 6.1 *Outline of the international postal regime*

Principles

Free movement of commerce: obligation of states to reduce impediments to the free movement of goods and services.

Free flow of information: obligation of states to allow the flow of information among peoples of different states.

Efficiency: obligation of states to provide goods and services to their populations at lowest possible cost.

Transnational damage control: obligation of states to prevent activities of their nationals from imposing damages on the nationals and property of other states and to provide compensation for any damages.

Internal political control: right of states to assert jurisdiction and control over activities within their territories.

Norms

Jurisdictional rights

Within-state carriage: right to exclude foreign postal firms and to carry foreign mails within or through own territory.
- Relevant principles: internal political control
- Strength: strong

Internal surveillance: right of states of origin and destination to open and interrupt foreign mails in accord with national laws.
- Relevant principles: internal political control
- Strength: strong

Transit passage (or innocent passage): obligation to allow transit of foreign mails (unopened) through own territory unless there are good grounds for believing that mail items threaten the security of transit states in war time or contain material forbidden under international law.
- Relevant principles: free flow of information, free movement of commerce, internal political control
- Strength: strong

Table 6.1 (*cont.*)

Damage control problems

Mail protection: obligation to assure that letters and packages mailed between states are not lost, damaged, or stolen.
- Relevant principles: transnational damage control, free flow of information, free movement of commerce
- Strength: strong

Mail handler protection: obligation to prevent individuals handling the mails from being hurt by contents.
- Relevant principles: transnational damage control, free movement of commerce
- Strength: strong

Smuggling/counterfeiting prevention: obligation to prevent smuggling contrary to UPU or national regulations and counterfeiting of stamps.
- Relevant principles: transnational damage control, internal political control
- Strength: moderately strong

Reasonable compensation: obligation to compensate individuals for damage to, loss of, or theft of valuable (i.e. insured or registered) letters and parcels.
- Relevant principles: free movement of commerce, transnational damage control
- Strength: strong

Technical and procedural barriers

National treatment: obligation to give the same treatment to foreign mail that is given to own mail.
- Relevant principles: free flow of information, free movement of commerce
- Strength: strong

Minimum standard: obligation to treat foreign mail with a minimum quality of service so as to assure speedy delivery.
- Relevant principles: free flow of information, free movement of commerce
- Strength: moderately strong (problems in some LDCs)

Table 6.1 (*cont.*)

Standardization (technical interconnection): obligation to promote uniformity of postal technical standards.

- Relevant principles: free flow of information, free movement of commerce, efficiency
- Strength: strong
  (**Note:* The national treatment and minimal standard norms would fall completely within the facilitation norm as defined in the other regimes covered in this book; regulations that promote the standardization norm would fall in the facilitation norm as defined in the other regimes, and others would fall under the technical interconnection norm.)

Prices and market shares

Cartel: obligation of state postal administrations jointly to control market shares, postal rates, and sharing of revenue.

- Relevant principles: internal political control, freedom of commerce, efficiency
- Strength: moderately strong until 1980s; weakening gradually since then

Some important general rules:
(1) The UPU should establish international postal rates (medium to weak).
(2) The UPU should establish fees that states of origin should pay for services performed by other states and commercial firms (i.e. transit fees, terminal fees, and ship and air conveyance dues) (moderately strong to medium).
(3) Postal administrations should not try to take business and revenue from each other (strong to medium).
(4) Postal administrations should not interconnect with private postal companies (strong to medium).

Limited competition: obligation to support open competition in all postal service markets except basic lettermail and to accept states' preferences for control over international lettermail service.

- Relevant principles: free flow of commerce, internal political control
- Strength: very weak before 1980s; weak to medium since 1980s

---

envelope or parcel contains substances forbidden by the UPU.[27] There is another exception that is contained in an arbitral decision and has generally been accepted in state practice, and it is that transit can be interrupted in times of war.[28] In fact, interruptions of mail flows through transit states and the opening of mail items are very infrequent outside of war conditions and situations where banned substances are suspected,[29] and the norm is seen as a bedrock of the international postal system. One way of looking at the norm is to view it as comparable to the innocent passage norm with regard to ocean navigation – namely, that states have an obligation to allow the transit of foreign mail items unless they have grounds for believing that they threaten their peace, good order, or security.

The norms and rules that have evolved in the jurisdictional area serve states' interests in their political control of their own societies and the free flow of information and commerce. The principle of promoting states' internal political control is given legal precedence in the shaping of the regime norms, but at the same time states have been quite liberal in granting a right of innocent passage for transit mail. Looking at the UPU regime injunctions pertaining to free transit from the perspective of reducing market failures, they have served to reduce impediments to the free flow of goods and services, uncertainty of costs, and trans-action costs.

Damage control problems

Since the formation of the UPU its member states have been very concerned with minimizing damages to mail items, mail senders and receivers, and mail handlers, and to realize these ends the UPU has promulgated a broad range of regulations. The purposes of the regulations are captured by the norms of the regime which are analyzed below: mail protection, smuggling/counterfeiting prevention, mail handler protection, reasonable compensation, dispute settlement, and national enforcement. There have been relatively minor conflicts over the prominence that should be given to different principles in developing the norms and rules. Central to the formulation of the damage control norms have been states' commitments to transnational damage control and the free flow of information and commerce, and of lesser relevance have been states' concerns to maintain their own internal political control.

The key norm is the *mail protection norm* or the obligation of states to assure that mail items are not damaged, lost, or stolen. It encompasses both accident and crime prevention. If such things occurred frequently, not only would the flow of information and commerce be curtailed but the financial viability of postal administrations would be undermined by the refusal of parties to use the public mails and by the need to pay compensation to some of the aggrieved parties. Of great importance is the need for commercial parties to have certainty concerning the reliability of their communications in order for international commerce to thrive. There have always been a large number of obligations concerning mail security that states have included in the Convention, special agreements, and detailed regulations, and these have grown over the years – with little political controversy. The regulations include matters such as the quality of packaging, procedures to follow in case of incorrect or changed addresses, and procedures to follow to prevent losses, damages, and theft. When conflicts arise between states concerning the interpretation of the rules, there is quite a highly developed system for settling differences. Also, the UPU holds meetings and symposia devoted to disseminating information on how postal administrations can improve security of the mails. At the 1989 Congress the member states asked the Executive Council to create a group of experts to develop a coordinated program to address problems of mail security. This UPU Postal Security Action Group is now active in promoting meetings and formulating guidelines on a wide range of security matters.[30]

A second norm focuses on the *protection of mail handlers*. The main strategies involve banning the shipment of certain substances and requiring that other substances be packaged in certain containers. The substances range over a variety of biological, chemical, and radioactive materials, and the rules are often formulated after consultations with the World Health Organization and the International Atomic Energy Agency. The regulations actually encourage the shipment of some items by mail because they reduce the likelihood of harmful accidents, and they also assist states in protecting their nationals in line with national legislation.[31]

A third and minor norm is the *smuggling and counterfeiting prevention norm*. It does not concern damage to mail items, but the enforcement of certain state regulations concerning the use of the mails. States recognize that they need the cooperation of other states to prevent smuggling across their borders (particularly with regard to drugs), and at times they require the assistance of other countries in preventing counterfeiting of their stamps and apprehending the counterfeiters. In essence, states sometimes need the cooperation of other countries in maintaining compliance with their own national laws. The UPU regulations in this area of crime control are few in number,[32] but UPU member states engage in a great deal of consultation and collaboration. In developing coordinated and joint strategies the UPU works closely with the Customs Cooperation Council (CCC), the UN Fund for Drug Abuse Control, the International Narcotics Control Board, and Interpol. The main body through which crime control strategies are developed is the CCC–UPU Contact Committee.[33]

Another norm is the *reasonable compensation norm* which concerns compensation for the loss of, damage to, or theft of mail items. Provisions for liability, in fact, have been inserted in international postal agreements since the earliest postal accords in the seventeenth century.[34] The term "reasonable" is included because the UPU members have judged over the years that they should be liable solely for items that are registered or insured.[35] The reason is that the financial and administrative costs of being liable for financial losses with regard to all items would be greater than the benefits. Periodically national representatives argue that states should be liable for all lost, damaged, or stolen items, but this is rejected by the great majority of the UPU members.[36] UPU regulations encourage states to send certain valuable items through the public mails since they can purchase insurance, but the exclusion of most mail items from financial liability regulations also assures that costs for postal administrations are not too great and that postal rates are not raised significantly to cover compensation costs. In fact, some industrialized countries have insurance fees and compensation levels for national mail that are quite a bit higher than those for international mail, and this sometimes leads to misunderstanding and dissatisfaction.

The UPU regulations and consultations relating to damage control are extensive and quite effective. The regulatory and collaborative arrangements have been developed both to realize states' mutual economic interests in the free flow of information and their mutual political interests in promoting compliance with domestic legislation relating to customs and protection of mail handlers. With regard particularly to the regulations that have promoted mutual economic interests, the UPU regulations have reduced the market failures of uncertainty of costs, impediments to flow of commerce, and transaction costs for developing international rules.

Technical and procedural barriers

Aspects of the postal regime relating to reducing barriers to the flow of mail overlap with those concerning damage control. While they certainly have not been high-profile issues, they have still been quite important to the development of the industry for more than a century. The key issues and norms have concerned providing equal treatment to foreign and domestic mail, providing a minimum standard of service, and promoting technical standardization.

The *national treatment norm* refers to states' obligation to treat foreign and domestic mail equally, and it emerges in several contexts in the international postal regime. With regard to transit mail the norm emerges clearly in Article 1 of the Universal Postal Convention which states: "Freedom of transit . . . shall carry with it the obligation for each postal administration to forward always by the quickest routes it uses for its own items" all foreign mail.[37] One area where the 1989 Congress did impose requirements on states of destination was with regard to air and priority mail. The requirement reads: "Administrations of destination shall fix a service target for the handling of priority and airmail items addressed to their country. The target shall be no less favourable than those applied to comparable items in their domestic service."[38] The latter point concerns equal national treatment, but in fact the key motivation for the provision is the need for states to establish service targets for priority and airmail which will make these services competitive with private carriers. It was particularly the industrialized countries that were concerned that all states upgrade their expedited services so that state postal administrations do not lose an increasing share of this market to private carriers.

There is a related prescription that at least implicitly exists in international postal regulations, and it is the *minimum standard norm*. There are a host of references in the regulations that states should meet certain general standards in their treatment of foreign mail. Until the 1980s these standards had only a modest influence on states' behavior. The countries of the world have quite disparate levels of economic development and administrative efficiency, and their mail services reflect these. Regardless of what horatory standards might have been espoused in an international treaty, states paid little attention to these commitments *per se*. They basically treated foreign mail only as well as they treated the much larger volume of domestic mail. It should, however, be noted that the International Bureau consulted regularly with many members about procedures and technologies that they might employ, and these deliberations did promote a certain raising of national postal standards. Since the 1980s and more particularly since the Hamburg Congress in 1984 there has been a more high-profile and coordinated effort to improve postal standards throughout the world since speed and reliability are crucial to protecting postal administrations' roles from incursions from private carriers. As a result of monitoring mail flows, recommendations to national authorities, and increased technical assistance, it appears that the UPU is having a little more influence on quality of service and hence the speed of delivery.[39]

The single norm in this policy sector that has evoked the largest volume of regulations is the technical and *procedural standardization norm*. There are a variety of regulations in the Universal Postal Convention and the Parcel Post Agreement that deal with packaging requirements, equipment to be used, and handling procedures for facilitating the movement of the mails. The requirements concerning equipment deal with matters such as their ability to read international coding symbols, and those pertinent to procedures often concern the interchange of mails at gateways (e.g. airports). These standards are often developed in cooperation with the International Standards Organization and International Air Transport Association – particularly in the ISO–UPU and IATA–UPU Contact Committees. For example, it was in negotiations within the ISO–UPU Contact Committee that accords on standardized sizes of letters and packages were reached in the 1960s. A tremendous number of the regulations that are developed at the UPU and its congresses deal simply with allowing the mails to be transferred among countries in the most expeditious manner. In terms of the overriding principles of the postal regime standardization activities serve both to expedite the flow of information and commerce and to lower the cost of postal services.[40]

A standardization problem that has emerged quite recently does not involve letters or parcels per se but the exchange of information on postal flows by electronic means (known as electronic data interchange or EDI). Its importance is highlighted in the comment that "Electronic messaging through EDI offers the greatest opportunity this century to the Post to serve its customers, streamline and modernize its operations, and handle efficiently the increasing quantities of mail we all wish to see."[41] The standardization work in this area is now centered in the UPU Electronic Transmission Standards Group, and its work has greatly facilitated the rapid flow of mail items.

One standardization issue that the UPU regularly reviews is customs procedures. One way that the UPU seeks to mitigate interference from customs is to make sure that all countries publicize those substances or materials that they prohibit. All countries are obligated to send this information to the International Bureau in Berne, and the latter then distributes it to member states.[42] In cooperation with the Customs Cooperation Council the UPU seeks to standardize and simplify customs regulations for the mails and to develop faster methods such as the use of telematics for customs clearance. These accords are developed through the CCC–UPU Contact Committee. The UPU also seeks to promote states' ratification of the International Convention for the Simplification and Harmonization of Customs Procedures. This convention has, in fact, not obtained a large number of ratifications because states are very reluctant to sacrifice traditional customs practices and absorb additional financial costs.[43]

In the area of technical and procedures barriers the UPU has been quite successful in assuring national treatment and standardization and has made modest progress in assuring minimum standards. In so doing it has promoted the free flow of information and commerce – and consequently a lowering of barriers to economic exchange, greater certainty of costs in international commerce, and lower transaction costs in negotiating accords. Both states' realization of mutual economic gains from such regulations and the progress of the UPU in developing effective guidelines for state behavior are palpable.

Prices and market shares

Those aspects of the international postal regime relating to prices, revenue, and market shares may appear to be more stable than comparable regime dimensions in the shipping, air transport, and telecommunications industries. The differences, however, are not as striking as many might think. Technological and economic trends have gradually been promoting changes in commercial practices and consequently the nature of the international postal regime since the 1970s, and more dramatic changes are quite likely to occur in the next decade.

The *cartel norm* has been moderately strong in the international postal industry until quite recently, but the cartel has gradually weakened since the 1970s. State postal administrations are not cooperating as they once did to manage rates, revenues, and market shares. The UPU has always had a significant influence on the fees that states charge each other for services, and until recently states supported market sharing and the primacy of foreign postal administrations within their own markets. On the other hand, states have seldom cooperated very effectively in regulating the rates that they charge senders of mail. The character of the century-old cartel is analyzed by first looking at the key reasons why states supported it and then focusing on the key policy issues: the setting of postal rates, the setting of fees for services performed by other countries and industries, and the control of competition for revenues and markets. It is in the context of this last issue that the recent decline of the old order is discussed.

There are two key justifications for the traditional intergovernmental postal cartel – first, that it supports the monopoly position of state postal administrations and hence facilitates states' control over their economies and, second, that it realizes efficiency gains because there are economies of scale in international as well as in domestic postal services. Turning to the first point, as early as the seventeenth century European states created postal monopolies in order to monitor international communications into and out of their countries and in order to raise revenues. Often the revenues from international postal services were used to subsidize domestic postal services.[44] Then, in the nineteenth century states became interested in using postal monopolies to promote economic development and national integration by offering their citizens (especially those from rural areas) regular and inexpensive postal services. To quote a recent publication, state postal administrations were seen as "a powerful element of national unity and political cohesion . . . a direct and indirect promoter of economic development and the essential prelude to the development of backward areas."[45] With governments' political commitment to maintain domestic postal monopolies and the desire of many states to raise revenues from international mail services it was logical that they would judge that an intergovernmental cartel for dividing the international market and setting rates, service charges, and a division of revenues was in their interests.

The second major argument in favor of an intergovernmental cartel has been the economies of scale or natural monopoly argument. In other words, it was judged economically wasteful to have two or more pick-up, sorting, transportation, and delivery systems when a single one could provide services at lower rates. This, of course, justified both domestic postal monopolies and an intergovernmental cartel since they promoted lower rates for consumers.[46]

One area where the intergovernmental network of postal administrations has had a very modest impact on commercial postal relations is with regard to the setting of international postal rates. There are a variety of reasons why the UPU has only had a minor impact on unifying and lowering rates, and chief among them is that states vary in both their costs and their policies concerning the raising of revenues from international postal flows. These differences among states began to have a marked impact after World War I, and then became more accentuated with decolonization of Asia and Africa after World War II.

Most UPU congresses have devoted a great deal of time to international postal rates. There has always been a lot of conflict over postal charges, but agreement has always been reached because ever since 1874 states have been given considerable flexibility in setting their actual charges above and below the specified target rates. And, in fact, the flexibility has increased recently. In 1960 states were allowed to set letter rates 60 percent above and 20 percent below the target rates; by 1974 it was 70 and 50 percent; and by 1984 it was 100 percent and 70 percent. In the 1989 Convention the range was excluded, and it was stated that the target figures are solely "for guidance purposes."[47] The problem at the moment in achieving any discipline on postal rates is that many developing countries want to continue to use international mail flows to raise revenue and many developed countries want to keep rates low so as to prevent incursions into the market from private carriers. Despite the variations in state practices UPU members do take the process of setting charges for different types of mail quite seriously since many states are influenced by UPU guidelines when setting their own postal rates. Some states, like Japan, automatically adopt UPU target rates.[48]

One aspect of the international postal market where postal administrations have been quite cooperative over the years concerns compensation for services – the setting of transit fees, terminal dues, and air and ship conveyance dues. Compensation, needless to say, is paid by states of origin that collect postal fees from senders. In the early years of the UPU there was a reasonable amount of conflict concerning transit fees, and some countries pressed for their abolition. The major transit states such as France blocked that move. Now the issue of transit rates is less important because most long-distance international mail is transported by air. In looking at UPU politics over the past century it is clear that member states have accepted that transit countries should be compensated for costs that they absorb. Criteria for calculating transit fees have been specified in UPU regulations, and they are followed very closely by most states.[49]

At the time of the 1874 conference that created the UPU, it was agreed that states of destination would not charge terminal fees for mail that they received and delivered. It was assumed that letters were sent and received in approximately equal numbers, and therefore it was not worth the transaction costs of figuring out the flows between pairs of states.[50] There were some challenges to this practice in the early twentieth century, but they were rebuffed. In the 1960s the developing countries mounted a concerted drive against the past system, and in 1969 they succeeded in obtaining acceptance of the prescription that states that receive a much larger volume of mail than they send should be compensated for their efforts. Over time developing countries have been the major beneficiaries from this rule because many of them "import" much more mail than they "export."[51] For example, in 1989 India dispatched 148 million pieces of mail to foreign states but received 621 million. Similarly, for Ghana the respective figures were 17 million and 67 million, and for Zambia 3 million and 12 million. What makes these patterns of mail flows especially burdensome is that in the case of developing countries foreign mail is sometimes around 20 percent of all mail delivered.[52] Since 1969 statistics on bilateral flows, which are based on the periodic weighing of mail bags, have been kept, and compensation by the big mail exporters to the big importers has been paid.

A three-nation study in 1984 indicated that the costs of delivering different types of mail varied quite a bit, and that the larger the items in a bag, the lower the total delivery costs. The cost of handling a bag of big parcels was the lowest; the cost of a bag of printed papers and small parcels was in the middle; and the cost of a bag of letters was the highest. Therefore, the report recommended that compensation to terminal states be tied to the type of item in a bag rather than being based simply on the weight of the bag.[53]

In 1989 a two-tier system of terminal fees was accepted whereby bags of letters and bags of newspapers and small parcels were assigned different rates if total mail flows between two countries exceeded 150 tonnes annually. The developed countries wanted a three-tier system whereby newspapers and small parcels would be separated from large parcels, but the developing countries, realizing that this would lower their revenues, opposed it. Some developed countries such as Canada and Japan that import more printed papers than they export also opposed the three-tier system. A major concern of many developed countries was that a joint rate for printed papers and parcels encourages remailing (discussed below) and diverts business for parcels to private carriers, but they did not prevail.[54] One reason that the developed countries judged that they could compromise without serious loss is that many have special terminal rates for mail between themselves, especially with those countries with whom they exchange the largest number of items. In fact, in the late 1980s most developed countries adopted a common system for determining terminal rates to take into account the large number of letters they were receiving as a percentage of their total incoming mail. This was done to reduce the large volume of remailing to their countries. What now exists is a bifurcated system whereby there is one system of terminal rates for mail flows among most developed countries and a different system for other mail flows.[55]

A particular component of the cost of international mail transport that the UPU has regulated with varied impact is the fees that states of origin pay international transport operators – particularly shipping lines and airlines. Until World War II states often used postal carriage contracts to subsidize their shipping fleets, and this led them to set UPU sea conveyance dues rather high. In the postwar period sea conveyance dues have declined in importance because of the dominance of air and ground conveyance, and states now seldom use mail carriage contracts to subsidize shipping fleets. The UPU sea conveyance dues are now used largely as rough guides for the negotiation of contracts between states and shipping lines since costs vary among routes and over time.[56]

Air conveyance dues have been established by the UPU since the interwar period, and for some time states viewed them as quite important for the well-being of their national airlines. Until the 1970s most states used air conveyance contracts to provide subsidies to their airlines, and therefore they were willing to accept rather high UPU rates. Developed countries now seldom use contracts for the carriage of airmail to subsidize national airlines, and in fact they now frequently utilize foreign airlines to carry their mail.[57]

Regardless of their desire to assist national airlines, postal administrations have long been concerned by the rates that the airlines have charged for transporting mail. In the 1920s the International Chamber of Commerce said that rates varied dramatically and that this situation was causing considerable confusion as well as affecting the competitive advantage of firms in different states. The UPU responded in 1927 by prescribing basic air conveyance dues, and the UPU has been involved in setting rates ever since then – presently after meetings of the IATA–UPU Contact Committee. Until 1974 the UPU rate levels generally provided very high profits to the airlines, but in that year they were lowered after a serious conflict between the postal administrations and the member airlines of IATA. Since then the UPU rate levels have generally reflected the preferences of the postal administrations. Today most developed and many developing countries bargain with individual airlines over rates for mail carriage, and the agreed rates are usually below UPU recommended rates. UPU rates are often applied to low volume mail of developing countries between foreign cities. In fact, the UPU rates provide valuable protection for developing countries in their bargaining with the airlines.[58]

There are a variety of guidelines to discourage competition for revenue and market shares that postal administrations have developed because of a concern to protect their national monopolies and the intergovernmental cartel. The guidelines that have been in existence for some time are that postal administrations (1) should not negotiate different transit rates with different foreign administrations; (2) should not vary rates according to the routeing of the mail; and, most importantly, (3) should not try to take business and revenue from other state administrations by interconnecting with private carriers.

The first injunction that a state should not alter its transit fees so as to encourage foreign postal administrations to ship mail through its territory was meant to discourage competition for transit business and also a spirit of competition in the industry. It used to be a moderately important rule when a high percentage of international mail traveled across countries by train and truck and when transportation costs were much higher. Now that a significant percentage of international mail is sent by air and transportation costs have fallen, transit dues are not very important. Compliance with the rule is not particularly good now, but because of the previously noted decline in significance of transit fees the lack of compliance does not pose a serious problem. A second anti-competition guideline that is related to the one concerning uniform transit fees is that states should not vary international postal rates depending on the route that letters and parcels travel. This is meant to discourage postal administrations from trying to get intermediary states to lower their transit dues and hence introducing a spirit of competition into the industry. Postal administrations tend to comply with it, but largely for reasons of administrative convenience.[59]

The third and central guideline for the international postal cartel is that postal administrations should not compete for mail and revenues with other administrations by interconnecting with private carriers. In order to understand how interconnection with private carriers and competition among postal administrations developed (especially with regard to "remailing" and government–private firm cooperation in courier services) it is necessary to start with two very important developments in 1969. In that year international courier companies began to emerge to meet the demands of business for the rapid shipment of letters, documents, and packages. Governments did not act to close down such intrusions into the domain of the postal administrations and, in fact, in 1971 the US and UK administrations launched a competitive expedited mail service (EMS). In other words, state postal administrations entered into competition with the private courier firms rather than try to close down the courier firms.[60] The other major development in 1969 was the introduction of terminal dues by the UPU – and very importantly, dues based on the weight of bags regardless of the contents (i.e. letters, small packages and newspapers, and large packages). Of course, a bag of letters costs a great deal more to deliver than a bag of packages. Therefore, states of destination generally were not paid adequate terminal dues to cover their cost of handling and delivering bags of letters, and they were paid very high dues for bags of non-letter items.

The growing recognition that international private mail services could make money, the terminal dues problem described above, and some very significant differences in international postal rates soon combined to create the significant problem of remailing which included competition for market shares and revenue among state postal administrations. Remailing refers to the posting of mail in a country other than the country of the sender, and it can assume several patterns. First, mail can be carried by a private carrier from one country to another and then sent via the public mail system back to the country of origin (ABA). This is traditionally the form of remailing that postal administrations most dislike. Second, it can be carried by private carriers from one country to another and then mailed to someone in the latter country (ABB). Third, it can be carried by private carrier from one country to another and then mailed there to a party in a third country (ABC). Needless to say, for remailing to be beneficial for senders the cost of transportation via a private firm from A to B plus the postal charge in B must be less than the postal rate they would have to pay in their home country. For it to be beneficial for the B state it must receive more in postal charges than it has to pay out in terminal dues to the state of destination.

What private remailing companies soon realized was that there were a good number of countries in the world that had very low international rates, and therefore they could take bulk mail from one country and post it in the country with low rates – saving money for the sender and making money itself. In fact, the remailing company and the B state generally made more money if the bags just included lettermail since more money could be collected from senders for a large number of letter items and since the terminal dues paid to the state of destination were the same regardless of the type of item in the bag. After a while postal administrations (largely but not exclusively in the Third World) began to give remailing companies special rates for posting mail in their countries. Some postal administrations, in fact, send officials into foreign states to offer special deals to firms that mail large numbers of letters to their country. They say that if the firms contract with a remailing firm to have their mail sent to a post office in their country, they will offer rates at a certain percentage below their normal domestic rate. Both the US and Canadian postal administrations conduct such activities in the other country, and there are a good number of other postal administrations that do the same.[61]

Certain efforts have been made to stem remailing and hence competition among postal administrations, but they have by no means put a stop either to the practice or more broadly the willingness of administrations to take market shares and revenue from each other. In 1979 the UPU Congress gave states of destination the right to return mail that was remailed, but they have seldom done this. In 1988 the Conference of European Post and Telecommunications (CEPT) approved a set of terminal dues that differentiates between types of mail and assures that terminal dues provide reasonable compensation for the handling and delivery work of states of destination. Most developed countries follow this dues schedule with regard to mail flows amongst themselves, but it does not cover mail between developed and developing countries. In 1989 the developed countries were able to secure the approval of the UPU Congress for a two-tier dues schedule for terminal dues for all mail volumes above 150 tonnes annually between two states. This was meant to eliminate the largest flows of remailed items from Third World states since it would assure reasonable compensation to states of destination for their delivery of letters. However, since this new UPU schedule of terminal dues has come into effect in 1991, the remailing firms have skirted the rules by distributing their remailing among a larger number of countries. Once the annual flow of mail from one country to another reaches 150,000 tonnes a year, they move to another country. The developed countries are seeking a new UPU system of terminal dues at the 1994 Congress that will allow them to impose different terminal dues on bulk mail regardless of the volume of mail between two states and, if accepted, it could curtail remailing to a significant degree.[62] It is important to stress that with a few exceptions the postal administrations of states from which the remailing is occurring are cooperating explicitly or implicitly with the remailing firms – with the deliberate intention of taking market shares and revenues from the administrations of origin and destination. To quote a German official: "Remailing changes the world postal system. It injects competition into a system traditionally governed by monopoly and cooperation."[63]

Another development that has introduced an important dimension of competition into the international postal world is the formation of a joint venture between five national postal administrations and a major international courier firm, TNT, in 1992. As a prelude to describing this venture it is necessary to note that a good number of the postal administrations developed a courier network between themselves (generally referred to as expedited mail service or EMS) in the 1970s and 1980s, but they were only able to make a dent in the market share of the private companies because the quality of the pickup and delivery service in some countries was poor. Therefore, private firms tended to avoid the state postal administrations when they needed priority service. A good example of how marginalized the postal administrations became with regard to priority mail is that in the early 1990s the US Postal Service only had a 7 percent share of the US market.[64] In 1988 the postal administrations of most developed countries formed the International Postal Corporation to try to improve the priority mail network of the state postal administrations, but it did not have a major impact. After several years the postal administrations of Canada, France, Germany, the Netherlands, and Sweden judged that the only way they were going to secure good end-to-end capabilities throughout the world was to go into a joint venture with a private courier company. This venture with the courier company TNT is called GD Express Worldwide (GDEW).[65] A number of other postal administrations, as well as the UPU Director-General, have been very upset by GDEW which is competing with other postal administrations within their own territories (e.g. GDEW delivers and picks up priority mail in Japan in competition with the Japanese post office). However, their attempts to have GDEW disbanded have not succeeded to date.

The traditional role of the UPU in managing international postal rates and market shares is now under considerable strain as a result of "the near revolutionary changes in the delivery market over the past two decades."[66] It is quite possible that the international network of state postal administrations could disintegrate within a decade under the force of several developments.

First, international courier services have grown rapidly over the past two decades, and while they occupy a rather small segment of the market, it is a very lucrative segment and it may be the "thin edge of the wedge" in expanding the role of private carriers. After noting that courier services still account for a small percentage of all mail items, a Canadian postal official remarked: "when one looks at the high unit prices that can be demanded in the market place, and the high profit margins that can be achieved, one realizes that an effective competitor in the courier market can quickly accumulate the capital to invest in more effective competition on a grander scale."[67] If private carriers gain acceptance from commercial and political authorities of a particular market niche, other concessions could follow. The five-nation joint venture in courier services with TNT could increase these postal administrations' share of the courier market, but in this case the postal administrations have been brought into the commercial world to a greater extent than the commercial world has been brought into the intergovernmental world. The joint venture is likely to promote a general acceptance of competition among postal administrations. It is also important to recall that some states are cooperating with private carriers involved in remailing, and in so doing they undercut the business of other postal administrations.

Second, new forms of international communications have developed that are challenging traditional postal services – particularly e-mail. As one author notes: "There is . . . enormous potential for new technology (the 'electronic letter') to make the traditional mail monopoly ineffective. The advent of this competition introduces a new element into the politics of the post as it seems to give the postal service a vested interest in meaningful reform – *unless* it seizes the opportunity to extend its monopoly to cover electronic mail."[68] While over a dozen postal administrations have started their own e-mail services,[69] they are not going to dominate the service. And given that one study has projected that up to one-half of all mail could someday be sent via e-mail,[70] the long-term threat is very real.

Third, economists are increasingly pointing out that the traditional justification of postal monopolies – namely, the existence of economies of scale – is not valid or is only valid for sparse local networks. Also, other economists are stating that even if economies of scale exist, it is not desirable for governments to allow state monopolies and inter-governmental cartels because they will not act efficiently without some competition. Some economists point out that if postal monopolies have a valid justification, it is a political one – namely, they cross-subsidize certain activities with the revenues from other activities (for example, the revenues from urban services to subsidize rural ones or from international services to subsidize national ones).[71] Economists are not particularly sympathetic to arguments about the existence of economies of scale in postal services, cross-subsidizations, or postal administrations' condemnations of "cream-skimming" by new entrants in the market. One author stated that "virtually no evidence suggests postal services enjoy significant economies of scale," and "The notion that a natural monopoly should *require* legal barriers against competitors in order to survive is equally absurd."[72] While academic economists may be disdainful of postal monopolies and may believe that rural areas will receive reliable and reasonable service in a purely competitive environment, politicians often disagree with these views. They are sensitive to political pressures from rural areas, and they are likely to support postal monopolies for regular mail services – at least in the medium term. In the longer term the prospect for the lettermail monopolies may not be very favorable.

The extent to which public thinking on this issue is evolving is indicated by a recent editorial in the leading Canadian newspaper, the *Globe and Mail*:

> A competitive postal service may strike some readers as a new and
> bizarre idea. In truth it is neither. Letter delivery is not a "natural
> monopoly." The surest proof of this is the statute itself. The post
> office has remained a monopoly around the world only by the most
> ruthless suppression of attempts to defy it . . . The key argument
> against removing the monopoly unconditionally is that competition
> would mean an end to universal service at universal rates. Charging
> everyone the same price for a letter, regardless of cost, is a form of

cross-subsidization . . . There is a compelling social basis for redistribution from rich to poor; no such argument applies to redistribution
from town to country.[73]

It is virtually inconceivable that this 1991 editorial would have been
written even back in the mid-1980s. The nature of the public policy
dialogue on postal services is changing dramatically.

Postal administrations have gradually responded to technological
and commercial changes in international communications. Some
Western governments have separated the regulatory and operational
functions of their postal services and have also made their administrations responsible for their financial viability.[74] As a part of this
general strategy, there is also a movement in many postal administrations to eliminate cross-subsidizations among services and to charge
clientele at cost. [75]A large number have developed priority service and
facsimile service and, as noted, a modest number are offering e-mail.[76]

At the UPU level some important changes have occurred since
the 1984 Congress and its approval of the Hamburg Declaration. The
essence of this Declaration was that the UPU was going to undertake a
concerted effort to get states to improve the quality of their postal
services and was going to establish service standards and monitor
states' activities. For the first time it appeared that postal administrations were "running scared" as a result of the increasing roles of
courier services and new electronic forms of communication. In
addition, the Congress gave the Executive Council greater leeway in
revising the conventions and detailed regulations between its sessions
every five years. (This leeway was expanded yet again at the 1989
Congress.)[77] One of the impressive things about the new attitudes of
many postal authorities is the recognition that the competition has
grown because of their own failures. As the Assistant Director-General
of the UPU remarked: "The setbacks are mainly due to the inadequate
quality of the postal service and to its inability to detect new customer
requirements sufficiently early and address them promptly."[78] This
same official was quite open to having the UPU withdraw from
establishing price ranges for postal rates in order to promote greater
competitiveness among postal administrations. In fact, with the UPU's
recommendation of rates solely "for guidance purposes" at the 1989
Congress it has moved decisively in this direction.

The momentum toward change within the UPU that started with the
Hamburg Congress continued at the Washington Congress in 1989.

Indicative of the new approach was the approval of the "permanent project . . . to modernize the international postal service" as well as an absence of regulations concerning priority and e-mail (hence allowing postal administrations to try to compete with private firms).[79] The output of the Congress as well as subsequent developments indicate that the UPU is definitely moving in the direction of giving postal administrations more commercial freedom, although postal administrations will fight to maintain monopoly control of regular lettermail service.[80] An indication of the sense of threat that exists as well as the pessimism that some officials feel was a comment by the UPU Deputy Director-General: "Although an optimist by nature, I must admit that some observations made in the field have me somewhat worried: indeed the Post seems to me to be on the decline, to the point of disappearance in many countries. Hence the special, even vital, need for urgent and vigorous action by the administrations – which in the last resort are responsible for their own future."[81]

The intergovernmental cartel that has dominated international postal services for over a century is still reasonably strong in non-priority lettermail service, but in package, priority, and electronic services there is increasing acceptance of competitive international markets. Once private firms acquired prominent positions in the priority mail and electronic services markets and governments refused to protect the monopoly positions of postal administrations, there was very little prospect that the UPU could extend the cartel into these realms. Now the issue is whether competition will spread into traditional postal service areas and the cartel will further lose its authority. The recent launching of the five-state/TNT joint venture in priority mail and the termination of the lettermail monopolies of the postal administrations in Argentina and Sweden may be signs of future trends. Also, studies that point to the absence of economies of scale in postal services and which posit that postal services are presently not important for national integration could seriously undercut political support for the old national monopolies and the intergovernmental cartel.[82]

The traditional postal regime relating to prices and market shares had at its heart, first, a tacit accord that postal administrations should only interconnect with other postal administrations (a *de facto* market sharing system) and, second, agreements on "reasonable" service charges that transit and terminal states had to pay to states of origin. Of some importance have been UPU guidelines on air conveyance rates and formerly ship conveyance rates. There have, however, only been very loose strictures on the postal rates that states could charge their own nationals. The regime has been based on concerns to facilitate commerce and to keep interstate financial obligations reasonably close to cost, but it has also been based on the right of states to enhance their own revenues by charging their nationals and businesses above cost. This latter policy approach is increasingly being challenged.

A variety of factors have acted to erode the economic and political mutualities of interest that sustained the traditional cartel regime. Particularly in the developed world the maintenance of state monopolies over all postal services is not regarded as politically important as it once was because governments recognize that private firms can provide key services to the entire population at reasonable rates. If they conclude that private firms can provide regular lettermail to all segments of the population at politically acceptable prices, the state postal administrations are likely to disappear. Also, the economic rationale for national postal monopolies over domestic and international mails is being gradually undermined. An increasing number of economists and state officials reject the existence of economies of scale in postal services.

In the short run postal administrations will tend to limit interconnections in regular mail services to other state postal monopolies except for some limited cooperation with remailing firms. However, this form of intergovernmental collaboration will probably not last very long. It is probably the case that the five-nation joint venture with TNT in courier services is the thin end of the wedge in states' acceptance of new forms of international competition. The next big change is likely to be allowing private postal firms into regular mail delivery and then allowing them to interconnect internationally with each other – as has recently occurred in Argentina and Sweden. To what extent the ongoing developments are a product of a decline in the value that states attach to governmental and national control over the national postal industry and to what extent they are a product of changing judgments of national economic interests is difficult to say. Both factors appear to be playing a role.

Conclusion

The international postal regime has been quite stable for over a century, and even now it is only in the area of prices and market shares that some important changes are occurring. In the cases of jurisdictional rights, damage control problems, and technical and procedural barriers, the long-standing regime norms give a high priority to the principles concerning the free flow of information, free movement of commerce, and economic efficiency while at the same time recognizing states' right to control the flow of information and the quality of services in their own societies. While most states have occasionally interrupted transit mail for political or security reasons, it has not occurred often. Overall the norms and implementing rules in the three policy sectors of jurisdictional rights, damage control problems, and technical barriers are likely to remain strong because of states' concerns to reduce impediments to the flow of commerce, uncertainty of costs, and transaction costs.

With regard to prices and market shares there was until quite recently a strong consensus on an intergovernmental cartel for all postal services, and to a significant extent it still prevails for lettermail services. The only significant weakness of the traditional cartel regime prior to the 1970s was that states did not agree on the postal rates that states of origin should charge. What have begun to undermine the dominance of state postal administrations domestically and the cartel arrangements internationally are new means of communication, the emergence of private delivery services, and a greater acceptance of international economic competition. With the expansion of alternative means of international communication pressure has developed on postal administrations to become more competitive, and this has meant that the old disciplines are breaking down. There is little accord on rules of the game in the areas of priority mail and e-mail, and there is unlikely to be additional cooperation since alternative carriers have secure places in the market. Also, some postal administrations are finding it quite lucrative to work with courier services in remailing large volumes of mail, and they are encouraging a more open competitive environment which may someday promote their demise. One important official has, in fact, declared that postal administrations are fighting a losing battle and that "The international mail market will be open for full competition."[83]

The traditional support for state monopolies and an intergovernmental cartel was based significantly on states' mutual interest in maintaining control over an industry that was viewed as crucial to their ability to shape national economic and political developments. In the case of the developed countries this perception is fading because of the virtual achievement of universality in postal service, the development of competitive services and alternative carriers, the rejection of natural monopoly arguments, a growing faith in market forces, and probably a declining valuation of state autonomy in this sector. Future international postal regulations concerning prices and market shares may be confined to some accords on transit and terminal fees.

In concluding this brief analysis of the factors that sustained and still sustain a vast body of UPU regulations, particular note should be paid to states' interest in reducing the transaction costs attendant on the regulation of the international postal industry. A major motivation for the establishment of the UPU commercial regulations in 1874 was to lessen the transaction costs attendant on the multiplicity of accords and standards. At that time Germany had seventeen different postal agreements, France sixteen, and Great Britain twelve. Also, there were three different units of weight, and rates often differed by route. A US Postmaster-General in the 1860s commented that "the complicated accounts necessary to be kept with the several foreign countries with whom we had postal treaty relations, and each of which had to be credited with its portion of the sum prepaid on each article (not on the aggregate weight of the mails), and the minute details required to be entered in the Letter Bill sent with each mail, are almost beyond belief."[84] It cannot be overstressed that crucial motivations for the development of international postal regulations have been and still are the mitigation of the transaction costs and in addition the reduction of uncertainty of costs caused by a patchwork pattern of bilateral or minilateral accords. On the other hand, as the above analysis indicates, at least with regard to prices and market shares, conflicting economic interests in regulation have come to dominate past perceptions of mutual interests in uniform international rules.

7   Normative continuities and international regime theory

The descriptive focuses of this study are the norms of the four international regimes and their strength. The explanatory focuses are the assertions that mutual interests among states have sustained the four regimes and that these economic and political mutual interests are generated by the existence of "market failures" and certain conditions that impinge on the autonomy of all or most states. At a theoretical level the book generally supports a neoliberal perspective that mutual interests can form the basis of important international regimes, but it also stresses that neorealists have overlooked the possibility that regime norms based on the protection of state policy autonomy may be quite compatible with its assumptions and its views on obstacles to cooperation.

This concluding chapter first looks at the norms, the principles that they promote, and the conditions that generated mutual interests in the norms in the four policy sectors (jurisdictional rights, damage control problems, technical and procedural barriers, and prices and market shares). It then turns to general indicators of the importance of mutual interests to regime development and general theoretical perspectives on international cooperation.

Similarities in norms across the four industry regimes

There have been significant similarities in the norms governing international shipping, air transport, telecommunications, and postal services. This should not surprise us since they are all international service or infrastructure industries on which other international industries depend. The efficient operation of the entire global economy

212

depends on them. To use a biological analogy, transportation and communications industries are the arteries that carry goods and information throughout the body of the global economy and keep it alive. The norms and rules of the four industrial regimes constitute the genetic programs that assure the orderly and efficient flow of goods and communications throughout the arteries of the economic body. Without at least some norms and rules the economic body would die.

Jurisdictional rights

There are three jurisdictional norms that cut across all four international issue areas that this book has examined. They are states' right of free access to international space, their right of innocent passage through other states' sovereign jurisdictional spheres, and their right to exclude foreign services and firms from their sovereign territories. There has been little dispute over access to international spaces, and the same is basically the case concerning control by states over entry of foreign commercial services and firms into their sovereign territories, air space, adjacent inland waters, and territorial sea. The one issue area where there is some conflict over sovereign control of "foreign intrusions" concerns telecommunication transmissions into national airspace. Some states (especially those in the West) believe that states must give significant weight to the principle of the free flow of communications and permit reception of communications except under very threatening circumstances. Most countries (particularly developing countries), however, accept that states have a residual right to block communications if they think that important values are at stake.

There is some question concerning the strength of the norm of the right of innocent passage in some of the four issue areas, but a strong case can be made for its existence in all four. The norm basically stipulates that states must allow transit of carriers and communications *through* their areas of sovereign authority unless there is an immediate threat to their peace, good order, and security. It is most clearly accepted in the case of the law of the sea, but in varying degrees it is embedded in the regimes for the other three international services as well. In the case of air transport a majority of states accept the right of foreign aircraft to overfly their territories to shorten flying distances and to land for "technical" reasons. Most countries that reject the Air Transit Agreement do so because they want to use overflight rights in bargaining over the terms of bilateral accords. They do not in principle oppose flights over their territories by foreign aircraft. Concerning telecommunications most states do not interfere with transmissions passing through their air space unless they believe that citizen reception of such transmissions constitutes a serious political threat. The case of postal services is quite similar to telecommunications since states are committed not to interfere with foreign mail in transit unless they suspect that mail envelopes and packages carry goods forbidden by UPU regulations or they perceive a serious political threat (usually only in war time). The strength of the innocent passage norm in the four issue areas varies, but it is reasonably strong in all of them.

The two principles or values on which the jurisdictional norms are most clearly based are the desirability of state policy autonomy and the free flow of commerce. These principles have conflicting implications for certain policy issues that require either the preeminence of one or a tradeoff between them. State autonomy is, of course, promoted by the norms pertaining to the right to exclude foreign firms and services and the right to interrupt innocent passage if the carriers or messages threaten the peace, good order, and security of the state. The importance of the right of states to prevent foreign transportation and communications firms from entering their territories needs to be high-lighted because it provides the great majority of small and medium states with leverage in maintaining control of their own economies and protecting national firms. This point was made clearly in one analysis of the international air transport regime:

> the adoption of the principle of sovereignty may have placed the international community irrevocably on the path of seeking an inter-national legal framework for aviation which would be acceptable to both large and small states alike. A regime based on freedom of the skies might have facilitated unfettered unilateral action and a "power oriented approach" to international aviation, an approach that in the end would have benefited the large states and those with substantial aviation capacity at the expense of the small.[1]

In fact, states are more concerned about maintaining control over entry of foreign services than they are with regard to entry of manufactured goods because market access for services generally involves the right of foreign companies to establish subsidiaries and to enter into open competition with national firms. This, of course, is anathema to states that want to assure certain market shares for national firms.

While the jurisdictional norms do provide some protection for state

214

Table 7.1 *Main norms of the regimes for international service industries*

Norms	International industries			
	Shipping	Air transport	Telecommuni-cations	Postal services
Jurisdictional rights				
Open access to international space	Strong	Strong	Strong (with limited planning)	–
Innocent passage	Strong	Strong	Strong (with limited planning)	Strong
Exclusion of foreign firms and services	Strong	Moderately strong	Moderately strong (weakening on transmissions)	Strong
Damage control				
Accident prevention	Strong	Strong	Strong	Strong (mail and handlers)
Crime prevention	Moderately strong	Moderately strong	Medium	Strong
Pollution prevention	Moderately strong	Moderately strong	–	–
Reasonable compensation	Strong	Strong	–	Moderately strong
Technical and procedural barriers				
Technical interconnection	Strong	Strong	Strong	Strong
Facilitation	Moderately strong	Moderately strong	–	Moderately strong
Prices and market shares				
Cartel	Moderately strong to 1970s	Moderately strong to late 1970s	Moderately strong to 1970s	Moderately strong until 1980s; gradually weakening
Limited competition	Moderately strong to 1970s	Weak (growing support for competition)	Weak (growing support for competition)	Weak (except courier)

Note: Some of the norms for the telecommunications and postal services regimes have different titles to those of the shipping and air transport regimes, but the purposes are basically the same. In *telecommunications* there is "qualified open access" to international and national air spaces, instead of "open access" and "innocent passage." "Qualified" is inserted because of the obligation to accept certain forms of international planning. Also, in the telecommunications regime the "prior use" and "necessary planning" norms both concern "accident prevention," and the "restricted intentional interference" norm is basically equivalent to the "crime prevention" norm. In *postal services* the "within-state carriage" and "internal surveillance" norms both concern "the right to exclude foreign firms and services"; and the "mail protection" and "mail handler protection" norms both concern "accident protection." The "standardization" norm concerns both "technical interconnection" and "facilitation"; but the "national treatment" and "minimum standard" norms also concern "facilitation."

autonomy, their major impact is to promote the flow of international commerce and hence economic welfare. For private firms the global regimes reduce uncertainty as to what laws (national or international) must be obeyed, and for governments they reduce the transaction costs of having to negotiate jurisdictional agreements on a bilateral or mini-lateral basis.[2] To quote an international legal scholar:

> First. . . the law delimits the governmental and jurisdictional com-petence of States and thus provides the elementary basis for orderly living. Without the concepts of land boundaries, of maritime zones and delimitation of peripheral zones of jurisdiction and superadjacent airspace, the incidence of collisions between States and the danger which results from uncertainty . . . would increase greatly.[3]

By establishing that most of ocean space and the air space above it are common property resources open to all states, the jurisdictional norms also create pressures for developing one set of regulations for both international and national air and ocean space, and such uniform regulations reduce financial impediments to the flow of international commerce. There is, needless to say, a proclivity to have one set of regulations for international and national zones. Concerning this point Morton Kaplan and Nicholas Katzenbach commented that "it is administratively desirable to have the greatest amount of uniformity with regard to international problems, and it is complicated to administer a number of special legal regimes with substantially the same subject matter."[4]

In concluding this section on jurisdictional norms it is valuable to recall a statement by Ruth Lapidoth concerning the law of the sea: "the freedom of the high seas is not a self-contained legal principle, but is ancillary to and dependent upon another norm – the right to commerce and communication."[5] This statement can be applied equally well to the norms of open access to international space and innocent passage through territorial space for all four international service industries. The central thrust of these norms is keeping open the arteries of international commerce.

Damage control

There are great similarities among the norms concerned with damage control although the actual titles given to the norms vary somewhat. In particular, they focus on the prevention of accidents, crime, and pollution and compensation to those who suffer losses. The four regimes are quite strong with regard to prevention of accidents, crime, and to a lesser extent pollution, and moderately strong with respect to liability and compensation. In the case of the promotion of compliance with regime rules, the key weaknesses are that states will not accept particular penalties for certain crimes and that there are no institutionalized ways of exerting pressure on states that do not prosecute offenders. However, states are sufficiently active in sharing information, monitoring compliance, and prosecuting parties on their own initiative that commercial parties are generally deterred from flaunting international rules relating to damage control. Overall, the norms relating to damage control are quite robust and were developed to facilitate the free flow of commerce; but, as noted above, there are certain weaknesses that are derived from states' concern to protect an important element of state independence – namely, the autonomy of their criminal justice systems.

The extensive damage control regulations promote international commerce and hence the economic welfare of states because they correct a number of market failures. The regulations enhance greater certainty of costs and reduce barriers to international transportation and communications by reducing the frequency and scale of financial losses and the likelihood that states will legislate a patchwork pattern of national rules. Relevant to states' inclination to develop rules to prevent unexpected losses in international commerce is the evaluation that "Trade automatically creates pressure for codes of conduct that facilitate the process of exchange and protect those engaged in it. Without some assurances of security, trading activity would be severely restricted, or even extinguished, by piracy, theft or excess taxation."[6]

The development of multilateral regulations for damage control also saves money for both private firms and governments by reducing their transaction costs. If firms are subject to one set of international laws rather than a patchwork pattern of national regulations, their costs in negotiating contracts are reduced and, of course, in the case of governments they save money if they can negotiate a single set of international regulations rather than a series of bilateral and minilateral ones. A simple, but very important point, is that "Both general law and particular agreements avoid the need for negotiating anew in every new instance."[7] Multilateral regulations also remove important impediments to the flow of goods and services in the form of multiple national

217

or international regulations. Uniformity of rules is a great facilitator of commerce. A final benefit relevant particularly to pollution control is that regulation promotes economic efficiency by reducing negative externalities. In economics terminology regimes internalize the costs in requiring that the perpetrators of the damages take preventative measures and compensate foreign injured parties.

Technical and procedural barriers

In all four international infrastructure industries there has been a strong norm in favor of assuring technical interconnection among national industries and a reasonably strong norm for facilitating the flow of goods, services, and carriers when they reach their countries of destination. Technical standards and administrative procedures are sometimes used for protectionist purposes, but they are not used in this manner when they might jeopardize interconnection or major blockages in the movement of goods and services. All states have an interest in making international commerce possible, and they realize that impeding or seriously slowing down commercial exchanges could be counterproductive.

In the international shipping industry there is an extensive convention concerned with facilitation, and one of the annexes attached to the Convention of the International Civil Aviation Organization is concerned with the same issue. The matter is taken very seriously in the air transport industry because airlines know that the public's use of air transportation is affected by the speed of transit through airports. There are many more technical standards facilitating interconnection in air transport than in shipping, but in shipping there are important regulations relating to the size and movement of containers. In the international postal area there are also quite extensive UPU regulations that are concerned with the efficient shipment of mail through transit states and into terminal states (e.g. requirements for mail bags, packages, and sorting equipment). Probably in no international industry are technical interconnection standards more important than in telecommunications. In recent decades the growth of international telecommunications has required extensive standardization among national networks and terminal equipment as well as at gateways because of the dramatic changes in technology. Countries often find ways of protecting national equipment manufacturers by legislating certain national technical standards, but they do not do it at the cost of international interconnection. This is especially the case with regard to those devices that are used by international businesses (e.g. telephones) as opposed to those forms of equipment that are consumer end-products (e.g. television sets). The major failures in standard-setting have largely concerned consumer products such as television sets and videotext because the absence of accords, while imposing high prices on consumers does not block the flow of international communications among commercial firms. Business firms, for example, would not tolerate blockages in the international telephone network.

The norms and rules relating to technical interconnection and facilitation of transit are, of course, designed to promote the principle of the free movement of commerce. From the perspective of correcting market failures the regulations reduce impediments to the flow of factors of production, but they also reduce cost uncertainty and trans-action costs. If states know that technical systems will interconnect and that the movement of goods, information, and people will be expeditious at points of "landing," they will be more certain of their costs. In addition, if they can negotiate one multilateral agreement rather than many accords with different states, they reduce their transaction costs and uncertainty of costs. As Gilbert Winham argues, the reduction of uncertainty is perhaps the central motive for the many types of international trade regulation:

> What is the role of international trade agreements in the modern nation-state system? The answer is to reduce protectionist national regulation, but even more important to reduce the uncertainty and unpredictability of the international trade regime, and to promote stability.[8]

To rephrase this point, international regimes relevant to international commerce are based centrally on the importance of *order* – or the creation of a predictable environment in which business can operate. That this occurs at the international level should not be surprising since a large amount of a state's domestic legislation is aimed at providing a similar orderly environment within its national market.

Prices and market shares

Until very recently an important pillar of the international cartels in the air transport, postal, and telecommunications regimes was that they enhanced states' control of their economies. States wanted this control because these industries had widespread effects on their societies, their international revenues subsidized domestic networks, and their ownership by nationals was seen as an attribute of independent statehood. In fact, there was a general assumption in most publics that any self-respecting nation owned and controlled its air transport, telecommunications, and postal industries. Until very recently almost all countries in the world had government-owned airlines, telecommunications administrations, and postal administrations, and a majority still do have government-owned monopolies in these areas.

The intergovernmental cartels were also sustained by perceptions that they would enhance economic welfare because the industries constituted natural monopolies (air transport being an exception, although fears of "destructive competition" were mentioned occasionally). It was certainly assumed that economies of scale existed for domestic telecommunications and postal services, and no one basically questioned whether any other system than an intergovernmental cartel would be the best arrangement for interconnecting these national systems. In the case of shipping, the cartels of private firms (or shipping conferences) were viewed as the most economic way of providing regular and reliable service among the vast number of ports around the world. There was a fear that if competition were allowed to take its course, the periodic demise of firms would lead to interruptions of service as well as the emergence of monopolists on different routes. What eventually undermined the international cartels was a combination of technological change, academic studies decrying the economic costs of monopolies and cartels, a growing acceptance of "deregulated" markets, and pressure from certain countries (particularly the USA).

One of the leading students of regulation, Stephen Breyer, recently analyzed regulatory and deregulatory trends in a number of industries. His comments are relevant to this analysis.

> The "price and entry" regulation of airlines, trucking, and ocean shipping was often justified by the asserted need to control "excessive" competition – competition that allegedly would lead to unreasonably low prices, bankruptcies, and the survival of one or two firms, which would then set unreasonably high prices . . . Most economists [now] doubt that firms can readily set predatory prices in the transportation industry.
>
> They [reformers in the telecommunications field] lost confidence that "natural monopoly" – the market defect that allegedly required

regulation – in fact existed in these markets. They thought that both the telephone equipment manufacturing industry and the long-distance telecommunications service industry were large enough to support not just one, but several, competing firms of efficient size.[9]

There is sometimes a tendency to look back to the era when inter-governmental and interfirm cartels dominated the industries in question and attribute the arrangements to the self-serving motives of governments and officials that controlled these industries, but there was, in fact, a prevalent belief in the existence of economies of scale and the prospects of destructive competition.[10] The fear of destructive competition related not just to the likelihood of high prices imposed by the surviving firm, but also to periodic interruptions in the flow of commerce created by the financial collapse of firms. This issue came out particularly in the case of shipping which is responsible for the transportation of most traded goods.

An issue that is very important for the theoretical analysis in this study is why the cartels in the four industries have been disintegrating since the late 1970s. It is clear that a small number of countries realized that their economic interests would be better served by competitive markets, and their support for competitive practices fractured inter-national commercial relations into several systems. In the case of shipping it was the innovative and efficient East Asian firms that were more responsible than any other commercial actors for undermining the shipping conferences or cartels. As these East Asian companies began to expand their operations in the 1970s and as the shipping conferences gradually saw their shares of liner shipping markets and their control of rates decline, most countries soon indicated that they would go along with the commercial changes that new technologies and more efficient shipping firms made possible. To a significant extent a broad consensus has gradually developed in favor of reasonably open competition on most routes and the control by shipping conferences of a modest number of routes. Of course, there has always been an open competitive regime for bulk trades since a competitive market did not threaten disruption in service.

With regard to postal services there seems to be quite a similar development toward a broad acceptance of competitive practices in courier and electronic services and a retention of national monopolies and weak international cartel arrangements for most letter and small parcel mail. There are, however, growing strains on the relationships

among state postal administrations as a result of certain administrations' attempts to take business from each other (e.g. remailing and
the emergence of government/private courier firms), differences
among states in their insistence that postal administrations operate
according to commercial competitive criteria, and the growing inroads
of private postal enterprises. Therefore, postal services could follow
close behind shipping, air transport, and telecommunications
services in the implementation of greater international commercial
competition.

In both the international air transport and telecommunications
industries the international cartels were undermined in part by the
challenges by the USA, although in the former case the USA had some
Asian allies from the start. The USA was able to use its leverage to
pressure some foreign states into competitive arrangements, and its
example also encouraged some other states to follow. At the moment
the world is fractured into groupings of states that pursue different
practices, but the trend is definitely toward more open competition in
international telecommunications and air transport. While these trends
over the last two decades can be attributed in part to the policies of
the USA and a few other states, a stronger case can be made that the
fracturing of the cartels and the introduction of competition were
wrought largely by technological changes and that the USA and a few
other countries followed a course that others would have eventually
adopted on their own. The most important impacts of technological
change were that it created alternative means of transportation and
communication services that competed with each other and also
spawned a rapidly changing commercial environment that governments found difficult to regulate. It is difficult to prove that technological transformation as opposed to US pressure was the crucial source
of regime change in telecommunications and air transport since we
cannot know what others would have done without the leads of the
USA and a number of other states. However, it is hard to imagine that
the multiplication of modes of communication and transportation, their
increasing importance to business, and growing support for deregulation would not have driven these international industries down the
road of more open competition in the late twentieth and early twenty-
first centuries.

There has been a remarkable amount of similarity among the norms
in the four policy sectors of the four international service industries. It
is interesting that in the one sector (prices and market shares) in which

there has been a real decline in the strength of the core norm (the cartel norm), the serious weakening started at approximately the same time in all four industries – between the late 1970s and the mid-1980s. Technological change that increased modes of transportation and communication and a greater willingness in many countries to support "deregulation" were fundamental to the weakening of the cartels.

The norms of the four regimes are grounded in states' support for a number of principles, but at the heart of most of the norms is the concern to promote the free movement of international commerce. The norms of the regime do not mandate that commerce take place, but they keep the door open for international transactions. The one principle that rivals in importance the free movement of commerce within the four regimes is internal policy control or the right of states to control activities within or immediately adjacent to their territories. It has greatly influenced the norms relating to jurisdictional rights and to prices and market shares. However, in the area of prices and market shares the long-standing cartel norm has recently declined in importance, and the question as to why this has happened has implications for our understanding of international political change. In essence, states have moved away from their insistence on state control over these industries (and particularly their international dimensions) and have been more open to competitive market forces and the growth of international interdependencies. Robert Jackson has commented that "Historical change often is marked by a change of principled beliefs and the institutions that embody them."[11] It is quite possible that we are witnessing such a historical change in principled beliefs concerning the management of economic and political affairs, and it is having an impact on international institutions. Such a development supports a liberal theoretical notion of how the world is evolving.

The hypotheses that were presented in the first chapter have been corroborated by the subsequent empirical chapters. The existence of market failures and certain conditions affecting state autonomy have promoted international regulations with particular normative thrusts. A "functional" approach to understanding the content and strength of international regimes does appear to offer considerable insights into the dynamics of international cooperation.

Mutual interests and international relations theory

The central assertion of this book is that mutual interests among states provide the bases for the development of many important international regimes. The *importance of mutual interests is,* first of all, supported by the fact that most of the regime norms have been quite stable over approximately a century during which time there have been some dramatic changes in international power relations and axes of conflict. While aspects of the regimes were certainly disrupted during the world wars, the norms have had tremendous breadth of support and continuity of normative content over the twentieth century. Politically hostile powers have been very supportive, as is clear from the support of most norms by the Western and Soviet bloc countries during the post-1945 era. Also, there is little evidence that the powerful states had to apply sanctions to gain acceptance of the basic parameters of the regimes by the majority of weaker states. Sanctions had to be applied on occasion against recalcitrant states and commercial enterprises, but such states and enterprises were not large in number. Usually the recalcitrants tried to gain a competitive advantage by not adopting international regulations that firms in other states had to implement, but the great majority of countries, led by the major trading states, assured that they went along with "the greatest good for the greatest number" – i.e. that they did not "free-ride."

The nature and distributional implications of the regimes were certainly affected by the interests and power of the most important states, but there were broad consensuses with regard to central regime norms and functions. There were virtually no doubts at major international conferences dealing with these regimes as to whether accords would emerge. In fact, if any state had reservations about any norms of the regimes over the past half-century, it was the USA with regard to the cartel norm. However, it went along with the cartels for a mixture of political and economic reasons until the late 1970s when it began to change its policies.

In analyzing the salience of mutual interests, it is important to establish that the conditions that our theory indicated would generate mutual interests existed and that particular regime norms emerged in response to these conditions. The hypotheses relevant to mutual economic interests and regime functions drew largely on neoclassical economic theory's analysis of market failures. All of the international

224

service industries have faced problems of uncertainty of costs, high transaction costs, and most importantly impediments to the international flow of services, and virtually all regime norms and rules contribute to their reduction. Apropos this point, Craig Murphy has commented that "the greatest impact of the world organizations has been on industrial change. They have helped create international markets in industrial goods by linking *communication and transportation infrastructures*, protecting *intellectual property*, and reducing legal and economic barriers to *trade*."[12] The task of exploiting new technologies to further open the arteries of international commerce is still a central challenge for states today. Relevant to this challenge, Fred Smith, the founder of Federal Express, noted that "The distribution revolution is almost as profound as the computer revolution . . . It is the symbiotic relationship between improved information management systems and modern logistics systems which is fueling the continued, remarkable creation of jobs."[13] This book is very much about states' adjustment to the evolving "distribution revolution" and their cooperation to exploit its possibilities for mutual gain.

All of these concerns for reducing uncertainty, transaction costs, and impediments to the flow of services come into play in the area of defining property or jurisdictional rights. Without multilateral regime norms and rules relating to jurisdictions the world of international commerce would probably be chaotic and a lot less active than it is at the present.

> Defining and delimiting the property rights of states is as fundamental a collective task as any in the international system. The performance of this task on a multilateral basis seems inevitable in the long run, although in fact states appear to try every conceivable alternative first.[14]

States have often disagreed as to the precise character of jurisdictional norms and rules. However, their differences have seldom challenged their perceptions of the need for the free flow of transportation and communications in the global economy and the need for multilateral accords for realizing this goal. States want to assure that the doors to international commerce are open. They do not insist that firms have to walk through those doors, but they want to assure that if firms wish to do so, they face a congenial environment.

Another market failure with which all of the regimes have had to deal to one degree or another is negative externalities, such as marine pollution and unintended interference with radio transmissions. Since the early twentieth century there has been an important and growing body of telecommunications regulations to control radio interference, and in recent decades there has been a major growth in pollution regulations. A final market failure that has figured quite prominently in the regulation of prices and market shares is a natural monopoly or the existence of economies of scale. The existence of the cartels for international shipping, telecommunications, and postal services cannot be accounted for without understanding that states and firms thought that cartels promoted economic welfare because of economies of scale. The fact that they also regarded the cartels for telecommunications and postal services as enhancing state policy autonomy does not negate their economic judgments of the impacts of cartels.

Now that the existence of natural monopolies is challenged in all four industries, it is possible that a new regime norm based on "limited competition" will emerge based on the prevention of collusion among firms and the reduction of barriers to the flow of goods and services. At the moment a large number of states are cross-pressured between fears of intrusions on their domestic policy autonomy and prospects of long-term economic gains. The momentum is toward broader acceptance of liberalization, but the world is still some way from stable consensuses on the management of the sectors concerned with prices and market shares. The general point to be drawn from this discussion is that the aspect of neoclassical economic theory dealing with market failures provides considerable insights into the analysis of international regimes and that in this study its application substantiated the argument concerning the importance of mutual interests underlying regime development.

While most of the norms in the four industries have been grounded in mutual economic interests, some have been based on mutual interests in state policy autonomy. The key norms have been the jurisdictional right to exclude foreign services and firms and the cartel norm that dominated the sector concerning prices and market shares until very recently. Whether neorealists would regard such regimes as unimportant "particles of government" is unclear. They should not be regarded in this way. States' agreements to respect each other's jurisdiction over activities on and around their territories are very important in that they establish a considerable degree of order in international relations. Such regimes upholding property rights of sovereign states were, of course, some of the first important regimes to develop in the interstate system. As was indicated in chapter 2, regimes of this type seem quite compatible with the views of neorealists, although some adherents to the international society school provide a better understanding of such regimes that support the international system of sovereign states.[15]

An important point to recall concerning regime norms based on the protection of state autonomy is that they generally do not require strong international monitoring and enforcement mechanisms because states are able to perform these functions effectively within and around their own territories. Also, problems of relative gains generally do not arise for such regimes. If regimes based on mutual respect for states' internal political control assist any particular group of states, it is the non-great powers which are most likely to be the victims of external intervention. However, the great powers often have strong interests in supporting internal political control for all states because it prevents challenges by other great powers to their own control. States do not like to live with uncertainty on such matters.

An interesting issue that concerns states' support for state autonomy and which has clear theoretical implications is why the cartel norm governing prices and market shares in the four industries has been seriously weakened in the past several decades. Part of the answer certainly lies in the impact of changing technologies and economic studies concerning the disappearance of "natural monopolies" in several of the industries. However, there is another development at work that is partially captured by Peter Cowhey's observation that we are witnessing "a redefinition of the public sector" that is a product of "a shift in political economic interests and a transformation of the epistemic community."[16] To this redefinition of the public sector one could add as well a redefinition of "the national sector" or rules concerning foreign ownership. What the redefinition of the public and national sectors entails is a belief that states and their nationals should not maintain control over certain economic activities if there are significant losses in economic welfare attendant on their maintaining control. In other words, states are gradually accepting constraints on their autonomy or internal political control as a result of participation in international regimes whose central purpose is to capture mutual economic gains. Implications of these developments are, of course, that regimes based on the maintenance of a high level of state policy autonomy are weakening and that economic nationalist forces are losing to transnational firms and groups. Both commercial and affective political interests are at stake.

A very good indication of this change in thinking is a 1994 editorial in *The Economist* concerning the decreasing importance of national ownership of major industries. While the editorial focused on the car industry, it commented on others as well.

> It may stir the patriotic blood to think of a national car-maker, airline or steel firm (even if they lose money and jobs); but it is more rewarding in the long run to have secure jobs, high and rising living standards, and vibrant industries (even if foreign owned ones).
>
> . . . the car industry – along with such other areas of national championry as airlines, steel, chemicals, and even stock exchanges – now stands in the way of two winds of change: free trade and technology.[17]

The editorial recognized that many "politicians and pundits are outdated about the industries they choose to make objects of national virility," but its general line of argument indicates that government and business officials are increasingly becoming less obsessed with state and national ownership of many industries. States are allowing foreign intrusions into some of their previously sacrosanct spheres of national control. What was once an inviolable preserve of state autonomy is increasingly open to foreign business.

If states are increasingly willing to sacrifice some control over certain economic spheres because they do not want to abjure economic gains, this is consistent with a liberal theoretical projection of the evolving state of international relations. Economic liberalism has long argued that states enhance the economic welfare of their populations if they withdraw from markets (apart from providing order and assuring fair competition) and allow private commercial actors free rein. This is, of course, why international liberalism is associated with free trade.[18]

In the case of the international industries covered in this book, states certainly did not sacrifice any internal economic and political control as a result of the demise of the shipping conferences. However, in the other three issue areas they certainly did suffer attenuations in their internal political control as a result of the significant weakening of the cartels. In the international air transport industry, many states have lost control over fares and to a limited degree market shares on certain routes, and there are indications that states may sacrifice more control, even their possession of national airlines, in the future. There have been share purchases and association agreements among some national airlines, and this could be a precursor to the emergence of a number of global megacarriers. In the area of telecommunications, most state monopolies do not control non-basic services, and competition within states to provide international telephone services and international alliances among national telecommunication firms are developing. State postal administrations have, of course, lost significant shares of the international communications market to telecommunications companies (e.g. data transmission and e-mail), and courier services have intruded into their traditional domain of the carriage of letters and documents. Postal administrations are also acting in more competitive ways toward each other, and it is quite likely that the postal services industry will move along the same path of deregulation that the telecommunications industry is following. Whether these trends are precursors of the emergence of a widely accepted open competition norm in the four industries is unclear, but there is a good chance that such a development will occur.

There is a neorealist riposte to a neoliberal argument concerning the recent and ongoing weakening of the cartels and the movement toward deregulated international markets, and it is that these developments have been products of the changing interests and power of a hegemonic state (the USA) or a small group of hegemonic states. To deal with this argument it is necessary to review briefly some developments in the four industries. In shipping, the long-standing US insistence on "open conferences" serving American ports may have had some negative impacts on the long-term decline of the shipping conferences, but it is very difficult to judge that US policy was a crucial factor in their dramatic decrease in strength starting in the mid-1970s. In fact, the USA became more protective of the conferences in the 1980s, as is revealed by the 1984 Shipping Act. In air transport the USA did play an important role although many states' support of charters and many Asian airlines' adoption of liberal policies before the late 1970s does indicate that the USA was not completely responsible for the fracturing of the IATA cartel. Still, both the pressure and example of the United States have to be given considerable weight.

An important role can be given to the USA in the case of the crumbling of the international telecommunications cartel. However, in this issue area a stronger argument can be made for the inexorable pressures of technology, which produced a multiplication of means of communication and an increasing importance of telecommunications services to businesses, and a growing belief in the value to deregulation. Finally, with regard to international postal services it is very difficult to argue that the explosion of courier services, the expansion of electronic substitutes for regular postal services, and more competitive practices among postal administrations (e.g. remailing) were due to US policy. In reviewing the four industries it is not easy to provide confident judgments as to what would have occurred in air transport and telecommunications if it had not been for the US pressure for deregulation. It is, however, probable that while the USA expedited the break-up of the cartels, it is not the crucial long-term determinant of commercial trends. Technological changes and an evolution in thinking about the role of government in the economy were largely responsible for undermining the traditional cartel arrangements and sowing the seeds for a possible redefinition of mutual interests along liberal economic lines.[19]

In conclusion, there are a number of findings in this book relevant to international relations theory, and more particularly regime theory, that deserve highlighting. First, there are some important regime norms that protect states' policy autonomy, which corroborate neorealism's perspective on state goals, but not its views on obstacles to cooperation. Neorealism is very pessimistic about the prospects for important regimes because of the dangers of cheating, the lack of monitoring institutions, and the impacts of regimes on relative gains. However, in the case of regimes that concern states' control over activities on or adjacent to their territories, these factors do not constitute serious obstacles. States can monitor and police their own territories, and relative gains are not generally a significant issue.

Second, while some regimes supportive of state autonomy can be reconciled with a modified form of neorealism, what is more difficult to reconcile with it is the changing weight that states are attaching to their own policy autonomy and to the acceptability of foreign intrusions into their societies and polities. This is most clearly seen in the demise of the cartels in recent decades, but it can also be seen implicitly in the degree to which states are consumed with opening the avenues of international commerce. States are maintaining their sovereign legal prerogatives for the most part, but they are accepting "the internationalization of the state."[20] What seems to be the case is that the extent of states' attachment to policy autonomy and their "operational sovereignty"[21] are weakening, and that the extent of their attachment is contingent on particular historical conditions rather than being a natural condition of anarchical international systems.[22] Such observations must be offered with a certain amount of circumspection because of the limited duration of the historical developments under study, but some historical corroboration does exist.

While neorealism is deficient in understanding the evolution of priorities among states' values and historical practices, the sparse literature on neoliberalism since the late 1980s has not delved into this area either. Neoliberalism has to be connected to its historical liberal roots and the multifaceted forces of political change that are addressed by writers associated with the liberal tradition.[23] While new research is required on the evolving character of important actors in world politics, a more immediate issue is the evolving interests and values of states. Our era is unquestionably one of significant transformations, and international relations theories must address these changes.

Third, in consonance with a neoliberal perspective, the four regimes and the meta regime for international service industries have been based on mutual interests, and the obstacles to cooperation cited by neorealists have been overcome. Disputes over the nature of regimes and the resultant benefits for states are generally resolved; greater interdependence through economic ties and regime obligations are increasingly accepted; and monitoring and enforcement problems are usually handled adequately through unilateral actions and coordination within international institutions. Pertinent to the resolution of relative gains problems, it is important to point out that while power relations affect gains, they do not dictate certain distributions of benefits. Smaller and weaker states have been major beneficiaries of the norms of the communications and transportation regimes that protected their autonomy and facilitated their participation in international commerce. The relationship between relative power and rewards from regimes is by no means clear. As Helen Milner has written:

> The joint gains . . . need not be equal . . . Indeed, the more asymmetric the power relationship, the more unequal the distribution of gains is likely to be. But it does not follow that the asymmetries of gains will always favor the stronger state; and . . . the opposite may well be true more of the time.[24]

In the international economic realm these joint or mutual gains are grounded significantly in the correction of market failures. A functional and neoliberal theoretical approach has a clear value in the analysis of international regimes. It does not explain all characteristics of regimes, including the distribution of benefits, and it does not account for the process of regime formation, including the use of some coercive bargaining. However, it does indicate under what conditions all or most states are likely to see regimes with certain functional or normative thrusts as favorable to their interests. This is not a minor accomplishment.

Fourth, while neorealists might judge that "it is not evident how power is relevant for solving problems of market failure,"[25] neoliberal scholars should retort that power relations and the use of coercion are important to regimes based on mutual interests. The correction of market failures increases global welfare and hence the probability that all or most states will realize gains. In order to make regimes effective, the few states that do not gain or actually lose have to be encouraged to comply with the rules by the use of negative or positive sanctions, and this pressure can generally be applied most effectively by a few major states. There are also almost always some states that seek to free-ride on a regime by accepting its benefits and refusing to contribute to its maintenance by complying with its injunctions. An example would be certain flag vessels' trying to avoid compliance with international safety and pollution laws in order to lower their costs vis-à-vis rival shipping firms. In such circumstances the major trading states generally insist that vessels servicing their ports comply with international safety and pollution standards, and their sanctions of excluding non-complying vessels from their ports or detaining such vessels in port have a major impact on ships' compliance with international maritime law.[26] If the major trading states did not adopt such policies in support of international law, non-compliance would soon be rife. Even regimes based on an increase in global welfare, and hence the probability that all states will realize absolute gains, need the political backing and coercive power of the major states. Their support can, however, usually be counted on because they reap some absolute gains.

Lastly, for many years states have crafted transportation and communications regimes that have been crucial for the operation and expansion of the international commercial system. These regimes have not been ephemeral to the large tides of global politics; they have been central to some of the most dramatic economic and hence political trends that have shaped our modern world.[27] A possible neorealist critique of these regimes as inconsequential technical regimes does not grasp how important orderly commercial relationships and the opening of the arteries of the international economy have been. Cobwebs of agreements have grown, and states have become more aware of the importance of both order and openness for national prosperity. In fact, technological change appears to be pushing states ever further and faster toward openness and new forms of international order. This is a decidedly *liberal* development in international relations. This image of the world should not, in fact, come as surprise to perceptive observers of international relations since there has been an extensive network of orderly law-based relations for many years. The British legal scholar Ian Brownlie has made this point very clearly in a review of the roles of international law:

> what coverage [of international relations] there is tends to be sensationalist and superficial, even when some kind of political objectivity is attained. The normal side of international relations is simply left out. The effect is unfortunate. The audience is given the impression that relations between States consist almost entirely of a drama consisting of breaches of the peace, massacres, and other disasters. The normal traffic of State relations is almost completely ignored. It is as though in the sphere of national life, the operation of the road traffic system were to be reported exclusively in terms of severe accidents, multiple collisions on motorways, and so forth, without an indication of the areas of relatively successful operation and normality.[28]

An important reality of international relations is that there are broad areas of cooperative and law-governed behavior based on mutual gains among states and commercial actors.

Notes

1 International regimes and global networks

1 Three monographs representative of the international society school are: Hedley Bull, *The Anarchical Society: A Study of Order in World Politics* (New York: Columbia University Press, 1977); David Armstrong, *Revolution and World Order: The Revolutionary State in International Society* (Oxford: Clarendon, 1993); Robert H. Jackson, *Quasi-States: Sovereignty, International Relations, and the Third World* (Cambridge: Cambridge University Press, 1990).

2 For two selections of articles on these theoretical approaches see David A. Baldwin (ed.), *Neorealism and Neoliberalism: The Contemporary Debate* (New York: Columbia University Press, 1993); and Charles Kegley (ed.), *Controversies in International Relations Theory: Neorealism and the Neoliberal Challenge* (New York: St. Martin's, 1995). There are additional citations in ch. 2.

3 The identity of the four policy sectors was derived inductively from a study of the literature on the regulatory arrangements in the four industries.

4 Several good discussions of the industry and regime are: Alan F. Cafruny, *Ruling the Waves: The Political Economy of International Shipping* (Berkeley, CA: University of California Press, 1987); Edgar Gold, *Maritime Transport* (Lexington, MA: Lexington Books, 1981); and Clyde Sanger, *Ordering the Oceans* (Toronto: University of Toronto Press, 1987). For additional sources see ch. 3.

5 The industry and regime are described in: Paul Stephen Dempsey, *Law and Foreign Policy in International Aviation* (Dobbs Ferry, NY: Transnational Books, 1987); Christer Jonsson, *International Aviation and the Politics of Regime Change* (New York: St. Martin's Press, 1987); *International Aviation: Trends and Issues* (Canberra: Bureau of Transport and Communications Economics, 1994). For additional sources see ch. 4.

6 The industry and regime are described in: Jonathan D. Aronson and Peter F. Cowhey, *When Nations Talk: International Trade in Telecommunications*

234

(Cambridge: Ballinger, 1988); George A. Codding and Anthony M. Rutkowski, *The International Telecommunication Union in a Changing World* (Dedham, MA: Artech, 1982); James G. Savage, *The Politics of International Telecommunications Regulation* (Boulder, CO: Westview, 1989). For additional citations see ch. 5.

7 Several good works on the postal industry and regime are: George A. Codding, *The Universal Postal Union* (New York: New York University Press, 1964); and Michael A. Crew and Paul R. Kleindorfer (eds.), *Competition and Innovation in Postal Services* (Norwell, MA: Kluwer Academic, 1991). For additional sources see ch. 6.

2 Mutual interests and international regime theory

1 Many studies have focused on international regimes and have cited the definition used in the 1982 volume *International Regimes*, but there have been very few attempts to structure descriptive analyses around "principles, norms, rules and decision-making procedures." For such attempts see Mark W. Zacher, "Trade gaps, analytical gaps: regime analysis and international commodity trade regulation," *International Organization*, 41 (Spring 1987), pp. 172–202; and Vinod Aggarwal, *Liberal Protectionism: The International Politics of Organized Textile Trade* (Berkeley, CA: University of California Press, 1986).

2 Stephen D. Krasner, "Structural causes and regime consequences: regimes as intervening variables," in Stephen D. Krasner (ed.), *International Regimes* (Ithaca, NY: Cornell University Press, 1983), p. 2.

3 Aggarwal, *Liberal Protectionism*, pp. 16–20. Aggarwal uses the term "meta-regime" in a somewhat different way in that he labels the principles and norms in any regime as its meta regime. He recognizes that they are generally shared with other regimes. Our definition highlights the sharing of the same or very similar norms among specific regimes.

4 Ronald Dworkin, "The model of rules," *University of Chicago Law Review*, 35 (1967–68), p. 27.

5 Ronald Dworkin, "Legal principles and the limits of the law," *Yale Law Journal*, 81 (1972), p. 844. Dworkin refers to all binding prescriptions and proscriptions as "rules" whereas we divide binding prescriptions into norms, rules, and decision-making procedures.

6 Dworkin, "The model of rules," p. 27. In another publication Dworkin states that "All that is meant, when we say that a particular principle is a principle of our law, is that the principle is one which officials must take into account, if it is relevant, as a consideration inclining in one way or another." *Taking Rights Seriously* (1977), p. 27.

7 Paul Freund, "Constitutional dilemmas," *Boston University Law Review*, 45 (Winter 1965), pp. 22–23. Also see Paul Freund, "Thomas Reed Powell," *Harvard University Law Review*, 69 (1965), pp. 800–3.

8 On the lack of clarity concerning the components of the regimes and the difficulties in differentiating among them, see Robert O. Keohane, *After*

Hegemony: Cooperation and Discord in the World Political Economy (Princeton, NJ: Princeton University Press, 1984), pp. 57–59; and Stephan Haggard and Beth A. Simmons, "Theories of international regimes," *International Organization*, 41 (1987), p. 493. Keohane comments that while classifying injunctions into the four categories is sometimes difficult, it is possible to identify a hierarchy among injunctions. We do not think that it is too difficult to classify the injunctions in the four categories – particularly since the most general ones that are binding on states are norms. Therefore, the other injunctions fall into either substantive rules or decision-making procedures.

9 We delineated these four policy sectors on the basis of our analysis of the international negotiations and regulations relating to the four international service industries. While the four categories are appropriate for a study of these service industries, they would not be appropriate for many others.

10 Aggarwal offers the following definitions. "Nature refers to the objects promoted by regime rules and procedures." "Strength refers to the stringency with which rules regulate the behavior of countries." Aggarwal, *Liberal Protectionism*, pp. 20–21, 32–33. Haggard and Simmons identify strength as a characteristic of regimes, but substitute "organizational form" and "allocation mode" for nature. Haggard and Simmons, "Theories of international regimes," pp. 496–98. Also see Zacher, "Trade gaps, analytical gaps," pp. 174–78.

11 John Gerard Ruggie and Friedrich V. Kratochwil, "International organization: a state of the art on the art of the state," *International Organization*, 40 (1986), p. 764.

12 Robert Gilpin, "The richness of the tradition of political realism," in Robert O. Keohane (ed.), *Neorealism and Its Critics* (New York: Columbia University Press, 1986); Michael Joseph Smith, *Realist Thought from Weber to Kissinger* (Baton Rouge, LA: Louisiana State University Press, 1986); Joel H. Rosenthal, *Righteous Realists: Political Realism, Responsible Power, and American Culture in the Nuclear Age* (Baton Rouge, LA: Louisiana State University Press, 1991); Terry Nardin and David R. Mapel, *Traditions of International Ethics* (Cambridge: Cambridge University Press, 1992) – especially the articles by Steven Forde, Jack Donnelly, and Michael Joseph Smith; Mark W. Zacher and Richard A. Matthew, "Liberal international theory: common threads, divergent strands," in Charles Kegley (ed.), *Controversies in International Relations Theory: Realism and the Neoliberal Challenge* (New York: St. Martin's Press, 1995), pp. 107–50.

13 Kenneth N. Waltz, "Reflections on *Theory of International Politics*: a response to my critics," in Keohane (ed.), *Neorealism and Its Critics*, p. 341.

14 Joseph M. Grieco, "Anarchy and the limits of international cooperation: a realist critique of the newest liberal institutionalism," *International Organization*, 42 (Summer 1988); Robert O. Keohane, "Neoliberal institutionalism," in Robert O. Keohane (ed.), *International Institutions and State*

Power (Boulder, CO: Westview, 1989); David A. Baldwin, "Neoliberalism, neorealism, and world politics," in David A. Baldwin (ed.), *Neorealism and Neoliberalism: The Contemporary Debate* (New York: Columbia University Press, 1993), pp. 3–28, and the other articles therein; Waltz, "Reflections on *Theory of International Politics*," and other articles in Keohane (ed.), *Neorealism and Its Critics*; Kegley (ed.), *Controversies in International Relations Theory*.

A weak area of both theories concerns the identification of states' goals or their utility functions. In the case of neorealism it is not completely clear about the meaning of survival and security, and it does not identify other goals. In neoliberal writings there is the largely implicit message that states have a variety of goals – with economic welfare being one of the most important.

15 Hedley Bull, *The Anarchical Society: A Study of Order in World Politics* (New York: Columbia University Press, 1977); A. Claire Cutler, "The 'Grotian tradition' in international relations," *Review of International Studies*, 17 (1991), pp. 43–63; David Armstrong, *Revolution and World Order: The Revolutionary State in International Society* (Oxford: Clarendon, 1993); Robert H. Jackson, *Quasi-States: Sovereignty, International Relations, and the Third World* (Cambridge: Cambridge University Press, 1990); and Barry Buzan, "From international system to international society: structural realism and regime theory meet the English school," *International Organization*, 47 (1993), pp. 327–52 and the citations therein.

16 Kenneth N. Waltz, *Theory of International Politics* (Reading, MA: Addison-Wesley, 1979), pp. 153–55 (hereafter cited as *Theory*).

17 Waltz argues that "in an unorganized realm each unit's incentive is to put itself in a position to be able to take care of itself since no one else can be counted on to do so. The international imperative is 'take care of yourself'." He also comments that "States strive to maintain autonomy" and "success is defined as preserving and strengthening the state." *Theory*, pp. 107, 204, 117. Also see Waltz, *Theory*, pp. 88–92, 126–27; Grieco, "Anarchy and the limits of international cooperation," pp. 497–500. On the statist orientation of realism see Stephen D. Krasner, *Defending the National Interest: Raw Materials Investment and US Foreign Policy* (Princeton, NJ: Princeton University Press, 1978), ch. 1.

18 Waltz, *Theory*, pp. 105, 123–28; Grieco, "Anarchy and the limits of international cooperation," pp. 487, 496, 501, 504.

19 Joseph M. Grieco, *Cooperation Among Nations: Europe, America, and Non-Tariff Barriers* (Ithaca, NY: Cornell University Press, 1990), and "Understanding the problem of international cooperation: the limits of neoliberal institutionalism, and the future of realist theory," in Baldwin (ed.), *Neorealism and Neoliberalism*, pp. 301–38. For the debate on relative gains see the articles in the Baldwin edited volume, and Robert Powell, "Anarchy in international relations theory: the neorealist–neoliberal debate," *International Organization*, 48 (Spring 1994), pp. 329–38.

20 Waltz, *Theory*, pp. 88–92, 102–28; Grieco, "Anarchy and the limits of international cooperation"; Charles Lipson, "International cooperation in economic and security affairs," *World Politics*, 37 (October 1984), pp. 1–23.

21 Waltz, *Theory*, p. 114.

22 Stephen D. Krasner, "Global communications and national power: life on the Pareto frontier," *World Politics*, 43 (April 1991), pp. 336–66. With regard to a focus on market failures Krasner argues that "The connotation of this research program is that power can be ignored," although he admits that Keohane accepts that power relations do affect the character of a regime (pp. 360–61). Perhaps a stronger case can be made that the "connotation" of his power-oriented approach is that regimes are not formed unless the most powerful state(s) gain more. Robert Powell argues that the two approaches are complementary, but it is unclear whether the two sides could agree on terms of complementarity. The most likely basis of complementarity is that regimes require both mutual interests and greater gains for the most powerful state(s). Some scholars on both sides of the neorealist–neoliberal debate would find it difficult to accept this requirement. Robert Powell, "Anarchy in international relations theory," p. 340.

On "hegemonic stability theory," see Keohane, *After Hegemony*, ch. 3; Robert Gilpin, *US Power and the Multinational Corporation: The Political Economy of Foreign Direct Investment* (New York: Basic Books, 1975); Robert Gilpin, *War and Change in World Politics* (Cambridge: Cambridge University Press, 1981); Stephen D. Krasner, "State power and the structure of international trade," *World Politics*, 28 (April 1976), pp. 317–47. Waltz does not accept hegemonic stability theory: "Reflections on *Theory of International Politics*," pp. 340–41.

23 For a general overview of liberal international theory see Zacher and Matthew, "Liberal international theory," pp. 107–50. Particularly on the relative-absolute gains debate between neorealists and neoliberals, see the articles in Baldwin (ed.), *Neorealism and Neoliberalism*.

On states' tolerance of interdependencies to realize mutual gains, even an important realist like Robert Gilpin thinks that many mercantilists or realists have gone too far in projecting states' resistance to interdependence. "One weakness of nationalism is its tendency to believe that international economic relations constitute solely and at all times a zero-sum game, that is, that one state's gain must of necessity be another's loss. Trade, investment, and all other economic relations are viewed by the nationalists primarily in conflictual and distributive terms. Yet, if cooperation occurs, markets can bring mutual (albeit not necessarily equal) gain, as the liberal insists. The possibility of benefit for all is the basis of the international market economy." *The Political Economy of International Relations* (Princeton, NJ: Princeton University Press, 1987), p. 47. Some figures on economic flows are in: Mark W. Zacher, "The decaying pillars of the Westphalian temple: implications for international order and governance," in James N. Rosenau and Ernst-Otto Czempiel (eds.),

Governance Without Government: Order and Change in World Politics (Cambridge: Cambridge University Press, 1992), pp. 58–101.

24 This is discussed at length in Zacher and Matthew, "Liberal international theory."

25 Robert O. Keohane, "Neoliberal institutionalism," p. 10. For a good statement that concern for relative gains depends on the strategic environment, see Powell, "Anarchy in international relations theory," pp. 329–38. On the debate on this issue, see Baldwin (ed.), *Neorealism and Neoliberalism*; and the separate statements by Joseph Grieco, Robert Powell, and Duncan Snidal, in "The relative-gains problem in international relations," *American Political Science Review*, 87 (September 1993), pp. 719–35.

26 Robert O. Keohane, "Reciprocity in international relations," *International Organization*, 40 (Winter 1986), pp. 1–28; John Gerard Ruggie, "Multilateralism: the anatomy of an institution," in John Gerard Ruggie (ed.), *Multilateralism Matters: The Theory and Praxis of an Institutional Form* (New York: Columbia University Press, 1993), pp. 3–50. Relevant to this point Helen Milner notes that the concept of cooperation implies that all parties gain: "The gains need not be the same in magnitude or kind for each state, but they are mutual." She also notes that it is very difficult for states or scholars to judge what are balanced gains (which Grieco recognizes as promoting cooperation). "International theories of cooperation among nations: strengths and weaknesses," *World Politics*, 44 (April 1992), p. 468.

27 For an excellent statement on this issue see Robert O. Keohane, "Institutionalist theory and the realist challenge after the Cold War," pp. 279–81 in Baldwin, *Neorealism and Neoliberalism*. Also see the Powell and Snidal articles in Baldwin, *Neorealism and Neoliberalism*; and Andrew Moravcsik, "Liberalism and international relations theory" (Working Paper, Center of International Affairs, Harvard University, 1992). Relevant to the claim that regimes are based on mutual interests and consent, the well-known international legal scholar Ian Brownlie has written that the "dictated treaty" is the exception, "not the rule." "The roles of international law," *Zin en Tegenzin in Internationaal Recht* (Deventer: Kluwer, 1986), p. 19.

28 The strongest advocate of this position has been Robert Keohane. See in particular his discussions of "the international organization model" in Robert Keohane (with Joseph S. Nye), *Power and Interdependence* (Boston, MA: Little, Brown, 1977), "functionalism" in *After Hegemony* (esp. ch. 6), and "neoliberal institutionalism" in "Neoliberal institutionalism." An article that *inter alia* discusses the gradations in governance in the international system is Milner, "The assumption of anarchy in international relations theory," in Baldwin, *Neorealism and Neoliberalism*, pp. 143–69. On the importance of international institutions see Zacher and Matthew, "Liberal international theory," pp. 133–37; and Mark W. Zacher, "Multilateral organizations and the institution of multilateralism," in Ruggie, *Multilateralism Matters*, pp. 399–443.

29 Oran Young, *International Cooperation: Building Regimes for Natural Resources and the Environment* (Ithaca, NY: Cornell University Press, 1989), p. 200.

30 Andrew Moravcsik, "Liberalism and international relations theory," p. 10.

31 The absence of overt coercive bargaining does not always indicate that power relations did not determine the existence of a regime since states' policies can be shaped by a recognition of certain parameters for agreement that are dictated by the power of different groupings. However, it is usually possible to tell whether states felt that they had to submit to something that they regarded as contrary to important interests.

32 On the neoclassical economic model see F. M. Bator, "The anatomy of market failure," *Quarterly Journal of Economics*, 72 (August 1958), pp. 351–79; Robin Boadway, *Public Sector Economics* (Cambridge, MA: Winthrop, 1979); Alfred A. Kahn, *The Economics of Regulation: Principles and Institutions* (New York: John Wiley, 1970); F. M. Scherer, *Industrial Market Structure and Economic Performance*, 2nd edn (Chicago: McNally, 1980).

The effect of government regulation becomes less determinate when more than one condition is violated at the same time. Kevin Lancaster and Richard Lipsey showed that when two or more conditions required for the efficient functioning of markets do not exist, then correcting them through government intervention may not necessarily improve the efficiency of the market. "The general theory of second best," *Review of Economic Studies*, 24 (1954).

33 On market failures (or market imperfections) see Armen A. Alchian, "Uncertainty, evolution, and economic theory," *Journal of Political Economy*, 58 (February 1950), pp. 211–21; S. N. S. Cheung, "Transaction cost, risk aversion, and the choice of contractual arrangements," *Journal of Law and Economics*, 12 (April 1969), pp. 23–42; Carl Dahlman, "The problem of externality," *Journal of Law and Economics*, 22 (1979), pp. 141–62; Harold Demsetz, "The cost of transacting," *Quarterly Journal of Economics*, 82 (1968), pp. 33–53; E. J. Mishan, "The postwar literature on externalities: an interpretative essay," *Journal of Economic Literature*, 9 (1971), pp. 1–28; Richard A. Posner, "Natural monopoly and its regulation," *Stanford Law Review*, 21 (February 1969), pp. 548–649; Paul A. Samuelson, "The pure theory of public expenditure," *Review of Economics and Statistics*, 36 (November 1954), pp. 387–89; Oliver Williamson, *Markets and Hierarchies* (New York: Free Press, 1975); Charles Wolf, "A theory of nonmarket failure: framework for implementation analysis," *Journal of Law and Economics*, 22 (1979), pp. 107–139.

34 In the economics literature transaction costs refer to costs for "private" parties involved (a) in negotiating the terms for the sale of a good or the terms for the performance of a service and (b) in settling any conflicts concerning the sales. The existence of negotiating forums and dispute settlement bodies and the specificity of the legal rules concerning the transactions are central to the magnitude of the transaction costs since

inadequate institutions and a lack of clarity in the relevant law require that the parties spend a great deal of time and resources on negotiations. Mark Casson, "Transaction costs and the theory of the multinational enterprise," in Alan Rugman (ed.), *New Theories of the Multinational Enterprise* (London: Croom Helm, 1982), pp. 24–43.

In the international relations literature the transaction costs to which some writers refer have largely been "public" in that they refer to the costs to governments of negotiating accords or regimes in particular issue areas. Here again, the existence of negotiating forums and specific laws is central to the magnitude of the transaction costs. Reductions of both private and public transaction costs are relevant to this study. Keohane, *After Hegemony*, ch. 6.

35 The need to regulate natural monopolies has been challenged by the theory of "contestable markets." Baumol, Panzer, and Willig have argued that as long as there are no sunk costs the possibility of potential competitors moving into the market provides discipline that leads monopolists to optimal pricing and production levels. However, high sunk costs are frequently associated with natural monopolies, negating the practical significance of this finding. See W. J. Baumol, J. C. Panzer, and R. D. Willig, *Contestable Markets and the Theory of Industry Structure* (San Diego, CA: Harcourt Brace Jovanovich, 1982).

36 In his seminal work Ronald Coase showed that misallocations caused by externalities can (but will not necessarily) be resolved through voluntary bargains providing there is perfect information among market partici-pants, the absence of transaction costs, and defined property rights. "The problem of social cost," *Journal of Law and Economics*, 3 (1960), pp. 1–44. However, there is a sense that the "Coasian" solution is of limited relevance since the conditions of no transaction costs (and perfect infor-mation for that matter) are unlikely to be met. See Maureen L. Cropper and Wallace E. Oates, "Environmental economics: a survey," *Journal of Economic Literature*, 30 (June 1992).

37 The theory of hegemonic stability is built on the notion that regimes are a public good that will only be provided when a single state is sufficiently large that it is in a position to capture benefits from the good that exceed the cost of providing it. Duncan Snidal, "The limits of hegemonic stability theory," *International Organization*, 39 (1985), pp. 579–614; Joanne Gowa, "Rational hegemons, excludable goods and small groups: an epitaph for hegemonic stability theory," *World Politics*, 41 (1989), pp. 307–24.

38 The international society or English school addresses this issue of states' cooperation to protect their sovereignty at a general level, but it does not address how specific conditions could lead to specific accords. Hedley Bull, *The Anarchical Society*, and Barry Buzan, "From international system to international society: structural realism and regime theory meet the English school," *International Organization*, 47 (1993), pp. 327–52 and the citations therein.

39 Terry Nardin, "International ethics and international law," *Review of International Studies*, 18 (1992), pp. 26.

40 David Armstrong, *Revolution and World Order*, p. 32.

41 Armstrong, *Revolution and World Order*, p. 15.

42 Inis L. Claude, *Swords into Plowshares*, 4th edn (New York: Random House, 1971), p. 6. This outlook is also consistent with Hedley Bull's views on the elementary purposes and goals that guide international society, in *The Anarchical Society*.

43 For a general evaluation of functional theories, see A. L. Stinchcombe, *Constructing Social Theories* (New York: Harcourt Brace, 1969), pp. 80–98.

44 Haggard and Simmons, "Theories of international regimes," pp. 508 and 506–8.

45 Krasner, "Global communications and national power," pp. 342 and 362.

3 The international shipping regime

1 UNCTAD, *Review of Maritime Transport, 1989*, pp. 37–39; *The Economist* (15 November 1986), p. 82.

2 Abbott P. Usher, "The growth of English shipping, 1572–1922," *Quarterly Journal of Economics*, 42 (1928), p. 469.

3 UNCTAD, *Review of Maritime Transport, 1989*, p. 6.

4 Ibid.

5 UNCTAD, *Review of Maritime Transport, 1989*, pp. 6–25.

6 Interviews, April and May 1988; OECD, *Maritime Transport, 1986*.

7 UNCTAD, *Review of Maritime Transport, 1989*, p. 24; OECD, *Maritime Transport, 1989*, pp. 43–86, 95–107; J.W. Doerffer, "IMO and shipbuilding at the turn of the centuries," *IMO News*, 4 (1990), p. 7; Janet Porter, "P&O chief credits TAA for trans-Atlantic revival," *Journal of Commerce* (25 March 1994).

8 For summaries of past and present technological trends see OECD, *Maritime Transport, 1989*, pp. 122–25; UNCTAD, *Review of Maritime Transport, 1989*, pp. 40–50; Federal Maritime Commission, *Section 18 Report on the 1984 Shipping Act* (Washington, DC: 1989), pp. 46–52.

9 G. J. van de Ziel, "Competition policy in liner shipping: policy options," paper presented at the Workshop on Competition Policy in Liner Shipping, University of Antwerp, Belgium, 11 February 1994.

10 Elliot Schrier, Ernest Nadel, and Bertram E. Rifas, "Forces shaping international maritime transport," *World Economy*, 7 (March 1984), p. 88.

11 Schrier et al., "Forces shaping international maritime transport," p. 88; S. G. Sturmey, *The Open Registry Controversy and the Development Issue* (Bremen: Institute of Shipping Economics, 1983); van der Ziel, "Competition policy in liner shipping"; interviews with government officials.

12 The charter of the IMO, initially known as the Intergovernmental Maritime Consultative Organization (IMCO), was formulated in 1948, but the organization did not become operative until ten years later. (The name IMCO was changed to IMO in 1982.) The delay resulted from the concern of the traditional maritime states that the IMO would become involved in

commercial issues. It was not until these states were assured that the IMO would restrict its activities to technical issues that the convention establishing the IMO received enough support for it to enter into force. See R. Michael M'Gonigle and Mark W. Zacher, *Pollution, Politics, and International Law: Tankers at Sea* (Berkeley, CA: University of California Press, 1979), ch. 3.

13 Only the International Convention for the Safety of Fishing Vessels (1977), the International Convention for the Suppression of Unlawful Acts Against the Safety of Maritime Navigation (1988), and the International Convention on Oil Pollution Preparedness, Response and Co-operation (1990) have not yet entered into force.

14 Edgar Gold, *Maritime Transport* (Lexington, MA: Lexington Books, 1981), pp. 126–31 and *passim*.

15 O. Stemmer, "A new order for postwar shipping and the liner conference system: the International Maritime Conference, 1984," *Maritime Policy and Management*, 14 (1987), p. 25; B. Obinna Okere, "The technique of international maritime legislation," *International and Comparative Law Quarterly*, 30 (July 1981), p. 525; Sturmey, *The Open Registry Controversy and the Development Issue*; Stephen D. Krasner, *Structural Conflict: The Third World Against Global Liberalism* (Berkeley, CA: University of California Press, 1985), pp. 215–25.

16 A. Mankabady, "International and national organizations concerned with shipping," *Lloyd's Maritime and Commercial Law Quarterly*, 3 (1974); K. A. Bekiashev and V. V. Serebriakov, *International Marine Organizations*, trans. V. V. Serebriakov (The Hague: Martinus Nijhoff Publishers, 1981).

17 Paul W. Gormley, "The development and subsequent influence of the Roman legal norm of 'freedom of the seas'," *University of Detroit Law Journal*, 30 (June 1963), pp. 561–95; Edgar Gold, *Maritime Transport*, pp. 30–33; John C. Colombos, *The International Law of the Sea*, 2nd edn (London: Longmans, Green, 1951), pp. 39–41

18 Hugo Grotius, *The Freedom of the Seas (Mare Liberum)*, trans. Ralph Van Deman Magoffin (New York: Oxford University Press, 1916); Pitman B. Potter, *The Freedom of the Seas in History, Law, and Politics* (New York: Longmans, Green, 1924), pp. 57–78; Ruth Lapidoth, "Freedom of navigation – its legal history and its normative basis," *Journal of Maritime Law and Commerce*, 6 (1974–75), pp. 263–71; Gormley, "The development and subsequent influence of the Roman legal norm of freedom of the seas," pp. 586–70.

19 Bruce Farthing, *International Shipping* (London: Lloyd's of London Press, 1987), p. 2.

20 Potter, *The Freedom of the Seas in History, Law, and Politics*, pp. 84–90; T. W. Fulton, *The Sovereignty of the Sea: An Historical Account of the Claims of England to the Dominion of the British Seas, and of the Evolution of the Territorial Waters* (Edinburgh: William Blackwood, 1911), pp. 54–75; Gold, *Maritime Transport*, p. 62.

21 Gold, *Maritime Transport*, p. 99.
22 R. P. Anand, "Freedom of navigation through territorial waters and international straits," *Indian Journal of International Law*, 14 (1974), p. 149. Also see Anand, "Freedom of navigation," pp. 131–53; Gold, *Maritime Transport*, p. 98; Bernard G. Heinzen, "The three-mile limit: preserving the freedom of the seas," *Stanford Law Review*, 11 (May 1959), pp. 614–34; Lapidoth, "Freedom of navigation," pp. 418–19; Farthing, *International Shipping*, pp. 8–11.
23 Richard B. McNees, "Freedom of transit through international straits," *Journal of Maritime Law and Commerce*, 6 (1974–75), p. 175.
24 Farthing, *International Shipping*, p. 40.
25 D. P. O'Connell, *The Influence of Law on Seapower* (Manchester: University of Manchester Press, 1975), p. 796.
26 J. H. W. Verzijl, *International Law in Historical Perspective*, vol. IV (Leyden: A. W. Sijthoff, 1971), p. 40. Also see pp. 41–45.
27 N. J. J. Gaskell, C. Debattista, and R. J. Swatton, *Chorley and Giles' Shipping Law*, 8th edn (London: Pitman, 1987), p. 19.
28 Bernard G. Heinzen, "The three-mile limit: preserving the freedom of the seas," pp. 639–40; Gold, *Maritime Transport*, pp. 205–6.
29 Clyde Sanger, *Ordering the Oceans* (Toronto: University of Toronto Press, 1987), pp. 15–16; Gold, *Maritime Transport*, pp. 265–66; Ann L. Hollick, *US Foreign Policy and the Law of the Sea* (Princeton, NJ: Princeton University Press, 1981), pp. 144–47; Barry G. Buzan, *Seabed Politics* (New York: Praeger, 1976), pp. 30–52.
30 UN Doc. A/CONF.62/122 (1982).
31 Parts II, III, IV, VII, and XII of the 1982 treaty, UN Doc. A/CONF.62/122 (1982); Seyom Brown et al., *Regimes for the Ocean, Outer Space and Weather* (Washington, DC: Brookings, 1977), pp. 43–45; Hollick, *US Foreign Policy and the Law of the Sea*, pp. 235–36; Anand, "Freedom of navigation through territorial waters and international straits," pp. 180–89; Lapidoth, "Freedom of navigation"; Morris F. Maduro, "Passage through international straits: the prospects emerging from the Third United Nations Conference on the Law of the Sea," *Journal of Maritime Law and Commerce*, 12 (1980), pp. 65–95; John Norton Moore, "The regime of straits and the Third United Nations Conference on the Law of the Sea," *American Journal of International Law*, 74 (January 1980), pp. 77–121.
32 Lapidoth, "Freedom of navigation," p. 271.
33 Farthing, *International Shipping*, p. 11.
34 Ross D. Eckert, *The Enclosure of Ocean Resources: Economics and the Law of the Sea* (Stanford, CA: Hoover Institution Press, 1979), p. 85.
35 Farthing, *International Shipping*, p. 26.
36 Okere, "The technique of international maritime legislation," p. 517.
37 This was partly as a result of the findings of Samuel Plimsoll, a Member of Parliament who in 1868 published an account of the poor construction and substandard operational practices of the British fleet. A Royal Commission

established in 1874 confirmed Plimsoll's findings, and the UK Board of Trade was thereafter charged to ensure the safety of ocean vessels. The concept of the load line was developed at this time.

38 William McFee, *The Law of the Sea* (Philadelphia, PA: J. B. Lippincott, 1950), pp. 267–70; Arthur A. Kuhn, "International aspects of the *Titanic* case," *American Journal of International Law*, 9 (April 1915), pp. 336–51; John Warren Kindt, *Marine Pollution and the Law of the Sea*, Vol. 1 (New York: William S. Hein, 1986), p. 272.

39 *IMO News*, 2 (1987), pp. 2–3

40 "Aids to navigation," *Law Times*, 221 (March 1956); T. S. Busha, "Monitoring and surveillance: navigation," in E. M. Borgese and N. Ginsburg (eds.), *Ocean Yearbook* (Chicago, IL: University of Chicago Press, 1982); "IMO and the safety of navigation," mimeo (London: IMO, September 1985); "The facilitation of maritime travel and transport," mimeo (London: IMO, July 1986); Samir Mankabady, *The International Maritime Organization. Volume I: International Shipping Rules* (London: Croom Helm, 1986); Dion D. Raymos, "Liability of the government for improper placement of aids to navigation," *Journal of Maritime Law and Commerce*, 4 (October 1986), pp. 517–30; K. Sutton-Jones, *Pharos: The Lighthouse Yesterday, Today and Tomorrow* (Great Britain: Michael Russell Publishers, 1985).

41 W. W. Barrow, "Consideration of the new International Rules Preventing Collisions at Sea," *Tulane Law Review* (June 1977); J. H. Beattie, "Traffic routeing at sea, 1857–1977," *Journal of Navigation* (1978); S. T. Harley, "The Collision Regulations 1972," *Lloyd's Maritime and Commercial Law Quarterly*, 2 (1977), p. 178; Louis Franck, "Collision at sea in relation to international maritime law," *Law Quarterly Review*, 12 (1986); A. N. Crockroft and J. N. Lameijer, *A Guide to Collision Avoidance Rules*, 3rd edn (London: Stanford Maritime, 1983); David R. Owen, "The origins and development of marine collision law," *Tulane Law Review*, 51 (1977), pp. 759–813.

42 Charles H. Alexandrowicz, "The Convention on Facilitation of International Maritime Traffic and International Technical Regulation: a comparative study," *International Comparative Law Quarterly*, 15 (1966), pp. 621–59; Edgar Gold, "Vessel traffic regulation: the interface of maritime safety and operational freedom," *Journal of Maritime Law and Commerce*, 14 (January 1983), p. 1; "The facilitation of maritime travel and transport," mimeo (London: IMO, July 1986); G. Plant, "International traffic separation schemes in the new law of the sea," *Marine Policy* (April 1985), pp. 134–47.

43 "An international loadline," *Solicitors' Journal and Weekly Reporter*, 74 (5 April 1930), pp. 209–10; David B. Bannerman, "Highlights of the Load Line Conference, 1966," *Marine Technology*, 3 (1966); Richard Jiemenez, "The evolution of the load line," *American Bureau of Shipping Surveyor* (May 1976), pp. 7–13; Lester Kushner, "The 1966 International Load Line Convention: compatibility of greater carrying capacity with safety of life and property," *Journal of Maritime Law and Commerce*, 3 (January 1972), pp. 375–83; David Masters, *The Plimsoll Mark* (London: Cassell, 1955).

44 S. W. Doyle, "INMARSAT: the International Maritime Satellite Organization – origins and structure," *Journal of Space Law*, 5 (1977), p. 45; P. K. Menon, "The International Maritime Satellite Organization: an important milestone in maritime communications service," *Revue Belge de Droit International*, 13 (1977), p. 279; P. K. Menon, "International maritime satellite system," *Journal of Maritime Law and Commerce*, 8 (October 1976), pp. 95–106; H. H. M. Sondaal, "The current situation in the field of maritime communication satellites: INMARSAT," *Journal of Space Law*, 8 (1980), pp. 9–39; M. E. Volosov, A. L. Kolodkin, and Y. M. Kososov, "International maritime satellite communication system: history and principles governing its functioning," in E. M. Borgese and N. Ginsburg (eds.), *Ocean Yearbook, 1978* (Chicago, IL: University of Chicago Press, 1978), pp. 240–70.

45 Everett P. Wheeler, "International Conference on Safety of Life at Sea," *American Journal of International Law*, 8 (October 1914), pp. 758–68; Arthur A. Kuhn, "Safety of Life at Sea," *Proceedings of the Academy of Political Science*, 6 (1915–16), pp. 97–112; Arthur A. Kuhn, "International Convention for Safety of Life at Sea," *American Journal of International Law*, 24 (January 1930), pp. 133–35; Nagendra Singh, *International Maritime Law Conventions*, 4 vols., 3rd edn (London: Stevens, 1983); R. J. Slot, "National regulation of maritime transport and international public law," *Netherlands International Law Review*, 26 (1979), pp. 329–46; R. M. Stopford and J. R. Borton, "Economic problems of shipbuilding and the state," *Maritime Policy and Management*, 13 (1986), pp. 27–44; Joseph C. Sweeney (ed.), *Annual Proceedings of the Fordham Corporate Law Institute: International Regulations of Maritime Transportation* (New York: Mathew Bender, 1978).

46 "Global co-operation for the training of maritime personnel," mimeo (London: IMO, February 1985); "The International Convention on Standards of Training, Certification and Watchkeeping for Seafarers, 1978," mimeo (London: IMO, October 1986); P. K. Menon, "The World Maritime University: an attempt to train specialist maritime personnel," *Journal of Maritime Law and Commerce*, 17 (October 1986), pp. 585–96; Douglas Phillips-Birt, *A History of Seamanship* (London: Allen and Unwin, 1971).

47 "Piracy and other crimes," *IMO News*, 1 (1993), p. 13; Peter Kapoor and Richard Grey, "Maritime fraud: an overview," Plymouth Polytechnic Working Paper no. 9 (September 1985), p. 1. On the nature of the problem see Peter D. Clark, "Criminal jurisdiction over merchant vessels engaged in international trade," *Journal of Maritime Law and Commerce*, 11 (January 1980), pp. 219–37; B. H. Dubner, *The Law of International Sea Piracy* (The Hague: Martinus Nijhoff, 1980); Eric Ellen and Donald Campbell, *International Maritime Fraud* (London: Sweet and Maxwell, 1981); D. P. O'Connell, *The International Law of the Sea, Volume II* (Oxford: Clarendon, 1984), pp. 967–83; B. A. H. Parritt, "Maritime terrorism and the law," *Lloyd's Maritime and Commercial Law Quarterly* (February 1987), pp. 18–21; Barry A. K. Rider, "Combating international commercial crime – a

commonwealth perspective," *Lloyd's Maritime and Commercial Law Quarterly* (May 1985), pp. 217–40; Barry A. K. Rider, "The promotion and development of international cooperation to combat commercial and economic crime," Meeting of the Commonwealth Law Ministers, Barbados, April–May 1980; T. S. R. Topping, "International action against maritime fraud," in E. M. Borgese and N. Ginsburg (eds.), *Ocean Yearbook, 1985*, Vol. V (Chicago, IL: University of Chicago Press, 1985), pp. 102–8.

48 Rider, "Combating international commercial crime," pp. 229–30.

49 Interview with a governmental official, April 1988.

50 Malvina Halberstam, "Terror on the high seas: the *Achille Lauro*, piracy and the IMO Convention on Maritime Safety," *American Journal of International Law*, 82 (April 1988), pp. 269–310.

51 UN Doc. TD/B/C.4/AC.4/5 (1985), p. 4; Rider, "The promotion and development of international cooperation to combat economic and commercial crime," pp. 23–31; Ellen and Campbell, *International Maritime Fraud*, pp. 78–79.

52 UN Doc. TD/B/C.4/314 (1987), pp. 24–26.

53 Norman Howard-Jones, *The Scientific Background of the International Sanitary Conferences, 1851–1938* (Geneva: WHO, 1975); Neville M. Goodman , *International Health Organizations and Their Work* (Baltimore: Williams and Wilkins, 1955); David M. Leive, *International Regulatory Regimes: Volume I* (Lexington, MA: Lexington, 1976), pp. 1–152; C. A. Pannenborg, *The New International Health Order: An Inquiry into the International Relations of World Health and Medical Care* (Alphen aan den Rijn: Sijthoff and Noordhoff, 1979); Richard N. Cooper, "International cooperation in public health as a prologue to macroeconomic cooperation," Discussion Paper in International Economics, no. 44 (Washington, DC: Brookings, 1986).

54 M'Gonigle and Zacher, *Pollution, Politics and International Law*, esp. chs. 6 and 8; Kindt, *Marine Pollution and the Law of the Sea*, 4 vols. (New York: William S. Hein and Co., 1986); Sonia Zaide Pritchard, *Oil Pollution Control* (London: Croom, Helm, 1987); Jesper Grolin, "Environmental hegemony, maritime community, and the problem of oil tanker pollution," in Michael Morris (ed.), *North–South Perspectives on Marine Policy* (Boulder, CO: Westview Press, 1988); David M. Collins, "The tanker's right of harmless discharge and protection of the marine environment," *Journal of Maritime Law and Commerce*, 18 (April 1987), pp. 275–91; Gregorios J. Timagenis, *International Control of Marine Pollution*, 2 vols. (New York: Oceana Publications, 1980); "Resolutions emphasize importance of implementation" and "Port state control", *IMO News*, 4 (1991), pp. 8–9 and 14–15; "Marine environment and development: the IMO role," *IMO News*, 3 (1992), pp. 2–12; Ronald B. Mitchell, "Regime design matters: intentional oil pollution and treaty compliance," *International Organization*, 48 (Summer 1994), pp. 425–58.

55 M'Gonigle and Zacher, *Pollution, Politics, and International Law*, p. 261.

56 M'Gonigle and Zacher, *Pollution, Politics, and International Law,* ch. 4; Eric Nalder, *Tankers Full of Trouble* (New York: Grove, 1994), pp. 216–20.

57 Gaskell et al., *Chorley and Giles' Shipping Law,* 8th edn (London: Pitman Publishing, 1987), pp. 394–96.

58 Gaskell et al., *Chorley and Giles' Shipping Law,* p. 394.

59 M'Gonigle and Zacher, *Pollution, Politics, and International Law,* pp. 145 and 143–99. Also see Gold, *Maritime Transport,* p. 338; Farthing, *International Shipping,* pp. 47–50; Timagenis, *International Control of Pollution,* Vol. I, pp. 62–65.

60 Robert Hellawell, "Allocation of risk between cargo owner and carrier," *American Journal of Comparative Law,* 27 (1979), p. 357; John D. Kimball, "Shipowner's liability and the proposed revision of the Hague Rules," *Journal of Maritime Law and Commerce,* 7 (October 1975), p. 217; UNCTAD, "Bills of lading," UN Doc. TD/B/C.4/ISL/6/Rev. 1 (1971), p. 14.

61 For a general discussion of bargaining on liability see M'Gonigle and Zacher, *Pollution, Politics, and International Law,* ch. 5; UNCTAD, "Bills of lading," pp. 11–16.

62 Sweeney, *International Regulations of Maritime Transportation,* p. 74. See also UNCTAD, "The economic and commercial implications of the entry into force of the Hamburg Rules and the Multimodal Transport Convention," UN Doc. /B/C.4/315/Part I (1987).

63 M'Gonigle and Zacher, *Pollution, Politics, and International Law,* ch. 5.

64 "The facilitation of maritime travel and transport," mimeo (London: IMO, July 1986), pp. 3–4; Alexandrowicz, "The Convention on Facilitation of International Maritime Traffic and International Technical Regulation," p. 627.

65 Alexandrowicz, "The Convention on Facilitation of International Maritime Traffic and International Technical Regulation," pp. 628–29.

66 Alexandrowicz, "The Convention on Facilitation of International Maritime Traffic and International Technical Regulation," p. 629. It closely resembled the 1963 American Convention.

67 Alexandrowicz, "The Convention on Facilitation of International Maritime Traffic and International Technical Regulation," p. 641; "The facilitation of maritime travel and transport," p. 6.

68 Gold, *Maritime Transport,* p. 341; Alexandrowicz, "The Convention on Facilitation of International Maritime Traffic and International Technical Regulation," p. 627; interviews.

69 UN Doc. TD/B/C.4/302 (1986), pp. 23–27.

70 M. W. Wefers Bettink, "Open registry: the genuine link and the 1986 Convention on the Registration Conditions for Ships," *Netherlands Yearbook of International Law,* 18 (1987), pp. 74–77.

71 I. M. Sinan, "UNCTAD and flags of convenience," *Journal of World Trade Law,* 18 (1984); S. G. Sturmey, "The United Nations Convention on Conditions for Registration of Ships," *Lloyd's Maritime and Commercial Law Quarterly* (February 1987), pp. 97–117; Mervyn Rowlinson, "Flags of

convenience: the UNCTAD case," *Maritime Policy and Management,* 12 (1985), pp. 241–44; UNCTAD, "Economic consequences of the existence or lack of a genuine link between vessel and flag of registry," UN Doc. TD/B/C.4/168 (1977).

72 Sinan, "UNCTAD and flags of convenience," pp. 95–96; interviews.

73 Elliott Schreier et al., *Outlook for the Liberalization of Maritime Transport* (London: Trade Policy Research Centre, 1985), p. 23; Sinan, "UNCTAD and Flags of Convenience"; interviews.

74 Federal Maritime Commission, *Section 18 Report on the 1984 Shipping Act,* chs. 9 and 10; OECD, *Maritime Transport, 1989,* pp. 63–64; interviews with government and private shipping officials.

75 van der Ziel, " Competition policy in liner shipping," p. 7.

76 The nature of the bulk fleets and their markets are described in: UNCTAD, *Review of Maritime Transport, 1989,* pp. 9–10, 17, 64–67; OECD, *Maritime Transport, 1989,* pp. 69–75, 95–105. UN Doc. TD/B/C.4/203 (1980) analyzes the role of multinational corporations in bulk trades.

77 B. N. Metaxas, *The Economics of Tramp Shipping* (London: Athlone, 1971), p. 19. On the bulk sector see Metaxas, *The Economics of Tramp Shipping;* Alan F. Cafruny, *Ruling the Waves: The Political Economy of International Shipping* (Berkeley, CA: University of California Press, 1987), ch. 10; annual editions of the OECD's *Maritime Transport* and UNCTAD's *Review of Maritime Transport.*

78 Peter Faust, "The United Nations Convention on a Code of Conduct for Liner Conferences," *UNCTAD Review,* 1 (1) (1989), p. 121; interviews.

79 Cafruny, *Ruling the Waves,* ch. 10; UN Doc. TD/B/C.4/234 (1981). Also see the annual reports between 1979 and 1986 of the UNCTAD Committee on Shipping to the Trade and Development Board. There are a small number of cargo limitation schemes among developed countries. The USA, for example, has such an arrangement with Russia in the grain trade and with Japan in the car trade (interviews).

80 Cafruny, *Ruling the Waves,* pp. 250–55; E. A. Gdeorgandopoulos, "The proposed international regulations in the dry bulk markets," *Maritime Policy and Management,* 13 (1986), pp. 223–33.

81 Schreier et al., *Outlook for the Liberalization of Maritime Transport,* p. 23.

82 Daniel Marx, *International Shipping Cartels: A Study of Industrial Self-Regulation by Shipping Conferences* (Princeton, NJ: Princeton University Press, 1953), pp. 45–47; I. A. Bryan and Y. Kotowitz, *Shipping Conferences in Canada* (Ottawa: Department of Consumer and Corporate Affairs, 1978), p. 5.

83 Marx, *International Shipping Cartels,* pp. 45–47; Amos Herman, *Shipping Conferences* (Deventer, Netherlands: Kluwer, 1983), p. 10; G. K. Sletmo and E. W. Williams, *Liner Conferences in the Container Age: US Policy at Sea* (New York: Macmillan, 1981); Krasner, *Structural Conflict,* pp. 202–4; Federal Maritime Commission, *Section 18 Report on the 1984 Shipping Act,* p. 24.

84 Gunnar K. Sletmo, *Liner Conferences: International Aspects* (Ottawa: Transport Canada, 1982), p. 6.

85 Marx, *International Shipping Cartels*, pp. 201–22; Herman, *Shipping Conferences*, pp. 59–75.

86 UNCTAD, "The liner conference system," UN Doc. TD/B/C.4/62 (1970); Federal Maritime Commission, *Section 18 Report on the 1984 Shipping Act*, p. 24; Sletmo, *Liner Conferences: International Aspects*, pp. 7–8; Robert Ellsworth, "Competition or rationalization in the liner industry?," *Journal of Maritime Law and Commerce*, 10 (1979), p. 498; Cafruny, *Ruling the Waves*, pp. 73–88, 115–31, 180–82. On the impact of non-conference lines in promoting low profitability in liner shipping (a situation of market "contestability") see J. E. Davies, "Competition, contestability and the liner shipping industry," *Journal of Transport Economics and Policy*, 20 (September 1986), p. 311; and Federal Maritime Commission, *Section 18 Report on the 1984 Shipping Act*, pp. 155–205 and *passim*; van der Ziel, "Competition policy in liner shipping."

87 US legislation does ban a variety of practices that are tolerated by many other states. R. D. Hughes, "Tacking in stormy weather: the Shipping Act of 1984," *Georgia Journal of International and Comparative Law*, 15 (Summer 1985), pp. 260–62. The USA is actually the only developed state that actively regulates conference practices, although Canada does to an extent. B. J. Abrahamsson, *International Ocean Shipping: Current Concepts and Principles* (Boulder, CO: Westview, 1980), p. 126.

88 OECD, *Maritime Transport*, 1982, pp. 101–2

89 Sletmo, *Liner Conferences*, pp. 5, 26–41; Schreier et al., *Outlook for the Liberalization of Maritime Transport*, p. 37.

90 F. Scherer, *Industrial Market Structure and Economic Performance*, 2nd edn (Chicago, IL: Rand-McNally, 1970), pp. 198–216; Federal Maritime Commission, *Section 18 Report on the 1984 Shipping Act*, pp. 23–24.

91 G. K. Sletmo and E. W. Williams, *Liner Conferences in the Container Age*, ch. 8; Ellsworth, "Competition or rationalization in the liner industry?," pp. 497–506.

92 Studies supportive of closed conferences are: UK, *Report of the Royal Commission on Shipping Rings* (Cd. 4668) (London: 1909); *Report on Steamship Agreements and Affiliations in the American Foreign and Domestic Trade*, Proceedings of the House Committee on the Merchant Marine and Fisheries in the Investigation of Shipping Combinations, 63rd Congress (1914); UK, *Report of the Inquiry into Shippping* (The Rochdale Report) (Cmnd. 4337) (London: 1970); Marx, *International Shipping Cartels*; B. M. Deakin, *Shipping Conferences: A Study of Their Origins, Development and Economic Problems* (Cambridge: Cambridge University Press, 1973); Sletmo and Williams, *Liner Conferences in the Container Age*; Sletmo, *Liner Conferences*; I. A. Bryan and Y. Kolowitz, *Shipping Conferences in Canada* (Ottawa: Department of Consumer and Corporate Affairs, 1978).

93 Federal Maritime Commission, *Section 18 Report on the 1984 Shipping Act,* p. 24.

94 UNCTAD, "The liner conference system"; United States Department of Justice, *The Regulated Ocean Shipping Industry* (Washington, DC: US Government Printing Office, 1977).

95 UN Doc. TD/B/C.4/154 (1976); UK, *Report of the Inquiry into Shipping,* p. 135; Marx, *International Shipping Cartels,* p. 93; Federal Maritime Commission, *Section 18 Report on the Shipping Act of 1984,* pp. 143–49.

96 R. B. C. Farthing, "UNCTAD code of practice for the regulation of liner conferences: another view," *Journal of Maritime Law and Commerce,* 4 (1973), p. 468; Lawrence Juda, *The UNCTAD Liner Code: United States Maritime Policy at the Crossroads* (Boulder, CO: Westview, 1983), p. 7; W. J. Boises and W. G. Green, "The Liner Conference Convention: launching an international regulatory regime," *Law and Policy in International Business,* 6 (1974), pp. 540–41; Sletmo and Williams, *Liner Conferences in the Container Age,* pp. 287–88; UN Doc. TD/104/Rev. 1 (1972), pp. 6–7. CENSA refers to the Council of European National Shipping Associations. It includes the Japanese association.

97 Juda, *The UNCTAD Liner Code;* Lawrence Juda, "World shipping, UNCTAD and the new international economic order," *International Organization,* 35 (Summer 1981), pp. 493–516; Stephen C. Neff, "The UN Code of Conduct for Liner Conferences," *Journal of World Trade Law,* 15 (September/October 1980), pp. 409–10; S. G. Sturmey, "The Code of Conduct for Liner Conferences: a 1985 view," *Maritime Policy and Management,* 13 (1986), pp. 189ff.

98 OECD, *Maritime Transport, 1989,* pp. 63–64. Also see Lawrence Juda, "The UNCTAD Liner Code: a preliminary examination of the implementation of the Code of Conduct for Liner Conferences," *Journal of Maritime Law and Commerce,* 16 (April 1985), p. 183. The figures for US trades provide a more complicated picture. Federal Maritime Commission, *Section 18 Report on the Shipping Act of 1984,* pp. 245 and 329. The 1992 and 1993 *Annual Report* of the US Federal Maritime Commission indicate that on most routes conferences represent about 50–60 percent of capacity (see surveys of different regions).

99 van der Ziel, "Competition policy in liner shipping," p. 10.

100 Karl-Heinz Sager, "How to cure container shipping? Abolish the 'old' conferences," World Freight and Distribution Conference (Brussels, Belgium, 11 June 1991), p. 10.

101 Elizabeth Canna, "Consortia: what's the best way?," *American Shipper* (August 1993), p. 40-F; OECD, *Maritime Transport, 1989,* pp. 115–16; Federal Maritime Commission, *Section 18 Report on the Shipping Act of 1984,* esp. ch. 8 on rates and chs. 36–40 on independent action by conference members.

102 Interview with a government official. *Annual Report* of the Federal Maritime Commission (various issues); Sager, "How to cure container

shipping"; Elizabeth Canna, "Tough sell," *American Shipper* (June 1992), pp. 8–13; Elizabeth Canna, "TAA in fight for its life," *American Shipper* (June 1993), pp. 40B-40C; Janet Porter, "Atlantic ship pact violates EC law, official says," *Journal of Commerce*, 23 August 1993; Tony Beargie, "FMC cannot jump through the EC hoop," *American Shipper* (August 1993), pp. 14–15; Peter Tirschwell, "Atlantic lines battle over '94 rate structure," *Journal of Commerce*, 9 September, 1993; Janet Porter, "EC leaves door open to talk to TAA if shippers can prove it's injurious," *Journal of Commerce*, 26 October 1993; Janet Porter, "P&O chief credits TAA for trans-Atlantic revival," *Journal of Commerce*, 25 March 1994. The US Federal Maritime Commission launched a study of the TAA in the summer of 1994.

103 Mark Magnier, "Rates, rivalry, recession top shippers' agenda in Tapei," *Journal of Commerce*, 10 September 1993.

104 *Annual Report* of the Federal Maritime Commission (various issues); Terry Brennan, "Independents gain westbound Pacific cargo," *Traffic World*, 26 July 1993; Mark Magnier, "Pacific lines to withhold more capacity," *Journal of Commerce*, 21 September 1993.

105 Schrier et al., *Outlook for the Liberalization of Maritime Transport*, p. 9; Federal Maritime Transport, *Section 18 Report on the Shipping Act of 1984*, pp. 46–52.

106 UN Doc. TD/B/C.4/186 (1979), p. 3

107 Juda, *The UNCTAD Liner Code*, pp. 183–85; Sletmo and Williams, *Liner Conferences in the Container Age*; Herman, *Shipping Conferences*. LASH (lighter on board) allow the shipment of barges with goods on board. Neo-bulk can take certain types of cargo that can also go by liner vessels. RO-ROs (roll-on, roll-off) are containerized but allow trucks to be driven on board to pick up containers.

108 Sletmo, *Liner Conferences*, pp. 18–36; OECD, *Maritime Transport, 1989*, pp. 40–50, 110–17; Trevor D. Heaver, "Workable competition, politics, and competition policy in liner shipping," paper presented to the International Conference on Current Issues in Maritime Economics, Erasmus University, Rotterdam, The Netherlands (20–22 June 1991), pp. 10–14.

109 van der Ziel, "Competition policy in liner shipping," pp. 8–10.

110 Sager, "How to cure container shipping?," p. 10.

111 Susan Strange, "Who runs world shipping?," *International Affairs*, 52 (July 1976), p. 347.

112 Ernest G. Frankel, "Competition in liner shipping: an economic debate," paper presented at the Workshop on Competition Policy in Liner Shipping, University of Antwerp, Belgium, 11 February 1994, p. 1.

113 Strange, "Who runs world shipping?," pp. 356–58; OECD, *Maritime Transport, 1989*, p. 40; Schreier et al., *Outlook for the Liberalization of Maritime Transport*, p. 11; Cafruny, *Ruling the Waves*, p. 196; "Reading between the lines," *Containerization International*, 24 (March 1990), pp. 29–35; "The challenge of the '90s," *Containerization International Yearbook*, 1990, p. 6.

114 Sager, "How to cure container shipping?," pp. 3–4.

115 While conference firms controlled close to 50 percent of the traffic on the US's North Atlantic and North Pacific routes, the number of independent firms was about three times their number. Federal Maritime Commission, *Section 18 Report on the 1984 Shipping Act*, pp. 53–54.

116 Canna, "Consortia," p. 40-F.

117 Ellsworth, "Competition or rationalization in the liner industry?," pp. 513–14; Herman, *Shipping Conferences*, pp. 99–102; Christopher Hayman, "International shipping," in R. P. Barston and Patricia Birnie (eds.), *The Maritime Dimension* (London: George Allen and Unwin, 1980), pp. 136–38; E. Schreier, E. Nadel, and B. C. Rifas, "Forces shaping international maritime transport," *World Economy*, 7 (1984), pp. 87–92; Trevor D. Heaver, "Liner freight rates: principles, practices, and prognosis," paper presented at the Workshop on Competition in Liner Shipping, University of Antwerp, Belgium, 11 February 1994. If one looks at the conference and non-conference shipping lines, it is clear that conference firms are largely from Europe, Japan, and the USA. Federal Maritime Commission, *Section 18 Report on the 1984 Shipping Act*, pp. 309–74; interviews with government shipping officials.

118 "Catch-22 in the struggle over the TAA," *American Shipper* (June 1993), p. 40-D.

119 Juda, "The UNCTAD Liner Code," pp. 210–11; Sletmo, *Liner Conferences*, pp. 83–102; Ellsworth, "Competition or rationalization in the liner industry?," pp. 11–15; Cafruny, *Ruling the Waves*, pp. 128–67, 129–67, 221; Schreier et al., *Outlook for the Liberalization of Maritime Transport*, pp. 19–20, 38–41, 69; Federal Maritime Commission, *Section 18 Report on the 1984 Shipping Act*, pp. 81–99. Some developed countries have established ways to protect their national lines as well.

120 Federal Maritime Commission, *Section 18 Report on the Shipping Act of 1984*; Sletmo and Williams, *Liner Conferences in the Container Age*, pp. 299–313; US Department of Justice, *Analysis of the Impact of the Shipping Act of 1984* (March 1990), pp. 31–35; Bryan and Kotowitz, *Shipping Conferences in Canada*, pp. 69–74; Cafruny, *Ruling the Waves*, passim; Alan F. Cafruny, "The political economy of international shipping: Europe vs. America," *International Organization*, 39 (Winter 1985), pp. 79–120. For a comparative analysis of US and Canadian legislation, see D. Khosla, "Canada's new shipping conference legislation: provision for competition with the cartel system," *Canadian Competition Policy Record*, 9 (March 1988), pp. 49–67.

121 van der Ziel, "Competition policy and liner shipping," pp. 12–22; Sager, "How to cure container shipping?"; interviews with government and private shipping officials.

122 Leigh Stoner, "Ocean carrier antitrust immunity is target of new shippers' lobby," *Traffic World* (22 January 1990), p. 34.

123 Stoner, "Ocean carrier antitrust immunity is target of new shippers' lobby," pp. 34–35.

124 Faust, "The United Nations Convention on a Code of Conduct for Liner Conferences," pp. 114–15.

125 See Cafruny, *Ruling the Waves, passim*; and annual editions of the OECD's *Maritime Transport*.

126 Sager, "How to cure container shipping?"; Federal Maritime Commission, *Section 18 Report on the 1984 Shipping Act*, pp. 7–8 and *passim*.

127 Interviews with government shipping officials; OECD, *Maritime Transport, 1989*, p. 121.

128 Lapidoth, "Freedom of navigation," pp. 271–72.

129 M'Gonigle and Zacher, *Pollution, Politics, and International Law*, p. 261.

4 The international air transport regime

1 Nicholas M. Matte, *Treatise on Air/Aeronautical Law* (Toronto: Carswell, 1981), pp. 24–26; Christer Jonsson, *International Aviation and the Politics of Regime Change* (New York: St. Martin's Press, 1987), pp. 6–7, 26; David Corbett, *Politics and the Airlines: The Making of Airline Policy in Australia, Britain, Canada, India and the United States* (London: Allen and Unwin, 1965), p. 26.

2 Paul Stephen Dempsey, *Law and Foreign Policy in International Aviation* (Dobbs Ferry, NY: Transnational, 1987), p. 9; J.W.S. Brancker, *IATA and What It Does* (Leiden: Sijthoff, 1977), p. 7; Jonsson, *International Aviation and the Politics of Regime Change*, pp. 86–91; Ramon de Murias, *The Economic Regulation of International Air Transport* (Jefferson, NC: McFarland, 1989), pp. 20–38; Anthony Sampson, *Empires of the Sky: The Politics, Contests and Cartels of World Airlines* (London: Hodder and Stoughton, 1984), p. 55; Rigas Doganis, *Flying Off Course: The Economics of International Airlines* (London: Allen and Unwin, 1991), pp. 1–3; Alan H. Stratford, *Air Transport Economics in the Supersonic Era* (London: Macmillan, 1973), p. 6.

3 Martin Dresner, *The International Regulation of Air Transport: Changing Regimes and Price Effects* (Ph.D Dissertation, Faculty of Commerce and Business Administration, University of British Columbia, 1989), table 2.16. Dresner's data are from: ICAO, *Civil Aviation Statistics of the World 1991* (Montreal: ICAO, 1992); and IATA, *World Air Transport Statistics 1991* (Montreal: IATA, 1992). On developments in international aviation see Sampson, *Empires of the Sky*, pp. 123–25; Stephen Wheatcroft, *Air Transport Policy* (London: Michael Joseph, 1964), pp. 92–95; Doganis, *Flying Off Course*, pp. 1–3; Stratford, *Air Transport Economics in the Supersonic Age*, pp. 13, 175–76.

4 Sampson, *Empires of the Sky*, p. 224.

5 Dresner, *The International Regulation of Air Transport*, tables 2.2, 2.3, and 2.4; Daniel M. Kasper, *Deregulation and Globalization: Liberalizing International Trade in Air Services* (Cambridge, MA: Ballinger, 1988), pp. 11–12; IATA, *World Air Transport Statistics, 1991*, pp. 5, 10; Doganis, *Flying Off Course*, p. xv; "A survey of the airline industry," *The Economist* (12 June 1993), p. 2; *International Aviation: Trends and Issues* (Canberra, Australia: Bureau of Transport and Communications Economics, 1994), p. 42.

6 Dresner, *The International Regulation of Air Transport*, tables 2.8, 2.9, and 2.10; Kasper, *Deregulation and Globalization*, pp. 13–27; Doganis, *Flying Off Course*, p. 9; *International Aviation*, ch. 3.

7 Dresner, *The International Regulation of Air Transport*, table 2.7; Kasper, *Deregulation and Globalization*, p. 12; Doganis, *Flying Off Course*, pp. 11–17; *World Air Transport Statistics 1991*, p. 5; ICAO, *Civil Aviation Statistics of the World 1991*, pp. 16–17.

8 Stanley Rosenfield, "International aviation: a United States government–industry partnership," *The International Lawyer*, 16 (Summer 1982), p. 483; Betsy Gidwitz, *The Politics of International Air Transport* (Lexington, MA: D. C. Heath, 1980), pp. 6–13; OECD, *Deregulation and Airline Competition* (Paris: OECD, 1988), pp. 16–17; Doganis, *Flying Off Course*, pp. 17–22; Kasper, *Deregulation and Globalization*, pp. 113–22; ICAO, *Civil Aviation Statistics of the World 1991*, pp. 26–28; *International Aviation*, pp. 133–34 and 153–200.

9 Brancker, *IATA and What It Does*, pp. 6–10.

10 Thomas Burgenthal, *Law-Making in the International Civil Aviation Organization* (Syracuse, NY: Syracuse University Press, 1969), p. 221.

11 Eugene Sochor, *The Politics of International Aviation* (Iowa City: University of Iowa Press, 1991), pp. 22–31, 57–70; Gidwitz, *The Politics of International Air Transport*, pp. 82–83; *Memorandum on ICAO* (Montreal: ICAO, 1990), pp. 9–20; Burgenthal, *Law-Making in the International Civil Aviation Organization*, passim.

12 Brancker, *IATA and What It Does*, pp. 13–17, 35–42, 66–70; Richard Pryke, *Competition Among International Airlines* (Aldershot, UK: Gower for the Trade Policy Research Centre, 1987), p. 9; Dempsey, *Law and Foreign Policy in International Aviation*, pp. 281–85; Jacques Narveau, *International Air Transport in a Changing World* (Dordrecht: Martinus Nijhoff, 1989), pp. 61–65, 127–28.

13 Brancker, *IATA and What It Does*, p. 13; Doganis, *Flying Off Course*, pp. 40–41, 63.

14 For a list of (and legal citations for) the international conventions concerning international air transport see "Table of international conventions and other agreements" at the beginning of I. H. Diederiks-Verschoor, *An Introduction to Air Law*, 2nd edn (Deventer, Netherlands: Kluwer, 1985). Almost all of them are mentioned in the context of this chapter.

15 Diederiks-Verschoor, *An Introduction to Air Law*, pp. 18–19, 25–26, 105–6, 152–64.

16 J. C. Cooper, *The Right to Fly* (New York: Henry Holt, 1947), pp. 18–22; J. W. Salacuse, "The little prince and the businessman: conflicts and tensions in public international law," *Journal of Air Law and Commerce*, 45 (1980), pp. 809–13; Jonsson, *International Aviation and the Politics of Regime Change*, pp. 26–22; C. H. Alexandrowicz, *The Law of Global Communications* (New York: Columbia University Press, 1971), p. 11.

17 On the establishment of these jurisdictions between 1919 and 1944 see

Salacuse, "The little prince and the businessman," pp. 814–16; de Murias, *The Economic Regulation of International Air Transport*, pp. 4–5; Jonsson, *International Aviation and the Politics of Regime Change*, pp. 86–91; Wencelas J. Wagner, *International Air Transport as Affected by State Sovereignty* (Brussels: Bruylant, 1970), pp. 40–51; Nicholas M. Matte, *Treatise on Air-Aeronautical Law* (Toronto: Carswell, 1981), pp. 105–7.

18 Kay Hailbronner, "Freedom of the air and the convention on the law of the sea," *American Journal of International Law*, 77 (July 1983), p. 490. It should, however, be noted that quite a few states do establish Air Defense Identification Zones (ADIZ) off their coasts, and they require permission to enter these zones. E. Cuadra, "Air Defense Identification Zones – creeping jurisdiction in the airspace," *Virginia Journal of International Law*, 18 (1978/79), pp. 485–512; J. Carroz, "International legislation on air navigation over the high seas," *Journal of Air Law and Commerce* (1959), pp. 231–60; Diederiks-Verschoor, *An Introduction to Air Law*, pp. 27–28; E. Cuadra, "Air Defense Identification Zones – creeping jurisdiction in the airspace," pp. 485–512. As noted in the following section, states through ICAO do prescribe navigation lanes in international airspace so there is some community management of this area.

19 Kasper, *Deregulation and Globalization: Liberalizing International Trade in Air Services*, p. 47. Also see Jonsson, *International Aviation and the Politics of Regime Change*, pp. 31–32; Betsy Gidwitz, *The Politics of International Air Transport*, pp. 47–48; Salacuse, "The little prince and the businessman," pp. 822–25; *Memorandum on ICAO*, pp. 26–27; Alexandrowicz, *The Law of Global Communications*, pp. 14–15. As of October 1994 there are 99 states that are parties to the agreement (information supplied by ICAO Legal Bureau).

According to the Transit Agreement states can designate the route of the overlying as well as the airports and facilities to be used if it thinks that the overflying airline is not complying with the laws of the state or the stipulations of the agreement. This has led some scholars to be very doubtful as to whether a right of innocent passage exists. Wagner, *International Air Transport as Affected by State Sovereignty*, pp. 141–42; Matte, *Treatise on Air-Aeronautical Law*, pp. 105–7, 132, 140–50.

20 Salacuse, "The little prince and the businessman," p. 814.

21 *International Aviation*, pp. 141 and 138–43.

22 Charles Perrow, *Normal Accidents: Living with High Risk Technologies* (New York: Basic Books, 1984).

23 Brancker, *IATA and What It Does*, p. 7; Matte, *Treatise on Air-Aeronautical Law*, pp. 112–18; Salacuse, "The little prince and the businessman," p. 81; Osborne Mance, *International Air Transport* (London: Oxford University Press, 1944), pp. 19 and 26; Vicki L. Golich, *The Political Economy of International Air Safety: Design for Disaster?* (New York: St. Martin's Press, 1989), p. 18; Vicki L Golich, "The politics and economics of the international commercial aviation safety regime" (unpublished Ph.D dissertation,

School of International Relations, University of Southern California, 1984), p. 157. (The book by Golich is based on her dissertation. Both, however, are cited in this chapter since the dissertation covers the issue more extensively.) Most cooperation within the Western Hemisphere was at the bilateral level.

24 One could make a case that the annex on national registration is concerned with accident control in that some political authority is required to assure compliance with the technical rules. Annex 7: Aircraft Nationality and Registration Marks (Montreal: ICAO, 4th edn, 1981).

25 For an extensive discussion of the intergovernmental and nongovernmental organizations involved in aircraft safety see Golich, "The politics and economics of the international commercial aviation safety regime," pp. 257–307.

26 Gerald F. Fitzgerald, "ICAO and the joint financing of certain navigation services," *Annals of Air and Space Law*, 11 (1986), pp. 17–54 and 12 (1987), pp. 33–60.

27 Eugene Sochor, "From the DC-3 to hypersonic flight: ICAO in a changing environment," *Journal of Air and Space Law*, 55 (Winter 1989), pp. 416–17; Jean Louis Magdelenat, "INMARSAT and the satellites for air navigation services," *Air Law*, 12 (December 1987), pp. 266–81.

28 Werner Guldimann, "Air transport in international law," in H. A. Wassenbergth and H. P. Van Fenema (eds.), *International Air Transport in the Eighties* (Boston: Kluwer, 1981) p. 161; Robert Thornton, *International Airlines and Politics* (Ann Arbor, MI: University of Michigan Press, 1970), p. 40; Thomas Burgenthal, *Law-Making in the International Civil Aviation Organization*, p. 101; H. H. Jones, "Amending the Chicago Conference and its technical standards: can consent of all states be eliminated?," *Journal of Air Law*, 16 (1949), p. 189.

29 Gidwitz, *The Politics of International Air Transport*, pp. 84–87.

30 Golich, "The politics and economics of the international commercial aviation safety regime," pp. 156–57, 264, 308. For a detailed discussion of the Bilateral Airworthiness Agreements see pp. 222–56. Also see Golich, *The Political Economy of International Air Safety*, pp. 32, 258, and 308.

31 Golich, *The Political Economy of International Air Safety*, pp. 26 and 8. The Europeans are beginning to establish greater independence in standard-setting recently (pp. 32 and 68)

32 Douglas W. Caves et al., "An assessment of the efficiency effects of US airline deregulation via an international comparison," in Elizabeth E. Bailey (ed.), *Public Regulation: New Perspectives on Institutions and Policies* (Cambridge, MA: MIT Press, 1987), p. 294.

33 Golich, "The politics and economics of the international commercial aviation safety regime," p. 314. She also observes interestingly that standards imposed by one state are likely to be qualitatively better than the products of compromise among many countries (p. 572).

34 Golich, "The politics and economics of the international commercial aviation safety regime," p. 257. Since 1972 ICAO has been more flexible on construction standards, and this does provide significant leeway for the key producer states.

35 *Memorandum on ICAO*, pp. 46–50; Sochor, "From the DC-3 to hypersonic flight," pp. 416–17; Jacques Naveau, *International Air Transport in a Changing World*, p. 55; Dennis B. Atchley, "Air transportation of radioactive materials and passenger protection under international law," *California Western International Law Journal*, 5 (1974/1975), pp. 425–45

36 Ghislaine Richard, "Air transport safety: prevention and sanctions," *Annals of Air and Space Law*, 9 (1985), p. 151; Gerald F. Fitzgerald, "The use of weapons against civil aircraft," *Annals of Air and Space Law*, 2 (Fall 1984), p. 7.

37 Golich, *The Political Economy of International Air Safety*, p. 4.

38 *Annex 16: Environmental Protection* (Vol. I: Aircraft Noise; Vol. II: Aircraft Engine Emissions) (Montreal: ICAO, 1st edn, 1981, 125 pp. and 60 pp.); S. Bhatt, *Aviation, Environment, and World Order* (New Delhi: Radiant, 1980), ch. 9; Brancker, *IATA and What It Does*, pp. 23–24; Diederiks-Verschoor, *An Introduction to Air Law*, pp. 108–13; "Balancing 'green' against growth," *IATA Review*, no. 3 (1991), pp. 11–12; "Air transport and the environment," *IATA Review*, no. 3 (1992), pp. 10–14; Carole Blackshaw, *Aviation Law and Regulation* (London: Longman, 1992), pp. 229–53; *International Aviation*, pp. 367–72.

Another externality that ICAO regulates to an extent is the transfer of diseases through air traffic although the International Health Regulations developed by the WHO also deal with it. Of particular importance are Article 14 of the Chicago Convention and *Annex 9: Facilitation*.

39 *IATA Review* (January–March 1984), p. 4.

40 Abraham Abramovsky, "Multilateral conventions for the suppression of unlawful seizure and interference with aircraft. Part I: The Hague Convention," *Columbia Journal of Transnational Law*, 13 (1974), p. 381. All hijackings between 1947 and 1971 are described in James A. Arey, *The Sky Pirates* (New York: Charles Scribner's, 1972), pp. 315–54.

41 Louis A. Tyska and Laurence J. Fennelly, *Controlling Cargo Theft* (Woburn, MA: Butterworth, 1983), p. 460; *IATA Review* (May–June 1979), p. 22 and (January–March 1984), p. 4.

42 Frederick C. Dorey, *Aviation Security* (London: Granada, 1983), pp. 106–9; *IATA Review* (March–April 1980), p. 20. For an extensive discussion of strategies for controlling crimes against aircraft see Kenneth C. Moore, *Airport, Aircraft, and Airline Security* (Boston: Butterworth-Neinemann, 1991).

43 R. Frilander, *Terrorism: Documents of International and Local Control* (Dobbs Ferry, NY: Oceana, 1984), p. 324; Joseph J. Lampbert, *Terrorism and Hostages in International Law* (Cambridge: Grotius Publications, 1990).

44 Alana E. Evans and John F. Murphy (eds.), *Legal Aspects of International*

Terrorism (Lexington, MA: D. C. Heath, 1978), p. 27; Paul Sheppard and Eugene Sochor, "Setting international aviation security standards," in Yonah Alexander and Eugene Sochor (eds.), *Aerial Piracy and Aviation Security* (Dordrecht: Martinus Nijhoff, 1990), pp. 3–20; *Security: Safeguarding International Civil Aviation Against Acts of Unlawful Interference* (Montreal: ICAO, 4th edn, 1989, 18 pp.); Gerald F. Fitzgerald, "Aviation terrorism and the International Civil Aviation Organization," *Canadian Yearbook of International Law*, 25 (1987), pp. 219–41.

45 ICAO doc. 8895 A17-Res. (1970); *IATA Review* (May–June 1979), pp. 20–21 and (July–September 1985), p. 4; Brancker, *IATA and What It Does*, pp. 75–76; Dorey, *Aviation Security*, pp. 8–9; "ICAO to concentrate on coping with major challenges," *ICAO Journal* (September 1992): 31; Briana Wall, "Security remains a top priority," *IATA Review*, no. 3 (1991), pp. 16–18; Naveau, *International Air Transport in a Changing World*, pp. 64–65; Trevor Chaseling, "Aviation security and airlines," in Alexander and Sochor, *Aerial Piracy and Aviation Security*, pp. 21–32.

46 Diederiks-Verschoor, *An Introduction to Air Law*, pp. 154–58.

47 Mark E. Fingerman, "Skyjacking and the Bonn Declaration of 1978: sanctions applicable to reluctant nations," *California Western International Law Journal*, 10 (1980), pp. 127–28; Abramovsky, "Multilateral conventions for the suppression of unlawful seizure and interference with aircraft," p. 401; Abraham Abramovsky, "The legality and political feasibility of a multilateral air security enforcement convention," *Columbia Journal of Transnational Law*, 14 (1975), pp. 452–55; Dempsey, *Law and Foreign Policy in International Aviation*, pp. 358–65; Diederiks-Verschoor, *An Introduction to Air Law*, pp. 151–65.

48 John F. Murphy, *Punishing International Terrorists* (Totowa, NJ: Rowman and Allanheld, 1985), pp. 18–20; Dempsey, *Law and Foreign Policy in International Aviation*, pp. 367–70.

49 "Convention on the marking of plastic explosives for the purpose of detection, March 1, 1991," ICAO doc. 9571 (1991); Michael Milde, "Draft convention on the marking of explosives," *Annals of Air and Space Law*, 15 (1990), pp. 155–79; Roderick D. van Dam, "A new convention on the marking of plastic explosives for the purpose of detection," *Air Law*, 16 (1991), pp. 167–77.

50 Dempsey, *Law and Foreign Policy in International Aviation*, p. 380 (also pp. 357–70, 376–82); Sochor, *The Politics of International Aviation*, pp. 163–80; Geoffrey M. Levitt, "Collective sanctions and unilateral action," in Alexander and Sochor, *Aerial Piracy and Aviation Security*, pp. 95–124.

51 Abramovsky, "Multilateral conventions for the suppression of unlawful seizure and interference with aircraft," p. 384.

52 Walter Guldimann, "A future system of liability in air carriage," *Annals of Air and Space Law*, 16 (1991), p. 94.

53 Diederiks-Verschoor, *An Introduction to Air Law*, p. 45 and *passim*. For a chart outlining the evolution of "the Warsaw system" see p. 82. Also see

Finn Hjalsted, "Passenger liability in international carriage by air: lines of development," in Arnold Kean (ed.), *Essays in Air Law* (Netherlands: Kluwer, 1982), p. 105; Sven Brise, "Some thoughts on the economic significance of limited liability in air passenger transport," in Kean, *Essays in Air Law*, pp. 19–26.

54 Diederiks-Verschoor, *An Introduction to Air Law*, pp. 71–75; Michael Milde, "ICAO work on the modernization of the Warsaw system," *Air Law*, 14 (1989), p. 198.

55 Guldimann, "A future system of liability in air carriage," p. 94.

56 Y. W. Kihl, *Conflict Issues and International Civil Aviation Decisions: Three Cases* (Denver: University of Denver, 1971), p. 67.

57 Diederiks-Verschoor, *An Introduction to Air Law*, pp. 76–81; Hjalsted, "Passenger liability in international carriage by air," pp. 95–106. The USA implemented higher liability limits funded by a surcharge on tickets in 1975. Robert P. Boyle, "The Warsaw Convention – past, present, and future," in Kean, *Essays in Air Law*, pp. 7–8. Four protocols dealing largely with the conversion of liability limits into SDRs were accepted in Montreal in 1975, but few states have ratified them. Many developing and socialist states oppose the high limits favored by the developed states.

58 Werner Guldimann, "Rebuilding the airline liability system," *IATA Review*, no. 4 (1989), pp. 11–14; Michael Milde, "ICAO work on the modernization of the Warsaw system," p. 206.

59 Guldimann, "Rebuilding the airline liability system," p. 12. Also see Guldimann, "A future system of liability in air carriage," pp. 95–99; L. R. Edwards, "The liability of air carriers for death and personal injury to passengers," *Australian Law Journal*, 56 (March 1982), p. 114.

60 Carole Blackshaw, *Aviation Law and Regulation* (London: Pitman, 1992), pp. 221–22 (and pp. 139–228 for a general analysis of the Warsaw system). A comparable evaluation is in Diederiks-Verschoor, *An Introduction to Air Law*, p. 81. Another indication of the stabilizing effect of the Warsaw system is the comment by Michael Milde that if the Montreal Protocols do not soon enter into force, "we may witness a trend to denunciation of the Warsaw System by several States with the ensuing chaotic conflicts of laws, conflicts of jurisdiction, unpredictably high compensation claims and skyrocketing increase in the insurance premiums." "ICAO work on the modernization of the Warsaw system," p. 206.

61 Diederiks-Verschoor, *An Introduction to Air Law*, p. 81.

62 There have also been some agreements on surface damage caused by planes, but there has not been strong backing for them. Diederiks-Verschoor, *An Introduction to Air Law*, pp. 93–116; ; G. F. Fitzgerald, "The Protocol to Amend the Convention on Damage Caused by Foreign Aircraft to Third Parties on the Surface (Rome, 1952) signed Montreal, September 23, 1978," *Annals of Air and Space Law*, 4 (1979), pp. 29–73; Bengt Nilsson, "Liability and insurance for damage caused by foreign aircraft to third parties on the surface – a possible new approach to a new problem,"

in A. Kean Amvid (ed.), *Essays in Air Law* (The Hague: Martinus Nijhoff, 1981), p. 181.

63 R. D. Margo, *Aviation Insurance*, 2nd edn (London: Butterworths, 1989), pp. 12–14; Nilsson, "Liability and insurance for damage caused by foreign aircraft to third parties on the surface," p. 185. The requirements of states vary considerably. For a good short analysis of airline insurance see Diederiks-Verschoor, *An Introduction to Air Law*, pp. 117–26.

64 ICAO, *Civil Aviation Statistics of the World 1980* and *1985* (Montreal: ICAO), p. 11 in each volume. Figures for the USSR and the Russian Federation are excluded.

65 Brancker, *IATA and What It Does*, pp. 84–86. Standardized waybills for cargo exist comparable to the standardized tickets that exist for passengers. Diederiks-Verschoor, *An Introduction to Air Law*, pp. 51–53; *IATA Review*, October/December 1982, p. 21.

66 Naveau, *International Air Transport in a Changing World*, pp. 112 and 215.

67 Brancker, *IATA and What It Does*, pp. 77–78; *IATA Review*, April/June 1984, pp. 10–13.

68 Naveau, *International Air Transport in a Changing World*, p. 215; "Streamlining travel," *IATA Review*, no. 3 (1992), pp. 19–20; *IATA Review*, April/June 1984, pp. 10–13.

69 Douglas W. Caves et al., "An assessment of the efficiency effects of US airline deregulation via an international comparison," p. 294.

70 *Annex 9: Facilitation*; "Streamlining travel," *IATA Review*, no. 3 (1992), pp. 19–20; R. I. R. Abeyratne, "Facilitation and the ICAO role – a prologue for the nineties," *Annals of Air and Space Law*, 15 (1990), pp. 3–14. IATA has formulated and periodically revised since the 1950s a Standard Ground Handling Agreement, and it has also published the IATA Airport Handling Manual. The articles of the convention also provide obligations concerning facilitation. Diederiks-Verschoor, *An Introduction to Air Law*, p. 32.

71 Brancker, *IATA and What It Does*, pp. 77–78; de Murias, *The Economic Regulation of International Air Transport*, pp. 16–18; Kasper, *Deregulation and Globalization*, pp. 65–68; ICAO doc. 9082/3 (1986); R. Katz, "The impact of computer reservation systems on air transport competition," in OECD, *Deregulation and Airline Competition* (Paris: OECD, 1988), pp. 85–102; Dempsey, *Law and Foreign Policy in International Aviation*, pp. 111–74, 269–302; Doganis, *Flying Off Course*, p. 94.

72 Dempsey, *Law and Foreign Policy in International Aviation*, p. 48–49.

73 For good analyses of interwar commercial developments see de Murias, *The Economic Regulation of International Air Transport*, pp. 19–43; Oliver Lissitzyn, *International Transport and National Policy* (New York: Council on Foreign Relations, 1942); E. Warner, "Airways for peace," *Foreign Affairs*, 22 (1943), pp. 11–27.

74 William O'Connor, *Economic Regulation of the World's Airlines* (New York: Praeger, 1971), pp. 20–30; Peter Haanappel, *Pricing and Capacity*

Determination in Air Transport (Boston: Kluwer, 1984), pp. 1–14; Harold Jones, "The equation of aviation policy," Journal of Air Law and Commerce, 27 (Summer 1960), pp. 227–29; E. Warner, "The Chicago conference: accomplishments and unfinished business," Foreign Affairs, 23 (1945), pp. 418–20.

75 Haanappel, Pricing and Capacity Determination in Air Transport, p. 17.
76 Sampson, Empires of the Sky, p. 92.
77 Wheatcroft, Air Transport Policy, p. 74; B. Diamond, "The Bermuda Agreement revisited: a look at the past, present and future of Bilateral Air Transport Agreements," Journal of Air Law and Commerce, 41 (1975), pp. 437–53; Haanappel, Pricing and Capacity Determination in Air Transport, pp. 28–32; O'Connor, Economic Regulation of the World's Airlines, pp. 27–28. The eight freedoms are described in de Murias, The Economic Regulation of International Air Transport, pp. 6–7. Dempsey wrote in 1987 that "many nations have rejected the Bermuda I capacity principles in favor of a system providing for the predetermination of capacity" (Law and Foreign Policy in International Aviation, p. 63). He should have replaced "many" with "the great majority of." In fact, this comes out in his discussion on pp. 62–65.
78 Richard Pryke, Competition among International Airlines, p. 9.
79 Doganis, Flying Off Course, pp. 27–41; Kasper, Deregulation and Globalization, pp. 52–55; Haanappel, Pricing and Capacity Determination in Air Transport, p. 35; A. Stoffel, "American Bilateral Air Transport Agreements on the threshold of the jet transport age," Journal of Air Law and Commerce, 26 (1959), pp. 127–32; Jones, "The equation of aviation policy," p. 231.
80 P. Harbison, "Liberal Bilateral Agreements of the United States: a dramatic new pricing policy" (unpublished LLM thesis, McGill University Law School, 1982), p. 9; R. Y. Chuang, The International Air Transport Association (Leiden: A. W. Sijthoff, 1972), p. 26; Leonard Bebchick, "The International Air Transport Association and the Civil Aeronautics Board," Journal of Air Law and Commerce, 25 (1958), p. 11; W. W. Koffler, "IATA: its legal structure, a critical review," Journal of Air Law and Commerce, 32 (1966), pp. 228–29.
81 J. H. Frederick, Commercial Air Transportation (Chicago: Richard D. Irwin, 1951), p. 238; Haanappel, Pricing and Capacity Determination in Air Law, p. 13.
82 Warner, "Airways for peace," pp. 419–20; Robert Thornton, International Airlines and Politics: A Study in Adaptation to Change, p. 23; de Murias, The Economic Regulation of International Air Transport, pp. 11–13.
83 Sochor, The Politics of International Civil Aviation, p. 183. Also see H. Stannard, "Civil aviation: an historical survey," International Affairs, 21 (1945), p. 500.
84 Sochor, The Politics of International Aviation, p. 204; Bruce Stockfish, "Opening closed skies: the prospects for further liberationalization of trade

in international air transport services," *Journal of Air Law and Commerce*, 57 (Summer 1992), p. 612.

85 Jonsson, *International Aviation and the Politics of Regime Change*, p. 157.

86 Robert Thornton, "Power to spare: shift in the international airline equation," *Journal of Air Law and Commerce*, 36 (1970), p. 682.

87 Jones, "The equation of aviation policy," p. 231; Stoffel, "American Bilateral Air Transport Agreements on the threshold of the jet transport age," p. 128.

88 Jack M. Goldklang, "Transatlantic charter policy: a study in airline regulation," *Journal of Air Law and Commerce*, 28 (1961), pp. 100–16; Peter Haanappel, "Ratemaking in international air transport," *Backgrounder* (Montreal: IATA, 1978), pp. 147–48.

89 Jones, "The equation of aviation policy," p. 234.

90 Thornton, *International Airlines and Politics*, p. 681; F. Thayer, *Air Transport Policy and National Security* (Chapel Hill: University of North Carolina Press, 1965), p. 79; Knut Hammarskjold, "Trends in international aviation since World War II and governmental policies with respect to routes, fares, charters, capacity, and designation, " in *Final Report of the International Aviation Symposium* (Kingston, Jamaica: 30 January–2 February 1979), pp. 46–48; Wheatcroft, *Air Transport Policy*, p. 89; K. G. J. Pillai, *The Air Net: The Case Against the World Aviation Cartel* (New York: Grossman, 1969), pp. 57–58; Malon R. Strazheim, *The International Airline Industry* (Washington, DC: Brookings Institution, 1969), pp. 39–41, 135–36.

91 Hammarskjold, "Trends in international aviation since World War II," p. 48. Also see Strazheim, *The International Airline Industry*, pp. 135–42; Doganis, *Flying Off Course*, pp. 41–47; ICAO, *A Review of the International Economic Situation of Air Transport, 1960–1970* (Montreal: ICAO, 1971), pp. 34 and 37; Haanappel, "Ratemaking in international air transport," p. 148.

92 The key non-IATA Asian airlines were Singapore International Airlines, Malaysian Airlines, Thai International Airlines, Cathay Pacific Airways, China Airways (Taiwan), and Korean Airlines. Often they received rights to routes when it appeared they would not fly many flights. Over time they flew an increasing number of customers because of their lower fares and the quality of their service. The socialist states did not belong to IATA, but they negotiated bilateral accords that strictly adhered to Bermuda capacity principles and that established high fares. Haanappel, *Pricing and Capacity Determination in Air Transport*, p. 118.

93 Thornton, *International Airlines and Politics*, pp. 681–82; F. Marx, "Non-scheduled air services: a survey of regulations on the North Atlantic routes," *Air Law*, 6 (1981), pp. 145–48; Haanappel, *Pricing and Capacity Determination in Air Transport*, pp. 122–23; *ICAO Bulletin*, May 1976, p. 26; Doganis, *Flying Off Course*, pp. 48–50; Nawal Taneja, *Airlines in Transition* (Lexington, MA: Lexington Books, 1981), p. 107; Diamond, "The Bermuda Agreement revisited," pp. 437–41.

94 Nawal Taneja, *US International Aviation Policy* (Lexington, MA: D. C. Heath, 1980), pp. 21–25; Paul B. Larsen, "Status report on the renegotiation of the US–UK Bilateral Air Transport Agreement (Bermuda Agreement)," *Air Law*, 3 (1977), pp. 85–88; Peter Haanappel, "Bermuda II: a first impression," *Annals of Air and Space Law*, 2 (1977), pp. 140–47. On US policy over the 1970s see Doganis, *Flying Off Course*, pp. 48–67.

95 Richard E. Caves, *Air Transport and Its Regulators: An Industrial Study* (Cambridge, MA: Harvard University Press, 1962); George W. Douglas and James C. Miller, *Economic Regulation of Domestic Air Transport: Theory and Policy* (Washington, DC: Brookings Institution, 1974); William A. Jordan, *Airline Regulation in America: Effects and Imperfections* (Baltimore: Johns Hopkins University Press, 1970).

96 Stephen G. Breyer, *Regulation and Its Reform* (Cambridge, MA: Harvard University Press, 1982), pp. 197–221.

97 Sampson, *Empires of the Sky*, p. 70; Jonsson, *International Aviation and the Politics of Regime Change*, p. 147; Gidwitz, *The Politics of International Air Transport*, p. 70. The chairman of the CAB appointed by President Ford, John Robson, had started the move toward liberalization. Also, the pressure in 1976 and 1977 from the scheduled airlines to receive the same advantages as the charter airlines with their ABC fares influenced the movement toward deregulation.

98 Kasper, *Deregulation and Globalization*, p. 78.

99 *ICAO Bulletin*, May 1978, p. 40.

100 Salacuse, "The little prince and the businessman," p. 834; Haanappel, *Pricing and Capacity Determination in Air Transport*, p. 165.

101 Thornton, *International Airlines and Politics*, p. 683.

102 Doganis, *Flying Off Course*, pp. 58–62; Taneja, *US International Aviation Policy*, p. 56; Haanappel, *Pricing and Capacity Determination in Air Transport*, pp. 51–53.

103 Harbison, "Liberal Bilateral Agreements of the United States," pp. 42–56; Haanappel, *Pricing and Capacity Determination in Air Transport*, pp. 140–41; Taneja, *US International Aviation Policy*, pp. 92–93; N. Shubat and R. Toh, "The impact and effectiveness of the International Air Transportation Competition Act of 1979," *Transportation Journal*, 25 (1985), p. 53; Jonsson, *International Aviation and the Politics of Regime Change*, pp. 39–54, 122–51; Kasper, *Deregulation and Globalization*, pp. 77–90.

104 Brancker, *IATA and What It Does*, pp. 66–70; Dempsey, *Law and Foreign Policy in International Aviation*, pp. 283–84; and Naveau, *Air Transport in a Changing World*, pp. 63–66, 111, 128.

105 *Aviation Week and Space Technology*, 6 September 1982, pp. 54–55. Even by the early 1990s the only non-national flag carrier with a significant role in intra-European scheduled traffic was Air Europe which operated out of Britain.

106 Sampson, *Empires of the Sky*, ch. 11; de Murias, *The Economic Regulation of International Air Transport*, pp. 177–79.

107 Martin Staniland, "The United States and the external aviation policy of the EU" (Graduate School of Public and International Affairs, University of Pittsburgh, 1994), p. 2.

108 *International Aviation*, pp. 119, 126, and 133–34; Staniland, "The United States and the external aviation policy of the EU," pp. 1–10; Kasper, *Deregulation and Globalization*, pp. 22–23; Doganis, *Flying Off Course*, p. 71; "Flight of the condors," *The Economist* (26 March 1994), pp. 79–80; Martin Dresner and Robert Windle, "The liberalization of US international air policy: impact on US markets and carriers," *Journal of the Transportation Research Forum*, 32 (1992), p. 282.

109 *The Economist* (28 September 1985), pp. 65–66; *Aviation Week and Space Technology*, December 1985, p. 36.

110 Doganis, *Flying Off Course*, pp. 79–106; OECD, *Deregulation and Airline Competition*, pp. 51–52; Sochor, *The Politics of International Civil Aviation*, pp. 184–94; Dempsey, *Law and Foreign Policy in International Aviation*, pp. 93–108; Michael W. Tretheway, "European air transport in the 1990s: deregulating the internal market and changing relationships with the rest of the world" (Working Paper 91-TRA-003; UBC Transportation and Logistics, Faculty of Commerce and Business Administration, University of British Columbia, June 1991), pp. 36–47; Staniland, "The United States and the external aviation policy of the EU," pp. 15–38; *International Aviation*, pp. 353–66.

111 Stockfish, "Opening Closed Skies," pp. 622 and 642; *International Aviation*, p. 147.

112 Tretheway, "European air transport in the 1990s," pp. 61–62.

113 Kasper, *Deregulation and Globalization*, p. 118. For an argument that international liberalization requires allowing open competition among suppliers of computer reservation systems in all countries see Chris Lyle, "Computer age vulnerability in the international airline industry," *Journal of Air Law and Commerce*, 54 (Fall 1988), pp. 161–78.

114 On likely regional developments see Stockfish, "Opening closed skies," pp. 643–46.

115 Daniel M. Kasper, "US–European air services in the 1990s," in *Industry, Services and Agriculture: The United States Faces a United Europe* (Washington, DC: AEI Press, 1992), p. 239.

116 *World Telecommunication Development Report* (Geneva: ITU, 1994), ch. 1. The study contrasts the situation in air transport with telecommunications where competition has not proceeded as far.

117 *International Aviation*, p. 265. See pp. 266–70 on globalization in the industry. On ownership regulations and their importance to future trends see pp. 129–31 as well as chs. 5, 6, and 8.

118 *International Aviation*, p. 168.

119 *International Aviation*, pp. 23–31 and 126 on impediments to competition and p. 274 on the likely decline of flag carriers ; Kasper, "US–European air services in the 1990s," pp. 242–43; Michael Westlake, "Fasten seat belts,"

Far Eastern Economic Review (26 August 1993), pp. 44–46; interview with Professor Michael Tretheway, January 1994.

120 Kasper, *Deregulation and Globalization*, p. 77.

121 Kasper, *Deregulation and Globalization*, p. 70.

122 Doganis, *Flying Off Course*, pp. 9 and 39. The importance of the Asian airlines is noted in *International Aviation*, p. 117.

123 Doganis, *Flying Off Course*, pp. 76–78.

124 Strazheim, *The International Airline Industry*, pp. 184–85.

125 OECD, *Deregulation and Airline Competition*, p. 22. On the issues of economies of scale and scope and contestable markets in civil aviation, see Ethan Weisman, *Trade in Services and Imperfect Competition: Application to International Aviation* (Dordrect: Kluwer Academic, 1990). For challenges to the existence of economies of scale and scope see Caves, *Air Transport and Its Regulators*; Alfred E. Kahn, "Deregulation and vested interests: the case of airlines," in Roger G. Noll and Bruce M. Owen (eds.), *The Political Economy of Regulation* (Washington, DC: American Enterprise Institute, 1983); O'Connor, *Economic Regulation of the World's Airlines*, pp. 9–10 and 116. Pryke, *Competition among International Airlines*, p. 97; David W. Gillen, W. T. Stanbury, and Michael W. Tretheway, "Duopoly in Canada's airline industry: consequences and policy issues," *Canadian Public Policy*, 14 (1988), p. 20. One study in the postwar years that did support the existence of economies of scale is John H. Frederick, *The Economics of Commercial Air Transport* (Homewood, IL: Richard D. Irwin, 3rd edn, 1951), esp. p. 113.

126 OECD, *Deregulation and Airline Competition*, pp. 19–20; Sampson, *Empires of the Sky*, p. 109; Pryke, *Competition among International Airlines*, p. 10.

127 Sampson, *Empires of the Sky*, p. 91.

128 Golich, *The Political Economy of International Air Safety*, p. 35.

129 Charles Perrow, *Normal Accidents: Living with High Risk Technologies*, p. 127. Central to Perrow's analysis is that the airlines support safety for their own economic self-interest.

130 Brancker, *IATA and What It Does*, p. 3.

5 The international telecommunications regime

1 George A. Codding, Jr., *The International Telecommunications Union: An Experiment in International Cooperation* (New York: Arno, 1972), pp. 6–9.

2 Codding, *The International Telecommunications Union*, pp. 10–11.

3 Codding, *The International Telecommunications Union*, pp. 81–82.

4 John Kench, "The convergence of technology: impact on public telecommunications broadcasting and television," *Law, Regulation, Standards of Global Communications* (Special Session, World Telecommunication Forum, Washington, DC, 18–19 April 1985), pp. 218–21; "The tangled webs they weave," *The Economist* (16 October 1993), pp. 21–24. A good discussion of technological changes is: Wilson P. Dizard, *The Coming Information Age* (New York: Longman, 1982), pp. 37–74.

5 "A Survey of Telecommunications," *The Economist* (23 October 1993).

6 R. E. Butler, "Multilateral co-operation on a global basis – the ITU," *Fifth World Telecommunication Forum: Part I* (Geneva: ITU, 1987), p. 107; Thomas Irmer, "Standardization in the changing world of telecommunications," in *The Telecommunications Industry* (New York: Economic Commission for Europe, UN, 1987), p. 44; Kench, "The convergence of technology," pp. 218–21; Andrew Adonis, "6,000 km under the sea," *Financial Times* (19 August 1993); *The Telecommunications Industry*, pp. 1–41; Jill Hills, *Deregulating Telecoms: Competition and Control in the United States, Japan and Britain* (Westport, CN: Quorum, 1986), ch. 1.

7 Dennis Gilhooly, "Telecom 87 – at the crossroads of change," *Telecommunications* (October 1987), p. 13; W. Poschenrieder, "Implementation of ISDN technology serving the telecommunications demand of the future," *Fifth World Telecommunication Forum: Part I* (Geneva: ITU, 1987), p. 92; "Survey of Telecommunications, " *The Economist* (10 March 1990), p. 12.

8 Hugo Dixon, "The phone redraws map of world," *Financial Times* (8 June 1990); *Yearbook of Public Telecommunications Statistics: Chronological Series, 1978–1989* (Geneva: ITU, 1990).

9 Peter F. Cowhey, "Telecommunications," in Gary Clyde Hufbauer (ed.), *Europe 1992: An American Perspective* (Washington, DC: Brookings, 1990), p. 161.

10 Geza Feketekuty, *Trade in Services: An Overview and Blueprint for Negotiations* (Cambridge, MA: Ballinger, 1988), p. 46; "International telephone service deficit remains a challenge for US," *FCC Week* (17 April 1989); Peter F. Cowhey and Jonathan D. Aronson, *Managing the World Economy: The Consequences of Corporate Alliances* (New York: Council on Foreign Relations, 1993), p. 185.

11 *World Telecommunication Development Report* (Geneva: ITU, 1994), chs. 1, 5, and 6; Jeffrey A. Hart, "The politics of competition in the global telecommunications industry," *The Information Society*, 5 (1988), p. 176.

12 George Codding and Anthony Rutkowski, *The International Telecommunications Union in a Changing World* (Dedham, MA: Artech, 1982), pp. 92–114; Jonathan D. Aronson and Peter F. Cowhey, *When Countries Talk: International Trade in Telecommunications* (Cambridge, MA: Ballinger, 1988), pp. 45–51; James G. Savage, *The Politics of International Telecommunications Regulation*, pp. 67–72; interviews.

13 Codding, *The International Telecommunications Union*, pp. 13–95; Savage, *The Politics of International Telecommunications Regulation*, pp. 28–33.

14 Robert Chapuis, "The CCIF and the development of international telephony, 1923–1956," *CCITT Reprint Series* (Geneva: ITU, 1976), pp. 23–24; Codding, *The International Telecommunications Union*, p. 122.

15 Codding, *The International Telecommunications Union*, pp. 146–56; John D. Tomlinson, *The International Control of Radio-Communications* (Ann Arbor, MI: J. W. Edwards, 1945), pp. 68–75; Savage, *The Politics of International Telecommunications Regulation*, pp. 34–36.

16 Codding and Rutkowski, *The ITU in a Changing World*, pp. 91–114; Savage, *The Politics of International Telecommunications Regulation*, pp. 14–19, 38–43. On the 1992 institutional changes see *Final Acts of the Additional Plenipotentiary Conference, Geneva, 1992* (Geneva: ITU, 1992); Alan Carter, "ITU reorganizes radio sectors," *Radio World* (22 July 1992); Andreas Evagora, "Standards cooperation?," *Communications Week* (11 November 1992); Andreas Evagora, "Standards Cooperation?," *Communications Week* (23 November 1992); George A. Codding, "After the December Plenipot: the new look for the ITU," *Intermedia* (March/April 1993); Edmund W. Beaty, "Standards regionalization – a threat to internetworking?," *Telecommunications* (May 1993).

17 William J. Drake, "The CCITT: time for reform?," in *Reforming the Global Network: The 1989 ITU Plenipotentiary Conference* (London: International Institute of Communications, 1989), pp. 34–35; Graham Finnie, "The spirit of Melbourne," *Telecommunications* (January 1989); Bob Horton, "Standardization and the challenge of global consensus," *Pacific Telecommunications Review*, 15 (September 1993), pp. 16–22.

18 Harvey J. Levin, *The Invisible Resource: The Regulation of the Radio Spectrum* (Baltimore: Johns Hopkins Press, 1971); J. M. Frost (ed.), *World Radio TV Handbook, 1983* (Hvidovre, Denmark: Billboard AG, 1983); Codding and Rutkowski, *The ITU in a Changing World*, pp. 246–47.

19 J. E. S. Fawcett, *Outer Space: New Challenges to Law and Policy* (Oxford: Clarendon, 1984), p. 88; Carl Q. Christol, "The Geostationary orbital position as a natural resource of the space environment," *Netherlands International Law Review*, 36 (1979), p. 5; interviews.

20 Nicholas M. Matte (ed.), *Space Activities and Emerging International Law* (Montreal: Centre for Research of Air and Space Law, McGill University, 1984), pp. 22–26; A. Chayes and L. Laskin, *Direct Broadcasting from Satellites: Policies and Problems* (St. Paul, MN: West Publishing, 1975); R. Davis, "Future trends in communication satellite systems," in D. J. Curtin (ed.), *Trends in Communication Satellites* (New York: Pergamon, 1979); Donna Demac, *Tracing New Orbits: Cooperation and Competition in Global Satellite Development* (New York: Columbia University Press, 1986); W. J. Howell, *World Broadcasting: The Age of the Satellite* (Norwood, NJ: Ablex, 1986); Martin A. Rothblatt, "New satellite technology, allocation of global resources, and the International Telecommunications Union," *Columbia Journal of Transnational Law*, 24 (1985), pp. 37–50.

21 Articles 79 and 112–15, United Nations Convention on the Law of the Sea (1982), *International Legal Materials*, 6 (November 1982).

22 Carl Q. Christol, *The Modern International Law of Outer Space* (New York: Pergamon, 1982), pp. 13–58; quote from Articles 1 and 2 of Outer Space Treaty.

23 D. M. Leive, *International Telecommunications and International Law: The Regulation of the Radio Spectrum* (Dobbs Ferry, NY: Oceana, 1970), pp. 41–42; Codding, *The International Telecommunications Union*, pp. 92–95; Codding

and Rutkowski, *The International Telecommunications Union in a Changing World*, pp. 117–18; Tomlinson, *The International Control of Radio-Communications*, pp. 25–26.

24 Codding, *The International Telecommunications Union*, pp. 119–50; Codding and Rutkowski, *The International Telecommunications Union in a Changing World*, pp. 189–91, 256–58; Leive, *International Telecommunications and International Law*, pp. 45–54.

25 H. Osborne Mance, *International Telecommunications* (London: Oxford University Press, 1943), pp. 36–37; Tomlinson, *The International Control of Radio-Communications*, pp. 303–4, 227–33.

26 Tomlinson, *The International Control of Radio-Communications*, p. 233.

27 Ranjan Borra, "The problem of jamming international broadcasting," *Journal of Broadcasting*, 9 (Fall 1967), pp. 358–60; Savage, *The Politics of International Telecommunications Regulation*, pp. 135–46.

28 This was reflected in the 1966 UN Covenant on Civil and Political Rights. Donald R. Browne, *International Radio Broadcasting: The Limits of the Limitless Medium* (New York: Praeger, 1982), p. 24.

29 Savage, *The Politics of International Telecommunications Regulation*, p. 156.

30 Savage, *The Politics of International Telecommunications Regulation*, pp. 157, 160.

31 During 1994 Iran outlawed satellite dishes; Singapore reaffirmed its ban and is rapidly wiring a national cable network to avoid satellites altogether; Canada restricted receiving equipment for DirecTv and other US systems; and China successfully pressured Hong Kong's AsiaSat to close down the Asian BBC television World Service. However, these have failed or are likely to fail. Personal communication from James Savage, November 1994.

32 E. D. du Charme, M. J. R. Irwin, and R. Zeitoun, "Direct broadcasting by satellite: the development of the international technical and administrative regulatory regime," *Annals of Air and Space Law*, 9 (1984), p. 270; Fawcett, *Outer Space*, p. 68; B. A. Hurvitz, "The labyrinth of international tele-communications law: direct broadcast satellites," *Netherlands International Law Review*, 35 (1988), pp. 158–60; Savage, *The Politics of International Telecommunications Regulation*, pp. 148–52; David E. S. Blatherwick, *The International Politics of Telecommunications* (Berkeley, CA: Institute of International Studies, University of California, 1987), pp. 37–44; UN General Assembly, Resolution 2916 (November 1972).

33 Hurvitz, "The labyrinth of international telecommunications law," p. 160.

34 The opposition of most Western states to the UNGA resolution was based on the judgment that a clause supporting the international flow of information should be added. Howard C. Anawalt, "Direct television broadcasting and the quest for communication equality," in *Regulation of Transnational Communications* (New York: Clark Boardman, 1984), pp. 364–69; Christol, *The Modern International Law of Outer Space*, pp. 648–49, 702–9; UN General Assembly, Resolution 3792 (February 1983);

Sharon L. Fjordbak, "The international direct broadcast satellite controversy," *Journal of Air Law and Commerce*, 55 (Summer 1990), pp. 903–38. On the Third World demand for a New World Information Order, see the McBride Commission report, *Many Voices, One World: Communication and Society Today and Tomorrow* (London: Kogan Page, 1980); Savage, *The Politics of International Telecommunications Regulation*, pp. 153–55.

35 Interviews with government and industry officials. In Europe SES-Astra from Luxembourg has an audience in England and the Low Countries, but Europeans are still wedded to their national networks. In Latin America DBS services are developing audiences very quickly. As satellites become more high powered and dishes are reduced in size and cost, regional satellites will proliferate.

36 For pre–1939 developments, see Codding, *The International Telecommunications Union*, pp. 113–14, 126, 147, 150, 157–60, 178–79; Tomlinson, *The International Control of Radio-Communications*, pp. 54, 179–223; Codding and Rutkowski, *The International Telecommunications Union in a Changing World*, pp. 267–68; Savage, *The Politics of International Telecommunications Regulation*, pp. 32–36, 67–71. On the resurrection of allotment plans after 1945, see Codding, *The International Telecommunications Union*, pp. 365–85.

37 Article 2 of the Outer Space Treaty; Christol, *The Modern International Law of Outer Space*, pp. 458–60; E. D. du Charme, R. Bowen, and M. J. R. Irwin, "The genesis of the 1985–87 ITU World Administrative Radio Conference on the Use of the Geostationary Satellite Orbit and the Planning of Space Services Utilizing it," *Annals of Air and Space Law*, 7 (1982), pp. 266–67; Larry F. Martinez, *Communication Satellites: Power Politics in Space* (Dedham, MA: Artech House, 1985), pp. 116–19. Also, all ITU conventions since the early 1970s have provisions concerning equal access and equitable sharing.

38 Codding and Rutkowski, *The International Telecommunications Union in a Changing World*, pp. 49–50; du Charme et al., "Direct broadcasting by satellite," p. 271; Martinez, *Communication Satellites: Power Politics in Space*, pp. 120–24; Jakhu et al., "The ITU regulatory framework for satellite communications," pp. 280–88; *ORB-88: A Pre-Conference Bulletin* (London: International Institute of Communications, 1987); George A. Codding, Jr., *The Future of Satellite Communications* (Boulder, CO: Westview, 1990), pp. 103–16.

39 Codding and Rutkowski, *The International Telecommunications Union in a Changing World*, pp. 15, 262–68; Tomlinson, *The International Control of Radio-Communications*, p. 48; Codding, *The International Telecommunications Union*, pp. 185–245, 344–45; Leive, *International Telecommunications and International Law*, pp. 55–65.

40 *Radio Frequency Use and Management: Impacts of the World Administrative Radio Conference of 1979* (Washington, DC: Office of Technology Assessment, US Congress, 1982), p. 10.

41 G. O. Robinson, "Regulating international airwaves: the 1979 WARC," *Virginia Journal of International Law*, 21 (1980), p. 45.

42 Codding, *The International Telecommunications Union*, pp. 91–95; Tomlinson, *The International Control of Radio-Communications*, pp. 25–26.

43 On the 1947 decision see, Codding, *The International Telecommunications Union*, p. 243. The provision is now in Article 12, paragraph 1506 of the 1982 Radio Regulations.

44 Leive, *International Telecommunications and International Law*, pp. 55–65; Codding, *The International Telecommunications Union*, pp. 185–245, 344–65.

45 R. J. Mayher, "World wide enhancement of national spectrum management systems," *Eighth International Zurich Symposium of Technical Experts on EMC, 7–9 March 1979*, p. 470; Abderrazak Berrada, "New approach to the international management of the spectrum and the geostationary-satellite orbit," *Eighth International Zurich Symposium of Technical Experts on EMC, 7–9 March 1979*, pp. 467–71; interviews.

46 G. A. Codding, *World Administrative Radio Conference for the Planning of HG Bands Allocated to the Broadcasting Service: A Pre-Conference Briefing Paper* (London: International Institute of Communications, 1983), p. 16; Codding and Rutkowski, *The International Telecommunications Union in a Changing World*, pp. 123–25, 252–53, 274–78; Savage, *The Politics of the International Telecommunications Regulation*, pp. 97–102; interviews

47 Codding, *The International Telecommunications Union*, pp. 92–95; Tomlinson, *The International Control of Radio-Communications*, pp. 25–26; Leive, *International Telecommunications and International Law*, pp. 41–42.

48 The head of the US delegation to the 1979 WARC wrote that "in the end these controversies typically were settled only when the developing countries realized that the United States and other countries were in a position to block effective use of the proposed allocations unless their existing services were accommodated." Robinson, "Regulating international airwaves," pp. 24–25.

   On the conflicts at the 1992 WARC, see "WARC begins, mobile telephone, Leosat service top agenda," *FCC Week* (10 February 1992); Hugo Dixon and Michiyo Nakamoto, "Making waves for the world," *Financial Times* (February 1992); "Hard WARC, but it was worth it," *Public Network Europe* (UK) (April 1992); C. Vishnu Mohan, "WARC-92, Spain," *Intermedia* (March/April 1992).

49 Codding, *The International Telecommunications Union*, p. 114; Tomlinson, *The International Control of Radio-Communications*, p. 54.

50 Since World War II global and regional maritime plans have been formulated in 1948, 1949, 1951, 1955, 1957, 1974, 1985, and 1987. Ones for aeronautical communications were adopted in 1948, 1949, 1951, 1964, 1978, and 1987.

51 In the postwar period regional allotment plans for Europe and/or Africa were adopted in 1949, 1952, 1961, 1963, 1966, 1974, 1983, and 1985. Western Hemispheric plans were adopted in 1981 and 1988.

52 Codding and Rutkowski, *The International Telecommunictions Union in a Changing World*, pp. 15, 262–68; Tomlinson, *The International Control of Radio-Communications*, p. 48; Codding, *The International Telecommunications Union*, pp. 185–245, 344–65; Leive, *International Telecommunications and International Law*, pp. 55–65; Savage, *The Politics of International Telecommunications Regulation*, pp. 67–91.

53 Robinson, "Regulating international airwaves"; George A. Codding et al., *ITU World Administrative Radio Conference for the Planning of HF Bands Allocated to the Broadcasting Service: A Pre-Conference Briefing Paper* (London: International Institute of Communications, 1983); interviews.

54 du Charme et al., "The genesis of the 1985–87 ITU World Administrative Radio Conference on the Use of the Geostationary Satellite Orbit and the Planning of Space Services Utilizing It," pp. 265–67; Donna Demac et al., *Equity in Orbit: The 1985 Space WARC* (London: International Institute of Communications, 1985), pp. 6–14; Codding and Rutkowski, *The International Telecommunications Union in a Changing World*, pp. 248–50; du Charme et al., "Direct broadcasting by satellite," pp. 271–77; Jakhu et al., "The ITU regulatory framework for satellite communications," pp. 280–88; Heather Hudson, "Mixed planning approach at Geneva," *Telecommunications Policy*, 9 (December 1985), pp. 270–72; *ORB-88*; "US pleased with WARC results," *Broadcasting* (October 1988); Christol, *The Modern International Law of Outer Space*, pp. 213–45; Articles 11–13 of the ITU Radio Regulations; Codding, *The Future of Satellite Communications*, pp. 99–116; Kim Degnan, "Orbital settlers shoot it out with space outlaws – where is the sheriff?," *Via Satellite*, 8 (September 1993), pp. 30–41; Jorn Christensen, "Orbital slot contention and the radio regulations," *Via Satellite*, 9 (June 1994); Roger Highfield, "Satellite's illegal orbit may start a jamming war," *The Daily Telegraph* (3 August 1994).

55 Christensen, "Orbital slot contention and the radio regulations."

56 Christol, *The Modern International Law of Outer Space*, pp. 59–151, especially p. 112. For a general study of the law relating to damages in outer space, see G. C. M. Reijnen and W. de Graaf, *The Pollution of Outer Space, in Particular of the Geostationary Orbit* (Dordrecht: Martinus Nijhoff, 1989). The Soviet Union claimed that the damage was not covered by the convention, and the convention was not mentioned in the settlement. However, acceptance of the norm did underlie the settlement.

57 Sylvia Ospina, "Piracy of satellite transmitted copyright material in the Americas: bane or boom," in Donna A. Demac (ed.), *Tracing New Orbits: Competition and Cooperation in Satellite Developments* (New York: Columbia University Press, 1986), pp. 166–98; Heather Dembert , "Securing authors' rights in satellite transmission: US efforts to extend copyright protection abroad," *Columbia Journal of Transnational Law*, 24 (1985), pp. 73–101; Fawcett, *Outer Space*, pp. 30–31; personal communication from James Savage, November 1994.

58 Borra, "The problem of jamming in international broadcasting," p. 346;

Julian Hale, *Radio Power: Propaganda and International Broadcasting* (London: Paul Elek, 1975), pp. 128 and 136; O. Mance, *International Telecommunications*, pp. 36–37; Tomlinson, *The International Control of Radio-Communications*, pp. 227–33, 303–04.

59 Browne, *International Radio Broadcasting*, p. 24; Borra, "The problem of jamming in international broadcasting," p. 358. In the early postwar years Third World states did back resolutions condemning jamming. UN General Assembly, Resolution 424 (14 December 1950).

60 Fawcett, *Outer Space*, pp. 68–77; Christol, *The Modern International Law of Outer Space*, pp. 613–49, 702–9; Blatherwick, *The International Politics of Telecommunications*, pp. 37–44; Anawalt, "Direct television broadcasting and the quest for communication equality," pp. 364–69.

61 Pekka J. Tarjanne, "Access to 1990s Telecom networks and markets," *Transnational Data and Communications Report* (February 1990).

62 D. M. Cerni, *The CCITT: Organization, US Participation, Studies toward the ISDN* (Washington, DC: Department of Commerce, 1982), p. 8.

63 Stanley M. Besen and Joseph Farrell, "The role of the ITU in standardization: pre-eminence, impotence, or rubber stamp?," *Telecommunications Policy* (August 1991), pp. 311–21; Philipp Genschel and Raymund Werle, "From national hierarchies to international standardization: historical and modal changes in the coordination of telecommunications" (Cologne: Max-Planck-Institut für Gesellschaftsforschung, February 1992), pp. 29–33; Beaty, "Standards regionalization"; Codding, "After the December Plenipot"; Evagora, "Standards cooperation?" Approximately 96 percent of all international technical standards come from the three Geneva-based organizations – the ITU, International Standards Organization, and International Electrotechnical Commission. Frances Williams, "Environment has been transformed," *Financial Times* (14 October 1994). Private firms have always been important participants in the deliberations of ITU standard-setting bodies, but they are now assuming a much stronger role in relation to governments.

64 Tomlinson, *The International Control of Radio-Communications*, pp. 25–36.

65 Tomlinson, *The International Control of Radio-Communications*, pp. 109, 86–96; Codding, *The International Telecommunications Union*, pp. 95–115; Codding and Rutkowski, *The ITU in a Changing World*, pp. 254–55; Savage, *The Politics of International Telecommunications Regulation*, pp. 172–77.

66 Codding, *The International Telecommunications Union*, pp. 83–96.

67 Interviews.

68 The CCIR has approved interconnection technologies for the three systems, but they are expensive and distort the picture. R. J. Crane, *The Politics of International Standards: France and the Color TV War* (Norwood, NJ: Ablex, 1979); Savage, *The Politics of International Telecommunications Regulation*, pp. 189–93.

69 Savage, *The Politics of International Telecommunications Regulation*, pp. 193–96; *The Economist* (1 October 1988), pp. 80–82; (27 May 1989),

pp. 67–68; (4 August 1990), pp. 58–60; Jeffrey A. Hart and Laura Tyson, "Responding to the challenge of HDTV," *California Management Review*, 31 (Summer 1989), pp. 132–45; "HDTV: a view of the 1990s," *Airwaves* (London, Summer 1988); Matthieu Joosten, "'Let the market decide' – but can it?," and Philip Carse and Mark Shurmer, "Why the US standard will have the clearest 'market focus'," *Intermedia* (March/April 1993); Andrew Hill and Andrew Adonis, "Turn on to the bigger picture," *Financial Times* (16 June 1993); Bill Powell, "Losing their lead," *Newsweek* (13 December 1993), p. 55. The USA in 1993 officially accepted a digital standard.

70 D. M. Cerni, *Standards in Process: Foundations and Profiles of ISDN and OSI Studies* (Washington, DC: Department of Commerce, 1984), pp. 22–23; interviews.

71 Savage, *The Politics of International Telecommunications Regulation*, pp. 196–98; Patrick Whitten, "Cellular: what need for European integration?," *Intermedia*, 14 (May 1986), pp. 36–38; interviews.

72 Codding, *The International Telecommunications Union*, pp. 13–21, 55, 65–67.

73 Codding, *The International Telecommunications Union*, pp. 32–36, 78; Codding and Rutkowski, *The ITU in a Changing World*, pp. 9, 84–85; Robert Chapuis, *The CCIF and the Development of International Telephony, 1923–1956* (Geneva: ITU, CCITT Reprint Series, 1976), p. 31.

74 Irmer, "Standardization in the changing world of telecommunications," p. 45.

75 Cerni, *The CCITT*, p. 48.

76 Interview with an ITU official; Irmer, "Standardization in the changing world of telecommunications," p. 28. Also, on the success of interconnection and the existence of multiple equipment standards, see William H. Melody, "Telecommunication – policy directions for the technology and information services," *Oxford Surveys and Information Technology*, 3 (1986), p. 92.

77 *Telecommunications Network* (Paris: OECD, 1988), pp. 58–61; Gregory Langford, "Planning the multinational network," *Telecommunications* (November 1989).

78 Poschenrieder, "Implementation of ISDN technology serving the telecommunications demand of the future," p. 94; M. E. Brenton, "The role of standardization and telecommunications," in *Trends of Change in Telecommunications Policy* (Paris: OECD, 1987), p. 196.

79 D. M. Cerni and E. M. Gray, *International Telecommunication Standards: Issues and Implications for the 80s* (Washington, DC: Department of Commerce, May 1983), pp. 57–59.

80 John J. Walsh, "Picturing an international standard," *Communications Week* (11 November 1988).

81 Savage, *The Politics of International Telecommunications Regulation*, pp. 201–10; Hussein Rostum, *Telidon and the Videotext Standard-Setting Process: Background Study Number 2* (Ottawa: Teega Research Consultants, 1985); E. O'Brien, *Final Report under DSS Contact OST83-00010 to Provide*

Technical Assistance to Study and Analyze Presentation Level Protocols (Ottawa: Department of Communications, 1984), pp. 4–6; M. Epstein, "Et voila! Le minitel," *New York Times Magazine* (9 March 1986), pp. 48–49.

82 Adrian Morant, "Dissent: screening the mail," *Intermedia* (August/ September 1990); "Developments in electronic messaging," *Computer Law and Security Report* (November 1990); "E-Mail connectivity," *Communications Week International* (18 February 1991); Harold B. Combs, "Future prospects for X.400," *Telecommunications* (July 1992).

83 ITU Doc. OCM XV-R 22-E, April 1987. This explicit statement of ITU policy is also generally followed by the International Standards Organization.

84 Rostum, *Telidon and the Videotext Standard-Setting Process*; Cerni and Gray, *International Telecommunication Standards*, pp. 48–49; Marvin A. Sirbu and L. Zwimpfer, "Standards setting for computer communication: the case of X.25," *IEEE Communications Magazine*, 23 (March 1985), pp. 35–44; S. M. Besen and L. L. Johnson, *Compatibility Standards, Competition, and Innovation in the Broadcasting Industry* (Santa Monica, CA: Rand, 1986); Aronson and Cowhey, *When Countries Talk*, p. 177.

85 Sirbu and Zwimpfer, "Standards setting for computer communication"; Lee McKnight, "The international standardization of telecommunication services and equipment," in E. J. Mestmaecke (ed.), *The Law and Economics of Transborder Telecommunications* (Baden-Baden: Momos Verlag, 1987), pp. 415–36; Cerni and Gray, *International Telecommunication Standards*, pp. 48–49; Aronson and Cowhey, *When Countries Talk*, p. 177.

86 Sirbu and Zwimpfer, "Standards setting for computer communication."

87 Sirbu and Zwimpfer, "Standards setting for computer communication"; McKnight, "The international standardization of telecommunications services and equipment"; Cerni, *The CCITT*, p. 48.

88 Sirbu and Zwimpfer, "Standards setting for computer communication"; McKnight, "The international standardization of telecommunications services and equipment."

89 Savage, *The Politics of International Telecommunications Regulation*, p. 217.

90 François Bar and Michael Borrus, *From Public Access to Private Connections: Network Policy and National Advantage* (Berkeley, CA: Berkeley Roundtable on the International Economy, University of California, 1987), Section I. On this point, see Cerni and Gray, *International Telecommunication Standards; Standards in Information and Communications Technology* (Paris: OECD, 1987).

91 Richard E. Butler, "Interconnection and trade," *Transnational Data and Communications Report* (October 1988).

92 M. E. Brenton, "The role of standardization and telecommunications," p. 166; "Survey of telecommunications," *The Economist* (5 October 1991), p. 16; Genschel and Werle, "From national hierarchies to international standardization," p. 27.

93 Albert Bressand, "Interconnection and the Think Net Process," *Interconnection: Vol. II* (Paris: Promethee, 1988), p. 293.

94 "ITU proposes global net," *Communications Week* (12 February 1990).

95 For an argument against the importance of mutual interests see Stephen D. Krasner, "Global communications and national power: life on the Pareto frontier," *World Politics*, 43 (April 1991), pp. 336–66.

96 Peter Cowhey refers to the cartel norm as the norm of "jointly provided services." "The international telecommunications regime: the political roots of regimes of high technology," *International Organization*, 44 (Spring 1990), pp. 177–79.

97 John Gerard Ruggie, "International regimes, transactions, and change: embedded liberalism in the postwar economic order," in Stephen D. Krasner (ed.), *International Regimes* (Ithaca, NY: Cornell University Press, 1982), pp. 195–232.

98 Good general analyses are in: Karl-Heinz Neumann, "The international system of telecommunications tariffs," in Mestmacker (ed.), *The Law and Economics of Transborder Telecommunications*, pp. 373–413; and Aronson and Cowhey, *When Countries Talk: International Trade in Telecommunications*. The ITU regulations are in General Tariff Principles (Geneva: ITU, 1985).

99 Wilson P. Dizard, "International regulation: telecommunications and information," in Carol C. Adelman (ed.), *International Regulation: New Rules in a Changing World Order* (San Francisco: ICS Press, 1988), p. 121.

100 Melody, "Telecommunication – policy directions for technology and information services," p. 79. Also, see Neumann, "The international system of telecommunications tariffs," p. 379.

101 Daniel R. Headrick, *The Invisible Weapon: Telecommunications and International Politics, 1851–1945* (New York: Oxford University Press, 1991), esp. chs. 2–4 and 10–11; Henry Ergas and Paul Paterson, "International telecommunications accounting arrangements: an unsustainable inheritance?" (mimeo, 1989).

102 Codding, *The International Telecommunications Union*, pp. 14–21, 57–58; Keith Clark, *International Communications: An American Attitude* (New York: AMS Press, 1931), p. 93.

103 Codding, *The International Telecommunications Union*, pp. 57–60; J. M. Herring and J. C. Gross, *Telecommunications: Economics and Regulation* (New York: McGraw-Hill, 1936), pp. 21–22; Mance, *International Telecommunications*, pp. 13–14; P. E. D. Nagle, *International Communications and the International Telegraph Convention* (Washington, DC: Government Printing Office, 1923), pp. 21–61. What frustrated both the Americans and Europeans about the British system was the routeing of telecommunications through Eastern/Cable and Wireless networks when the use of the American and European networks would have been more efficient. The USA finally succeeded in getting Britain to accept direct routeing prior to and during World War II.

104 Neumann, "The international system of telecommunications tariffs," p. 379.

105 Hart, "The politics of competition in the global telecommunications industry," p. 172.

106 Codding, *The International Telecommunications Union*, pp. 266, 273, 334; Clark, *International Communications*, pp. 110–22; G. Lloyd Wilson et al., *Public Utilities Industries* (New York: McGraw-Hill, 1933), p. 330; Henry Goldberg, "One hundred and twenty years of international communications, " *Federal Communications Law Journal*, 37 (1985), pp. 132–37. Canada tended to follow the US lead on policies toward the cartel, but its verbal opposition was never as strong.

107 *General Tariff Principles*, Section 2, Recs. 10–30; personal communication from James Savage. Only about 5 percent of all international calls go through transit states; for all others there are direct circuits.

108 *General Tariff Principles*, Section 3, Rec. 41; Neumann, "The international system of telecommunications tariffs," pp. 393–95; interviews. The sourcing of calls in lower-cost countries has actually only become quite common in recent decades.

109 *General Tariff Principles*, Section 1, Recs. 7 and 8.

110 Robert C. Fisher, "Telecommunications in transition: private transatlantic cables," *George Washington Journal of International Law and Economics*, 19 (1985), pp. 498–99; Goldberg, "One hundred and twenty years of international communications," pp. 138–39. Planning for transatlantic cables is done within the context of the North Atlantic Consultative Process. Melody has written that the cables constitute "simply an extension of national telecommunications systems to mid-ocean." Melody, "Telecommunication – policy directions for technology and information services," p. 102.

111 Jonathan F. Galloway, *The Politics and Technology of Satellite Communications* (Lexington, MA: D. C. Heath, 1972); Francis Lyall, *Law and Space Telecommunications* (Aldershot, Hants.: Dartmouth, 1989).

112 S. A. Levy, "INTELSAT: technology, politics and the transformation of a regime," *International Organization*, 29 (1975), p. 679.

113 Melody, "Telecommunication – policy directions for technology and information services," p. 102.

114 *General Tariff Principles*, Section 1, Recs. 7 and 8.

115 *General Tariff Principles*, Section 1, Rec. D.3.

116 *General Tariff Principles*, Section 1, Rec. 4; Cowhey and Aronson, *Managing the World Economy*, p. 167.

117 Fisher, "Telecommunications in transition," pp. 498–99; Goldberg, "One hundred and twenty years of international communications," pp.138–39.

118 Hugo Dixon, "Reconnecting charges with costs," *Financial Times* (3 April 1990); Hugo Dixon, "Telecoms practices to take centre stage at talks in Geneva," *Financial Post* (10 May 1990).

119 Peter F. Cowhey and Jonathan D. Aronson, "Trade in services and changes in the world telecommunications system," in Peter F. Cowhey et al. (eds.),

Changing Networks: Mexico's Telecommunications Options (LaJolla, CA: Center for US–Mexican Studies, University of California, San Diego, 1989), p. 7.

120 Hugo Dixon, "Reconnecting charges with costs"; "Survey of telecommunications," *The Economist* (5 October 1991), p. 31.

121 Elizabeth Johnson, "Telecommunications market structure in the USA: the effects of deregulation and divestiture," *Telecommunications Policy*, 10 (March 1986), pp. 59–60.

122 Aronson and Cowhey, *When Countries Talk*, chs. 1, 2, and 4.

123 Johnson, "Telecommunications market structure in the USA," pp. 60–64.

124 Jack E. Cole et al., *A Review of International Telecommunications Industry Issues, Structure, and Regulatory Problems* (Washington, DC: Office of Telecommunications, US Department of Commerce, 1977), pp. 2–6. While the dramatic change in US policy occurred with the 1980 court decision to break up AT&T, an important prelude to this was the FCC decision in 1976 to allow unlimited resale of circuits leased from AT&T – albeit still subject to FCC regulation. The FCC tried to extend this policy on resale to international circuits, but failed because of foreign opposition. Hart, "The politics of competition in the global telecommunications industry," pp. 173, 191.

125 Johnson, "Telecommunications market structure in the USA," pp. 60–64; Aronson and Cowhey, *When Countries Talk*, pp. 72–73.

126 Fisher, "Telecommunications in transition," pp. 499–520.

127 Jill Hills, *Deregulating Telecoms: Competition and Control in the United States, Japan and Britain* (Westport, CN: Quorum Books, 1986), pp. 158, 163, 170.

128 Chalmers Johnson, "MITI, MPT, and the telecom wars: how Japan makes policy for high technology," in C. Johnson, L. D'Andrea Tyson, and J. Zysman (eds.), *Politics and Productivity: How Japan's Development Strategy Works* (Cambridge: Ballinger, 1989), pp. 177–240; Hills, *Deregulating Telecoms*, p.189.

129 Peter F. Cowhey, "Public and private cooperation on the international informatics regime," in Eli Noam (ed.), *Pacific Basin Telecommunications* (New York: Oxford University Press, 1992); Hills, *Deregulating Telecoms*, pp. 19, 160, 177; Robert R. Bruce et al., *From Telecommunications to Electronic Services: A Global Spectrum of Definitions, Boundary Lines, and Structures* (London: Butterworth, 1986), pp. 136–138.

130 "Telecommunications survey," *The Economist* (5 October 1991); Charles Leadbeater, "Cut-off point for telecoms giants," *Financial Times* (15 January 1991); Giovanni Cordaro, "The telecommunications single market," *Telecommunications* (January 1991); Jonathan Aronson, "New directions in international telecommunications," *Transnational Data and Communications Report* (December 1990); Bruce et al., *From Telecommunications to Electronic Services*, ch. 4; Peter F. Cowhey and Jonathan D. Aronson, "Trade in services and changes in the world telecommunications system," and "Global diplomacy and national policy options for telecommunications,"

in Cowhey et al., *Changing Networks: Mexico's Telecommunications Options*, pp. 5–80; personal communication from James Savage, November 1994.

131 *World Telecommunication Development Report*, ch. 4.

132 "Telecommunications survey," *The Economist* (5 October 1991), p. 26.

133 Andrew Andonis and Andrew Hill, "Lifting the lid on liberalisation," *Financial Times* (10 May 1993); Andrew Adonis, "Whose line is it anyway?," *Financial Times* (11 October 1993). For a background to this decision see Wayne Sandholtz, "Institutions and collective action: the new telecommunications in Western Europe," *World Politics*, 45 (January 1993), pp. 242–70.

134 William Dawkins, "France Telecom enters the real world," *Financial Times* (22 July 1992). British Telecom is also creating another international entity (Cyclone) to offer other services. Hugh Dixon, "BT to spend $1bn on global telecommunications network," *Financial Times* (8 August 1992); Dawn Hayes, "BT taking US by storm," *Communications Week International* (10 August 1992).

135 The two largest private leased networks are the Society of Worldwide Interbank Financial Telecommunications (SWIFT) and the International Society for Aeronautical Telecommunications (SITA). Other industries are developing similar independent networks. *World Telecommunication Development Report*, ch. 2.

136 Interviews; Robin Mansell, *Telecommunication Network-Based Services: Implications for Telecommunications Policy* (Paris: OECD, 1988); Bruce et al., *From Telecommunications to Electronic Services*, ch. 4; Karl-Heinz Narjes, "EEC divided on free SATCOM market," *IPTC News*, no. 66 (February 1988), p. 8; Aronson and Cowhey, *When Countries Talk*, esp. chs. 2 and 8.

137 "'Calling home' sparks tariff row," *Communications International* (November 1992); Karen Lynch, "Calling card clash," *Communications Week* (10 May 1993); interviews with national officials.

138 "The privateers," *The Economist* (12 September 1992). There is a major problem with call-back services for countries like the USA. Because the calls are registered as being from the USA, the USA must pay the foreign country the settlement rate (one-half of the accounting rate) that was negotiated between the two carriers. Also, because of the use of call-back services there are more calls from than into the USA, and it must therefore pay larger sums to foreign countries than it receives from them. In the early 1990s the USA paid $2 billion more annually to foreign countries than it received. This is a major reason why the USA wants foreign states to lower their collection rates so as to reduce the financial outflow. I am grateful to James Savage for information on these issues.

139 *World Telecommunication Development Report*, ch. 2; Alan Crane, "AT&T aims to move in to UK telecom market," *Financial Times* (16 April 1993); Andrew Adonis, "Competition on the line," *Financial Times* (29 April 1993); Richard L. Hudson and Mary Lu Carnevale, "BT won't block AT&T

in Britain if it gets in US," *Wall Street Journal Europe* (April 1993); Martin Dickson, "MCI gains more firepower in telecoms war," *Financial Times* (16 June 1993); Andrew Adonis, "AT&T's hidden agenda, "*Financial Times* (6 June 1994).

140 A very good analysis of the growing impact of wireless technologies is "A survey of telecommunications," *The Economist* (23 October 1993). Information also obtained from interviews.

141 Drake, "The CCITT: time for reform," pp. 38–39; Jean-Luc Renaud, "North, South, and the CCITT," in *Reforming the Global Network*, p. 62; G. Russell Pipe, "WATTC agrees on new telecom rules," *Telecommunications* (January 1989); Peter Cowhey and Jonathan D. Aronson, "The ITU in transition," *Telecommunications Policy* (August 1991), pp. 305–6.

142 Alan Kamman, "The effects of WATTC on the user community," *Pacific Telecommunications* (May 1989).

143 "Private circuit liberalization," *Communications International* (January 1991); Hugo Dixon, "Telephones body to end curbs on international competition," *Financial Times* (3 December 1990); Hugo Dixon, "Cost of cross border calls to fall after telephone agreement," *Financial Times* (3 March 1991); "CCITT group backs cost-based international accounting rates," *FCC Week* (15 July 1992); "CCITT OKs Accounting Rate Pact," *FCC Week* (21 October 1992). This recommendation D. 140 was reconfirmed at the 1994 ITU Plenipotentiary.

144 Kenneth Leeson, "Policy debate shifting," *Communications Week International* (19 October 1992); Charles Leadbeater, "Intelsat says it will not invoke treaty to halt competition," *Financial Times* (5 December 1990); Codding, *The Future of Satellite Communications*, pp. 69–88; *World Telecommunication Development Report*, ch. 3.

145 Cowhey and Aronson, *Managing the World Economy*, pp. 24 and 213 and chs. 2–4 and 7; Cowhey and Aronson, "Global diplomacy and national policy options for telecommunications," pp. 64–72; Pipe, "Telecommunications services," pp. 88–101; G. Russell Pipe, "Trade of Telecommunications services: implications of a GATT Uruguay Round agreement for ITU and member states" (Geneva: ITU, May 1993); William J. Drake and Kalypso Nicolaidis, "Ideas, interests, and institutionalization: 'trade in services' and the Uruguay Round," *International Organization*, 46 (Winter 1992), pp. 37–100; Kalypso Nicolaidis, "International trade in information-based services: the Uruguay Round and beyond," in William Drake (ed.), *Governing the Global Information Structure* (forthcoming); John V. Langdale, "International telecommunications and trade in services," *Telecommunications Policy*, 13 (1989), pp. 203–21.

146 Hills, *Deregulating Telecoms*, pp. 5–6; Aronson and Cowhey, *When Countries Talk*, chs. 3 and 8; Marcellus S. Snow, "INTELSAT: an international example," *Journal of Communication*, 30 (Spring 1980); Marcellus S. Snow, "Regulation to deregulation: the telecommunications sector and industrialization: evidence from the Pacific rim and basin," *Telecommunications*

Policy (December 1985), pp. 281–318; Henry Ergas, "Regulation, monopoly and competition in the telecommunications infrastructure," OECD Doc. DSTI/ICCP/85.33 (1985).

147 Snow, "Regulation to deregulation," p. 284.

148 Donald W. Davies, "Telecommunications and government," *Intermedia*, 12 (July–September 1984), p. 68.

149 Cole et al., *A Review of International Telecommunications Industry Issues, Structure, and Regulatory Problems*, pp. 70–74.

150 Cole et al., *A Review of International Telecommunications Industry Issues, Structure, and Regulatory Problems*, pp. 80–130; Peter F. Cowhey, "The international telecommunications regime: the political roots of technological paradigms of world order" (paper presented to a conference at the University of Chicago, January 1989), p. 7.

151 Alan Altschuler, "The politics of deregulation," in Harvey M. Sapolsky et al. (eds.), *The Telecommunications Revolution* (New York: Routledge & Kegan Paul, 1992), p. 11 and *passim*.

152 Melody, "Telecommunication – policy directions for technology and information services," pp. 79 and 102.

153 Gerd Tenzer, "Deutsche Bundespost and telecommunications policy," *Law, Regulation, Standards for Global Communications* (Special Session, World Telecommunication Forum, Washington, DC, 18–19 April 1985), pp. 257–59. The public service and security motivations are also stressed in Geza Feketekuty, *International Trade in Services: An Overview and Blueprint for Negotiations* (Cambridge, MA: Ballinger, 1988), p. 163; and Claude Barfield and Robert P. Benko, "Trade policy issues in international communications," *Economic Impact*, 2 (1987), p. 20.

154 R. Brian Woodrow, "Telecom and trade in services – never the twain shall meet?," *Transnational Data and Communications Report* (April 1990), p. 15. Also see Aronson and Cowhey, *When Countries Talk*, p. 19.

155 Snow, "Regulation to deregulation," p. 284.

156 Aronson and Cowhey, *When Countries Talk*, p. 61.

157 Aronson and Cowhey, in fact, note these trends. *When Countries Talk*, p. 71.

158 Harold H. Greene, "Address," *Fifth World Telecommunication Forum: Part III* (Geneva: ITU, 1987). Also see Aronson and Cowhey, *When Countries Talk*, ch. 4; Narjes, "EEC divided on free SATCOMM market"; Hills, *Deregulating Telecoms*, ch. 1; Bruce et al., *From Telecommunications to Electronic Services*, ch. 4; "Survey of Telecommunications," *The Economist* (10 March 1990).

159 Cowhey, "The international telecommunications regime: the political roots of technological paradigms of world order," p. 18.

160 William J. Drake and Lee McKnight, "Telecommunications standards in the global information economy," *Deregulation in the 1990s* (Paris: Promethee, 1988), p. 21. The same points are made in Aronson and Cowhey, *When Countries Talk*, pp. 253–54.

161 Woodrow, "Telecom and trade in services," pp. 15–16 and *passim*.

C. Russell Pipe has written that "Telecommunications users have organized pressure groups in most developed countries, seeking greater deregulation and competition in all but basic residential telephone services. TNCs are at the forefront of the demand for liberalization of international services." "Telecommunications services: considerations of the developing countries in Uruguay Round negotiations," *Trade in Services: Sectoral Issues* (New York: United Nations, 1989), p. 63. Also see pp. 84–87.

162 Bruce et al., *From Telecommunications to Information Services*, pp. 10–11. Aronson and Cowhey, *When Countries Talk*, pp. 32–34, 135–41.

163 Bruce et al., *From Telecommunications to Information Services*, pp. 10–11, 156–58, 341; *The Telecommunications Industry: The Structure of Change* (Paris: OECD, 1987), p. 58; Hills, *Deregulating Telecoms*, p. 19; Cowhey, "The international telecommunications regime," p. 172; interviews with government officials.

164 Geza Feketekuty, "Negotiating the world information economy," in Sapolsky et al., *The Telecommunications Revolution*, p. 180.

165 "Telecommunications survey," *The Economist* (19 March 1990), pp. 6, 36. Also see Bruce et al., *From Telecommunications to Electronic Services*, pp. 345–46; *The Telecommunications Industry*, p. 37; Hills, *Deregulating Telecoms*, pp. 9–10. For a very good discussion of varied services and modes of interconnection and their impacts of competition, see "Refile and alternative calling procedures: their impact on accounting rates and collection charges", OECD Doc. DSTI/ICCP/TISP/AH(94)1 (Paris: Committee for Information, Computer and Communication Policy, OECD, May 1994).

166 Hugh Dixon, "Free the markets," *Financial Times* (19 April 1990), Sec. 3, p. 1.

167 "More freedom sought for world media," *Broadcasting* (19 September 1988).

168 *Radio Frequency Use and Management*, p. 108.

169 United States Congress, *World Administrative Radio Conference: Hearing before the Subcommittee on Communications and the Subcommittee on Science, Technology, and Space of the Committee on Commerce, Science, and Transportation*, US Senate (Ninety-ninth Congress) (Washington, DC: Government Printing Office, 1986), p. 39.

6 The international postal regime

1 George A. Codding, *The Universal Postal Union* (New York: New York University Press, 1964), p. 6.

2 Roger Sherman, "Competition in postal service," in Michael A. Crew and Paul R. Kleindorfer (eds.), *Competition and Innovation in Postal Services* (Norwell, MA: Kluwer Academic, 1991), pp. 194–95; Codding, *The Universal Postal Union*, pp. 12, 235; James D. Cotreau, "Historical development of the Universal Postal Union and the question of membership" (Ph.D dissertation, University of Fribourg, Switzerland, 1975), pp. 13–16; M. A. K. Menon, "The Universal Postal Union," *International Conciliation* (March 1965), pp. 5–6.

3 Codding, *The Universal Postal Union*, pp. 15–16; Cotreau, "Historical development of the Universal Postal Union," pp. 21–23.

4 Menon, "The Universal Postal Union," pp. 1–4; Cotreau, "Historical development of the Universal Postal Union," pp. 11–29; Codding, *The Universal Postal Union*, pp. 15–17; Paul S. Reinsch, *Public International Unions* (Boston: Ginn, 1911), pp. 21–28.

5 Roger Sherman, "Competition in postal service," pp. 195–96.

6 Cotreau, "Historical development of the Universal Postal Union," pp. 40–46; Codding, *The Universal Postal Union*, pp. 16–19; Menon, "The Universal Postal Union," pp. 6–7; Harold M. Vinacke, *International Organization* (New York: F. S. Crafts, 1934), pp. 402–3.

7 Codding, *The Universal Postal Union*, pp. 20–24; Cotreau, "Historical development of the Universal Postal Union," pp. 56–62; Gottfried North et al., *The Post: A Universal Link among Men* (Lausanne: VIE, ART, CITE, 1974), p. 135.

8 Vinacke, *International Organization*, p. 405.

9 Codding, *The Universal Postal Union*, pp. 25–34; Cotreau, "Historical development of the Universal Postal Union," pp. 73–78.

10 Cited in Roger Sherman, "Competition in postal service," p. 199.

11 Philip Dobbenberg, "The international mail market in the 1990s," in Michael A. Crew and Paul R. Kleindorfer (eds.), *Regulation and the Nature of Postal and Delivery Services* (Boston, MA: Kluwer, 1993), pp. 208–210.

12 The figures are taken from *Annual Report of the Postmaster General* (from 1980 to 1989) (Washington, DC: Office of the Postmaster General). As a percentage of total US mail it went down from 0.9 to 0.5 over this decade.

13 "The future of postal services," *Union Postale* (July/August 1981), pp. 91A–97A; Crew and Kleindorfer, *Competition and Innovation in Postal Services*; Barbara L. Krause, "Private international couriers: a challenge to the West German postal monopoly," *Cornell International Law Journal*, 19 (1986), pp. 35–63.

14 *1989 Statistique des Services Postaux* (Berne: UPU, 1990); *Annual Report of the Postmaster General: Fiscal Year 1988* (Washington, DC: Office of the Postmaster General, 1989), p. 2; *Annex to Circular Letter No. 0426 (M) 1558, 2 July 1992* (Berne: UPU). International mail as a percentage of total mail has remained stable in the 2–4 percent range over the twentieth century. James I. Campbell, "The future of the Universal Postal Union," in Crew and Kleindorfer, *Regulation and the Nature of Postal and Delivery Services*, p. 14.

15 European Commission, *Green Paper on the Development of the Single Market for Postal Services: Executive Summary* (Brussels: European Commission, 1992), p. 2; Douglas K. Adie, *Monopoly Mail: Privatizing the US Postal Service* (New Brunswick, NJ: Transaction Publishers, 1989), p. 1.

16 *1985 Statistique des Services Postaux* (Berne: UPU, 1986) placed the earnings of postal administrations at $63.5 billion. This did not include the earnings of some important states (China, Soviet Union) and of private carriers. The

estimate of $90 billion in revenues is conservative both because there has undoubtedly been significant growth since the mid-1980s and because a European Commission report recently noted that about 40 percent of postal revenues in Europe is accounted for by private mail services. European Commission, *Green Paper on the Development of the Single Market for Postal Services*, p. 2.

17 Menon, "The Universal Postal Union," pp. 23–48; Codding, *The Universal Postal Union, passim;* "1947–1987: the Executive Council is 40 years old," *Union Postale,* 112 (March/April 1987), pp. 27A–28A; "Organization and operation of Congress," *Union Postale,* 114 (January/March 1989), pp. 11A–14A; "The UPU adopts its workings to modern requirements," *Union Postale,* 114 (January/March 1989), pp. 15A–16A; Campbell, "The future of the Universal Postal Union," pp. 11–15. For the legal texts of the 1989 documents with commentaries on the historical background of each article, see *Constitution; General Regulations; Resolutions and Decisions, Rules of Procedure, Legal Status of the UPU: Valid at the Time Entry into Force of the Acts of the 1989 Washington Congress and Annotated by the International Bureau* (Berne: UPU, 1991) (hereinafter cited as *1989 Constitution, General Regulations, and Resolutions*); and *Convention: Revised by the 1989 Washington Congress and Annotated by the International Bureau* (Berne: UPU, 1991) (hereinafter cited as *1989 Convention*).

18 *1989 Convention*, Arts. 181–82, 192; Laurin Zilliacus, *From Pillar to Post* (London: William Heinemann, 1956), p. 188; Codding, *The Universal Postal Union*, pp. 111, 195; J. Ascandoni, "Technical assistance operation in the UPU," *Union Postale,* 111 (July/August 1986), pp. 97A–100A.

19 Codding, *The Universal Postal Union*, p. 111. Also see Menon, "The Universal Postal Union," pp. 16–17; Vinacke, *International Organization*, pp. 406–9.

20 Codding, *The Universal Postal Union*, pp. 227–29; Menon, "The Universal Postal Union," pp. 56–59.

21 Codding, *The Universal Postal Union*, pp. 75 and 229–34; Menon, "The Universal Postal Union," pp. 50–52; Otfried Braus-Packenius, "The nature of restricted postal unions," *Union Postale,* 87 (April 1962), pp. 55A–58A.

22 "Treaty concerning the formation of a General Postal Union" (signed at Berne, Switzerland, 9 October 1874), Art. 14; Codding, *The Universal Postal Union*, pp. 25–34.

23 *1989 Convention*, Art. 5. In Britain and the Commonwealth countries the tradition is to recognize that the mail item belongs to the recipient after it has been mailed, and these countries make reservations on this article. However, relevant to the point being made in this paragraph, these sending states assume the right to open and impede mail in keeping with their national legislation.

24 Edouard Weber, "Freedom of transit: a fundamental basis of the UPU," *Union Postale* (April 1962), p. 51A.

25 Codding, *The Universal Postal Union*, p. 74.

26 *1989 Constitution, General Regulations, and Resolutions*, Art. 1 (1). Also, see Art. 1 (1) in *1989 Convention*.

27 The Convention also recognizes the right of states of destination to impede delivery of the mail. *1989 Convention*, Arts. 1 (2), 2, and 23. The key provisions concerning transit are in Arts. 1–4.

28 Charles H. Alexandrowicz, *World Economic Agencies: Law and Practice* (London: Stevens, 1962), pp. 27–28, 33.

29 There are a few exceptions. Arab states have destroyed mail to or from Israel, and sometimes African states did the same with mail to or from South Africa. Interviews with government officials.

30 "1990 Executive Council Session," *Union Postale*, 115 (October/December 1990), p. 82A; "Resolution C 12/ 1989: Action to enhance the security and integrity of international mail," *1989 Constitution, General Regulations, and Resolutions*; "Security: bulwark of quality," *Union Postale*, 117 (January/February 1992), pp. 2A–6A. On dispute settlement see Zilliacus, *From Pillar to Post*, p. 188; "Treaty concerning the formation of a General Postal Union," Art. 16; *1989 Constitution, General Regulations, and Resolutions*, Arts. 32 and 127.

31 *1989 Convention*, Arts. 1 (2) and 23; Arts. 119–24 of Detailed Regulations. Comparable articles are found in the agreements on special services and their detailed regulations.

32 *1989 Convention*, Arts. 42–44.

33 "Drugs and the post," *Union Postale*, 112 (May/June 1987), pp. 54A–55A; Claude Montellier, "A turning point in cooperation with Customs," *Union Postale*, 114 (July/September 1989), pp. 71A–73A. The 1989 Congress resolution requesting the creation of a group of experts on mail security and proposing the adoption of a UPU action program at the next congress concerns protection of the mails from crime as well as accidents. Resolution C/12, *1989 Constitution, General Regulations, and Resolutions*.

34 Cotreau, "The historical development of the Universal Postal Union," pp. 22–23.

35 *1989 Convention*, Arts. 57–69. Comparable provisions exist in the agreements on special services.

36 *Acts of the Universal Postal Union, Volume III: Postal Parcels* (Revised at Hamburg in 1984) (Berne: UPU, 1985), p. 43.

37 *1989 Convention*, Art. 1 (1). A comparable stipulation is in Article 10 of the 1874 convention. Also see Edouard Weber, "Freedom of transit: a fundamental basis of the UPU," pp. 48A–52A. There are many standards of performance as well as procedural and technical standards in the International Postal Convention and the special agreements, but the most specific ones tend to be in the Detailed Regulations for each convention/ agreement.

38 *1989 Convention*, Art. 36 (1).

39 Robert Montandon, "Mail circulation – the basic task of the postal service," *Union Postale*, 113 (July/September 1988), pp. 66A–68; J. Ascandoni,

"Technical cooperation in the UPU," *Union Postale*, 111 (July/August 1986), pp. 97A–100A; Moussibahou Mazou, "Problems of postal management in the developing countries," *Union Postale*, 111 (July/August 1986), pp. 100A–103A; "Technical cooperation: overall picture, 1984–1989," *Union Postale*, 114 (April/June 1989), pp. 37A–42A.

40 Jean M. Milne, "The IATA-UPU Contact Committee – 30 years of cooperation," *Union Postale*, 111 (May/June 1986), p. 76A; Emile Buhler, "Towards normalization of the makeup of correspondence – the Contact Committee ISO–UPU," *Union Postale* (November 1961), pp. 146A–149A.

41 David G. Foot, "Postal electronic messaging – the work of the Electronic Transmission Group," *Union Postale*, 118 (January/February 1993), p. 11A.

42 *1989 Convention*, Art. 41 (5).

43 Articles in: *Union Postale*, 112 (May/June 1987), pp. 49A–61A; Claude Montellier, "A turning point in cooperation with Customs," *Union Postale*, 114 (July/September 1989), pp. 71A–73A.

44 See citations in the first section of this chapter on developments from the seventeenth through to the nineteenth centuries.

45 "Memorandum on the role of the post as a factor in economic and cultural development," *Union Postale*, 107 (May/June 1982), pp. 81–82; M. Rajasingham, "Whither postal monopoly? – From the perspective of a developing country," *Union Postale*, 107 (March/April 1982), pp. 30A–31A; Sherman, "Competition in postal service," pp. 194–206; Thomas Gale Moore, "The federal postal monopoly: history, rationale, and future," in P. J. Ferrara (ed.), *Free the Mail: Ending the Postal Monopoly* (Washington, DC: Cato Institute, 1990), pp. 61–64.

46 Alan L. Sorkin, *The Economics of the Postal System* (Lexington, MA: D. C. Heath, 1980), pp. 133–49; Robert Albon, *Private Correspondence: Competition of Monopoly in Australia's Postal Services* (Canberra: Centre of Independent Studies, 1985), pp. 1–74; Sherman, "Competition in postal service," p. 196; Ann Marie Hendricks, "Is there a natural postal monopoly?" (unpublished Ph.D dissertation, University of Michigan, 1982); Douglas K. Adie, *The Monopoly Mail: Analyzing Canadian Postal Service* (Vancouver: Fraser Institute, 1990), pp. 56–61.

47 *1989 Convention*, Art. 20. There are a variety of other rules concerning international rates and their payment which largely facilitate the operation of the postal system. Arts. 19–35.

48 For description of the debates on rates between 1874 and the early 1960s, see Codding, *The Universal Postal Union*, pp. 25–72.

49 *1989 Convention*, Arts. 71 and 72; Milomir Micic, "Transit charges and normal traffic," *Union Postale* (February 1963), pp. 27A–30A.

50 Charles H. Alexandrowicz, *World Economic Agencies: Law and Practice*, p. 33.

51 David E. Treworgy and James A. Waddell, "Postal service and less developed countries," in Crew and Kleindorfer, *Competition and Innovation in Postal Services*, pp. 253–56. In the case of European Community states they have abolished terminal dues for mail flows amongst each other.

Notes to pages 199–204

Some other developed states have signed bilateral agreements that set terminal dues below UPU standards. The key UPU rules are in *1989 Convention*, Arts. 73–75.

52 *1989 Statistique des Services Postaux*.

53 Luiz L. F. Pinerio, "Terminal dues study concluded," *Union Postale*, 109 (May/June 1984), p. 74A.There have always been terminal dues for large parcels. UPU guidelines on rates have had a limited impact. *Postal Parcels Agreement: Revised by the 1989 Washington Congress and Annotated by the International Bureau* (Berne: UPU, 1991); Sir Ron Dearing, "Foreword," in Crew and Klendorfer, *Competition and Innovation in Postal Services*, p. xiii.

54 *Documents of the 1984 Hamburg Congress, Volume 2: Discussions* (Berne: UPU, 1985), pp. 408–12; Campbell, "The future of the Universal Postal Union," pp. 12 and 18; Ulrich Stumpf, "Remailing in the European Community: economic analysis of alternative regulatory environments," in Crew and Kleindorfer, *Regulation and the Nature of Postal and Delivery Services*, pp. 179–204.

55 Interviews with government officials.

56 "Relations with postal administrations regarding sea conveyance of mail," *Union Postale*, 112 (November/December 1987), p. 120A; Erich Behnke, "Conveyance of postal items by sea," *Union Postale*, 112 (November/ December 1987), pp. 121A–123A.

57 A. V. Seshanna, "An air-mail argosy? Some thoughts," *Union Postale*, 102 (September/October 1977), p. 114A; Codding, *Universal Postal Convention*, p. 57; interviews with government officials.

58 Codding, *The Universal Postal Union*, pp. 65–67; Seshanna, "An air-mail argosy?," p. 112A; Jean M. Milne, "The airmail through the Airmail Provisions," *Union Postale*, 96 (February 1971), pp. 26A–29A; Jean M. Milne, "The IATA–UPU Contact Committee – Thirty Years of Cooperation"; ICAO Doc. 8240–AT/716 (1962); UPU Doc. 3410.1C 1025 (1985); UPU Doc. IATA-UPU/RATES/1 (1986); *1989 Convention*, Arts. 82–90 interviews with government officials.

59 Codding, *The Universal Postal Union*, p. 74; interviews with government officials.

60 Thomas E. Leavey, "Issues facing the international postal service," in Crew and Kleindorfer, *Regulation and the Nature of Postal and Delivery Services*, p. 1.

61 Some important remailing states in the last decade have been the Netherlands, Hungary, Singapore, Hong Kong, Dominican Republic, Venezuela, Panama, Morocco, and Zambia. Interviews with government officials.

62 Interview with government official.

63 Stumpf, "Remailing in the European Community," p. 179. Information on remailing obtained from interviews with government officials; Leavey, "Issues facing the international postal service," pp. 4–5; and Campbell, "The future of the Universal Postal Union," pp. 12–18.

64 Patrick M. McAfee and Elizabeth Reiland, "A step in the right direction: MAIS and the UPU," *Union Postale*, 118 (January/February 1993), p. 6A.

65 "Canada Post bets a bundle on TNT alliance," *Globe and Mail* (Toronto) (30 June 1992), p. C1; interviews.

66 Leavey, "Issues facing the international postal service," p. 1.

67 J. G. Halpin, "The courier business – what it takes to meet the competition," *Union Postale*, 112 (January/February 1987), p. 9A.

68 Albon, *Private Correspondence*, p. 3.

69 Angela Reeg-Muller, "Study 503: situation of the postal electronic mail services," *Union Postale*, 113 (October/December 1988), pp. 88A–92A; D. S. Smyth, "Postal public electronic text message services," *Union Postale*, 113 (October/December 1988), pp. 93A–95A.

70 Cited in Sherman, "Competition in postal service," p. 199. Some project that e-mail does not pose a serious threat to postal administrations, but this is probably wrong. Reeg-Muller, "Study 503," p. 89A.

71 Albon, *Private Correspondence*, pp. 1–72; Sorkin, *The Economics of the Postal System*, pp. 133–47; Sherman, "Competition in postal service," pp. 196–206; Moore, "The federal postal monopoly"; Hendricks, "Is there a natural postal monopoly?," esp. pp. 234–35; Adie, *Monopoly Mail: Privatizing the US Postal Service*.

72 Moore, "The federal postal monopoly," pp. 64–65.

73 "Questioning the Canada Post monopoly," *Globe and Mail* (Toronto), 27 August 1991, p. A14.

74 Sherman, "Competition in postal service," p. 196.

75 Dearing, "Foreword," p. xvii.

76 Special issue of *Union Postale*, 113 (October/December 1988) on e-mail; "Competition from private couriers: the reaction of the Post Office," *Union Postale*, 111 (January/February 1986), pp. 17A–18A; Halpin, "The courier business – what it takes to meet the competition," *Union Postale*, 112 (January/ February 1988), pp. 9A–10A; interviews.

77 On the Declaration of Hamburg and some of the follow-up activities, see "Declaration of Hamburg," *Union Postale*, 111 (November/December 1986), pp. 136A–141A; "Symposia at the International Bureau," *Union Postale*, 113 (April/June 1988), pp. 42A–43A; David G. Foot, "The acts of the UPU: a new perspective," *Union Postale*, 114 (July/September 1989), pp. 66A–67A; "A permanent activity: quality control," *Union Postale*, 114 (July/September 1989), pp. 68A–70A. On the 1989 expansion of the Executive Council's powers see "Resolution C1/1989: Immediate application of the new legislative powers of the Executive Council," *1989 Constitution, General Regulations, and Resolutions*.

78 E. Mostafa Gharbi, "Deregulation, a postal modernization factor," *Union Postale*, 112 (January/February 1987), p. 11A.

79 See in particular Resolutions C/5, 22, 67, 68, and 91: *1989 Constitution, General Regulations, and Resolutions*.

80 For examples of the new thinking and UPU policies see: Felix Ciceron (Deputy Director-General), "Parting thoughts," *Union Postale*, 114 (October/December 1989), pp. 99A–101A; A. C. Botto de Barros (Director-General), "Editorial," *Union Postale*, 116 (January/March 1991), pp. 2A–4A; Thomas E. Leavey (Chairman, Executive Council), "Five-point plan for UPU Executive Council action," *Union Postale*, 116 (January/March 1991), pp. 16A–19A.

81 Ciceron, "Parting thoughts," p. 101A.

82 Sherman, "Competition in postal service"; Adie, *The Monopoly Mail*; Moore, "The federal postal monopoly."

83 Dobbenberg, "The international mail market in the 1990s," pp. 211–12 and 215.

84 Gottfried North et al., *The Post: A Universal Link among Men*, p. 135.

7 Normative continuities and international regime theory

1 J. W. Salacuse, "The little prince and the businessman: conflicts and tensions in public international law," *Journal of Air Law and Commerce*, 45 (1980), pp. 14–15.

2 The term "minilateralism" refers to agreements among a modest number of countries to regulate or manage an international problem. It is sometimes used to refer to a controlling or coordinating role that a small number of countries perform within a global multilateral arrangement. It is not used in this latter sense here. See Miles Kahler, "Multilateralism with small and large numbers," *International Organization*, 46 (Summer 1992), pp. 681–708.

3 Ian Brownlie, "The roles of international law," in *Zin en Tegenzin in Internationaal Recht* (Deventer: Kluwer, 1986), p. 15.

4 Morton Kaplan and Nicholas Katzenbach, *The Political Foundations of International Law* (Chicago: Wiley, 1961), p. 26.

5 Ruth Lapidoth, "Freedom of navigation – its legal history and its normative basis," *Journal of Maritime Law and Commerce*, 6 (1974–75), p. 271.

6 Barry Buzan, "From international system to international society: structural realism and regime theory meet the English school," *International Organization*, 47 (1993), p. 341.

7 Louis Henkin, *How Nations Behave* (New York: Columbia University Press, 1968), p. 29

8 Gilbert R. Winham, *The Evolution of the International Trade Agreements* (Toronto: University of Toronto Press, 1992), p. 21.

9 Stephen Breyer, "Regulation and deregulation in the United States: airlines, telecommunications and antitrust," in Giandomenico Majone (ed.), *Deregulation or Re-Regulation?: Regulatory Reform in Europe and the United States* (New York: St. Martin's Press, 1990), pp. 11 and 22. Also see Dennis Swann, *The Retreat of the State: Deregulation and Privatization in the UK and US* (New York: Harvester Wheatsheaf, 1988).

10 For an overview of theories of regulation (including those focusing on

bureaucratic interests) see Barry M. Mitnick, *The Political Economy of Regulation: Creating, Designing, and Removing Regulatory Forms* (New York: Columbia University Press, 1980), ch. 3. Economic rationales are the focus of Stephen Breyer, *Regulation and Its Reform* (Cambridge, MA: Harvard University Press, 1982). Among the previous chapters the chapter on the international telecommunications regime best highlights the competing factors that affect regulation. A very good overview of some of the industries covered in this book is Breyer, "Regulation and deregulation in the United States."

11 Robert G. Jackson, "The weight of ideas in decolonization: normative change in international relations," in Judith Goldstein and Robert O. Keohane (eds.), *Ideas and Foreign Policy: Beliefs, Institutions, and Political Change* (Ithaca, NY: Cornell University Press, 1993), p. 114.

12 Craig N. Murphy, *International Organization and Industrial Change: Global Governance since 1850* (Cambridge, UK: Polity, 1994), p. 2. Italics in original.

13 Quoted in James I. Campbell, "The future of the Universal Postal Union," in Michael A. Crew and Paul R. Kleindorfer (eds.), *Regulation and the Nature of Postal Delivery Services* (Boston: Kluwer, 1993), p. 7.]

14 John Gerard Ruggie, "Multilateralism: the anatomy of an institution," in John Gerard Ruggie (ed.), *Multilateralism Matters: The Theory and Praxis of an Institutional Form* (New York: Columbia University Press, 1993), p. 21. Also see Mark W. Zacher, "Multilateral organizations and the institution of multilateralism: the development of regimes for nonterrestrial spaces," in Ruggie, *Multilateralism Matters*, pp. 399–42.

15 Hedley Bull, *The Anarchical Society: A Study of Order in World Politics* (New York: Columbia University Press, 1977); David Armstrong, *Revolution and World Order: The Revolutionary State in International Society* (Oxford: Clarendon, 1993).

16 Peter Cowhey, "The international telecommunications regime: the political roots of regimes of high technology," *International Organization*, 44 (Spring 1990), p. 18.

17 "The day of the national car industry is over," *The Economist* (5–11 February 1994), p. 14.

18 See the discussion of economic liberalism in Robert O. Keohane, "International liberalism reconsidered," in John Dunn (ed.), *The Economic Limits of Politics* (Cambridge: Cambridge University Press, 1989), pp. 165–94; and Mark W. Zacher and Richard A. Matthew, "Liberal international theory: common threads, divergent strands," in Charles Kegley (ed.), *Controversies in International Relations Theory: Neorealism and the Neoliberal Challenge* (New York: St. Martin's Press, 1995), pp. 107–49.

19 Reflective of the above judgment, Robert Keohane has written that the persistence of international monetary regimes "is partially accounted for by the continual strength of the United States, which had an interest in liberalism. But the persistence of cooperative regimes is also partially explained by the continuation of shared interests in the efficiency and

welfare benefits of international economic exchange." *After Hegemony: Cooperation and Discord in the World Political Economy* (Princeton, NJ: Princeton University Press, 1984), p. 209

20 Robert W. Cox, "Social forces, states and world orders: beyond international relations theory," in Robert O. Keohane (ed.), *Neorealism and Its Critics* (New York: Columbia University Press, 1986), p. 230. An indicator of the extent to which states are increasingly interdependent for their realization of crucial values is the growth of the transnational arms industry. Richard A. Bitzinger, "The globalization of the arms industry," *International Security*, 19 (Fall 1994), pp. 170–98.

21 Robert O. Keohane, "Sovereignty, interdependence, and international institutions," in Linda B. Miller and Michael Joseph Smith (eds.), *Ideas and Ideals* (Boulder, CO: Westview, 1993), p. 91. "Operational sovereignty" is states' effective freedom of decision-making, taking into account their international legal commitments. Keohane juxtaposes this with "formal sovereignty."

22 John Gerard Ruggie, "Territoriality and beyond: problematizing modernity in international relations," *International Organization*, 47 (Winter 1993), pp. 139–74; Alexander Wendt, "Anarchy is what states make of it: the social construction of power politics," *International Organization*, 46 (Spring 1992), pp. 391–26.

23 Zacher and Matthew, "Liberal international theory."

24 Helen Milner, "International theories of cooperation among nations: strengths and weaknesses," *World Politics*, 44 (April 1992), p. 471.

25 Stephen D. Krasner, "Global communications and national power: life on the Pareto frontier," *World Politics*, 43 (April 1991), p. 362.

26 R. Michael M'Gonigle and Mark W. Zacher, *Pollution, Politics, and International Law: Tankers at Sea* (Berkeley, CA: University of California Press, 1979), ch. 8.

27 Murphy, *International Organization and Industrial Change.*

28 Brownlie, "The roles of international law," p. 12. Brownlie also comments that "the dictated treaty" is the exception and not the rule. With regard to the importance of order and certainty to the growth of the international economy, the economist Jeffrey Sachs recently made a plea for expanding the scope and strength of international economic law since the lack of rules "threaten the global economic system." He asserted that "The world system relies increasingly on international rules to govern commercial relations." Jeffrey Sachs, "Beyond Bretton Woods: a new blueprint," *The Economist* (1 October 1994), pp. 23–27.

Index

Index